KT-369-667

FINANCIAL MANAGEMENT HANDBOOK

A Gower Press Handbook

FINANCIAL MANAGEMENT HANDBOOK

Gower Press

First published in Great Britain by Gower Press Limited
Epping, Essex

© Gower Press 1972

ISBN 0 7161 0070 3

Made and Printed in Great Britain by The Garden City Press Limited
Letchworth, Hertfordshire SG6 1JS

Contents

PART TWO: COSTING AND BUDGETARY CONTROL

Contents

Illustrations

Acknowledgement

The publishers would like to thank Michael Levete, Chief Marketing Executive at Charterhouse Finance Corporation for his assistance in the preparation of Chapter 15, Sources of Finance.

Notes on Contributors

P R Attwood, PhD, MSc, MS, BSc, MIIE, MORS, AMIWM, (Control of production) is a consultant in operational research and industrial engineering with C G Chantrill & Partners Limited. He specialises in the fields of distribution, production engineering and work organisation. His consulting assignments over the last twelve years have included training industrial engineers for the International Labour Office, Geneva; value analysis with the Indian Productivity Centre, Bombay; setting up a United Kingdom industrial engineering programme for Chrysler International; management development and training for AEI, London; establishing the industrial engineering function at Federal Motor Industries, Lagos. He has recently become Professor of Industrial Engineering, University of Benin, Nigeria.

At earlier stages in his career, Dr Attwood has been technical services manager for Caltex Oil Company in Nairobi, Kenya; Head of Engineering Department, University College of East Africa; and senior lecturer at Edinburgh University. Dr Attwood is retained as project survey director for the United Nations Industrial Development Organisation, Vienna. He is a committee member of the Institution of Works Managers, London and of the Institution of Industrial Engineers, Bombay Branch. He is author of *The Darsiri Method of Value Analysis*, *The Moore Manual of Management*, *Applying Commonsense*, and *Planning a Distribution System* (Gower Press).

Peter Baker (The Stock Market rating—Evaluating company share prices), in his capacity as Assistant Director of N M Rothschild and Sons Limited, has responsibility for managing £60 million of pension funds. He has an MA from Cambridge University and is an Associate Member of the Institute of Chartered Accountants, of which he is a member of the Earnings per Share Sub-committee. Mr Baker is also a member of the Council of the Society of Investment Analysts.

H W Calvert (Standard costing and marginal costing) was Principal Lecturer in Management Accountancy at North East London Polytechnic. After initially training in the production and marketing of linen products, Mr Calvert was a cost accountant with British Celanese Limited, Cost Accountant and Budget Accountant with Ilford Limited, and Senior Lecturer at South West Essex Technical College. He is an Associate Member of the Institute of Cost and Management Accountants; he was a member of the Institute's Education Committee from 1969 to 1971 and is currently a member of the Institute's Terminology Committee.

Geoffrey P E Clarkson (Managing working capital) is National Westminster Bank Professor of Business Finance at the Manchester Business School. He took his PhD at Carnegie-Mellon University and taught for several years at the Sloan School of Management, Massachusetts Institute of Technology. Among his many publications are *Theory of Consumer Demand* and *Portfolio Selection: A Simulation of Trust Investment* and (with Bryan J Elliott) *Managing Money and Finance*.
Bryan J Elliott (Managing working capital) is lecturer in finance at Manchester Business School and is a Social Science Research Fellow. He took his PhD at Manchester University and spent a number of years in industry and consultancy. He is co-author (with Geoffrey P E Clarkson) of *Managing Money and Finance* (Gower Press).

P C Elliott (The internal audit) is Manager, Corporate Accounts and Central Office Costs, Shell International Petroleum Company Limited, with experience in the Royal Dutch/Shell Group since 1950. He is responsible for the corporate accounts of various subsidiaries of the

Group and the administration of budgeting, accounting and cost control for the United Kingdom service companies. Mr Elliott is a Fellow of the Institute of Chartered Accountants in England and Wales, and a past President of the London Chapter of the Institute of Internal Auditors Incorporated.

Stanley Gale (The Stock Market rating—Enhancing the corporate financial image) is Managing Director of Shareholder Relations Limited. Before forming the company in 1958 Mr Gale was a financial journalist for twenty years, during which time he held appointments as Deputy City Editor of *The Evening Standard* and *The Daily Express*.

Eric Izod (Managing acquisition and merger situations) is Executive Director of Industrial Mergers Limited and Manager of the Merchant Banking Services of the Industrial and Commercial Finance Corporation Limited, which he joined in 1949. He is concerned with research and advice on mergers and new issues. Mr Izod is an external examiner for the British Institute of Management.

Alan R Leaper (Budgets and budgetary control) is Financial Controller of Hoover Worldwide's Eastern Region Headquarters, in which capacity he is responsible, at a regional level for reviewing and controlling the budgets of thirteen overseas subsidiaries. Mr Leaper's experience includes three years in Canada on cost and general accounting assignments, eleven years with the Frigidaire Division of General Motors Limited in various factory accounting positions and he has been with Hoover Limited for three years. During his career he has obtained considerable practical experience of budgeting and budgetary control in both manufacturing and commercial environments. Mr Leaper is a member of the Advisory Committee to the Management Division of Management Centre Europe where he is frequently invited to chair various seminars, courses and round table meetings.

R L Mansbridge (Forecasting financial requirements) is Controller, IMS International Inc. He is a chartered accountant. Until recently he was with Rank Xerox Limited where he spent five years in financial management in United Kingdom and European operating companies and five years in various senior planning and control functions at the company's international headquarters.

A J Merrett (The role of the finance director) is one of Britain's foremost financial experts with wide experience of financial management, consultancy, teaching and academic research. After working in industry for eight years, he took a First Class Honours Degree at the London School of Economics in 1955 and then lectured in Economics at Manchester University. From 1957 to 1963 he was a financial executive with Unilever, and, subsequently, Esso Petroleum. In 1963 he was appointed Professor of Applied Economics at Sheffield University and in 1966 he became the first Professor of Finance at the London Graduate School of Business Studies. Professor Merrett's publications include the classic *Finance and Analysis of Capital Projects* and *Capital Budgeting and Company Finance* (both with A Sykes) and *Equity Issues and the London Capital Market* (with M Howe and G D Newbould) and more recently *Valuation of Ordinary Shares* (Gower Press, 1970). He has also written several works on aspects of executive remuneration and taxation, including *Incentive Payment Systems for Managers* (with M White, Gower Press, 1968).

A W Pearson (Control of research and development) is Director of the Research and Development Research Unit of Manchester Business School. His industrial experience as a scientist was gained with Pilkington Brothers Limited and Henry Simon Limited before becoming Lecturer in Economic Statistics at Manchester University, Lecturer in Operational Research and Senior Lecturer in Decision Analysis at Manchester Business School. Mr Pearson has a BSc Degree from London University and is a Member of the Operational Research Society and the Institute of Physics. He has written articles on R and D management and is Editor of *R and D Management*.

John Reynolds (Managing corporate taxation) is Tax Adviser to Esso Petroleum Company Limited. Mr Reynolds was called to the Bar at

Gray's Inn in 1953 after training in management with Tillotson and Sons Limited. After practising at the Chancery Bar for two years he worked in the Office of the Solicitor of Inland Revenue, becoming a Senior Legal Assistant, before joining his present company in 1963. Mr Reynolds has an MA from Cambridge University and lectures on taxation.

Tessa V Ryder Runton (Capital investment planning) is a consultant and part-time lecturer on financial and corporate planning. She obtained an MA at Cambridge University in Natural Science and Law, and she studied Economics and Accountancy at the London School of Economics. She was formerly a Senior Financial Analyst, Group Planning, in the Rio Tinto Zinc Corporation where she spent six years, latterly as Administrative Secretary of the Capital Expenditure Committee.

Michael Springman (Sources of finance) is a consultant in executive recruiting at Heidrick and Struggles, with wide financial and marketing experience. This includes three years in a US venture capital company in the UK and five years at Hambros Bank, working on investments in private companies. More recently he was Marketing Director of Recording Designs, an EMI Subsidiary. Mr Springman has a BA from Oxford University and is a member of the Long Range Planning Society.

Guenter B Steinitz (Control of overheads) is a management consultant engaged in a wide range of consultancy work. He is a chartered accountant, an Associate of the Institute of Cost and Management Accountants and is a Member of the Institute of Management Consultants and a Committee Member of the North London Branch of the Institute of Cost and Management Accountants. Before becoming a consultant Mr Steinitz was Deputy Group Financial Accountant of Philips Industries Limited.

George R Thomson (Presentation of accounts) is a financial consultant engaged in advising companies on financial needs, methods of financing, acquisition opportunities and approaches; he is also concerned with grooming private companies for stock market flotation and advising on private portfolio investment. Mr Thomson's experience includes a period as a stockbrokers' investment manager prior to entering financial journalism, when he became City Editor of the *Sunday Express* and City Editor of the *Sunday Dispatch*; he has been a freelance financial journalist since 1961 and is the author of *The ABC of Investment*.

C Townsend (Profit planning) is Assistant Secretary to the British Sugar Corporation. In his capacity as Budget Accountant he was a member of a small team responsible for the design and implementation of a comprehensive system of budgetary control and its initial operation. His previous experience has been in posts as an internal auditor, a factory accountant and head of an organisation and methods department. He is a Member of the Institute of Cost and Management Accountants, the Institute of Chartered Secretaries and Public Administrators and the British Institute of Management. In addition, he is a member of the Advisory Committee to the Financial Management Division of the Management Centre Europe.

M T Wilson (Control of marketing and distribution) is Managing Director of Marketing Improvements Limited, a leading in-company marketing training, consultancy and staff selection organisation in the United Kingdom. After graduating with honours from Manchester University, Mr Wilson joined Ford Motor Company, eventually taking charge of commercial vehicle marketing in Britain. He joined the staff of the Institute of Marketing in 1962 and became Director of Residential Studies in the Institute's College of Marketing the following year. He formed Marketing Improvements Limited in 1964 to offer a more specific training service to industry. Since then his company has worked for over 200 companies throughout the world. He has personally lectured in 17 countries and has advised and trained well over 1000 sales managers. He is author of *Managing a Sales Force* (Gower Press).

R M S Wilson (Financial reporting systems and responsibilities) his previous experience has included posts as Management Services Adviser (engineering), Head of Product Management (consumer durables) and

Management Accountant (chemicals). In addition he is a former faculty member of the U of BMC and has also lectured on business administration at Bradford TC. Amongst his qualifications are MSc (management) and BCom degrees, plus the diploma in marketing of the Institute of Marketing which he holds with distinction and for which he was awarded the Rothman Prize in 1969. Mr Wilson is a member of ICMA, IM, BIM, MRS, IMRA, and TIMS. Included within his extensive range of publications are *Financial Control: A Systems Approach*, McGraw-Hill, *Management Control of Marketing*, Heineman, *Technological Forecasting* (joint authorship), Penguin and chapters in *Management Information and Control Systems*, (ed. R I Tricker and J A Payton), *Exploration in Marketing Thought*, (ed. by G S C Wills) and *Handbook for Managers*, (ed. by B Folkertsman).

PART ONE
Financial Planning

Chapter 1

The Role of the Finance Director

A J Merrett, Chairman, Xerox Education Group
(Eastern Hemisphere)

The scope and the very fact of publication of the present volume reflects the changing role of the finance director in post-war Britain. The role of the finance director more than any other has been developed and re-structured by the changing conditions of modern business and the development of modern methods of professional management. Following an older tradition and perpetuated by the cost-plus financial conditions of the war time period, the role of the finance director up to the 1950s was primarily narrow and functional and typically confined to statutory accounting, accounting administration and treasurership functions. These are functions which today would only describe—and narrowly at that—the role of the accountant. Essentially, in this traditional role the finance director performed much the same function as the eighteenth century "man of business," that of keeping the books and finding the funds.

This role was, however, appropriate only to the relatively small scale of organisation that could be controlled by personal review and intervention by the managing director using relatively simple statistical and accounting data. In a situation in which even a moderately successful growth rate of, say, seven per cent per annum would involve—quite apart from growth by merger and acquisition—a doubling in size in over ten years, management by personal inspection inevitably proved inadequate in scope, consistency and thoroughness. At the same time that this style of management was proving inadequate to cope with the sheer scale of modern enterprises it was also proving incapable of meeting the increasingly stringent conditions for financial viability as companies emerged from the cash surplus and excess demand conditions of the post-war to the cash stringency and excess capacity conditions of the 1960s and 70s.

The role of the finance director essentially arose from these conditions and the development of systematic—as opposed to personal—management of large companies. In essence, the systematic method of management is the creation of a system of procedures—policy directives, standard-setting, budgets and methods of reporting and action-taking—which is effectively the system which manages the company. The manager himself does not directly manage the company so much as manage the system which manages the company; in the same way that the crane driver manages the crane while it is the crane which actually does the lifting.

To a large extent the modern financial director is the designer and production controller of the management system. Breaking the role down into its component parts, it is seen from figure 1.1 that three of the eight activities (accounting, treasureship and budgeting) relate to specific functions. These in their turn break down into subsidiary functions of which only two—statutory accounting and capital raising—were common in the post-war years and earlier while the crucial activity of budgeting was relatively unknown.

Policy-making

The second major expansion of the role of the finance director is in policy-making, covering as it does credit policy, pricing, budget standards, performance assessment and planning. In credit control and pricing, the financial director counter-balances the entirely natural weight of the production and sales directors who are primarily concerned with output. In the areas of budget standards and performance assess-

4

ment the finance director performs the crucial role of advising the chief executive on the standards of financial performance that can be achieved and evaluates and reviews the subsequent analyses of the extent to which these standards were or were not realised.

FUNCTIONS	Accounting:	Statutory accounts and accounting procedures and credit control
	Treasurership:	Cash control, cash forecasting and capital raising
	Budgeting:	Cost and revenue budgets
POLICY-	Credit:	Customer and supplier credit policy
MARING	Pricing:	Pricing standards
	Budget Standards:	Recommended levels of costs and revenue performance
	Performance Assessment:	Review and analysis of actual performance against budget
	Investment Appraisal:	Pre- and post-sanction appraisal and recommendation on investment
	Planning?	

Figure 1:1   The role of the finance director

Essentially, in all these policy-making functions the finance director comes to represent the company's overall financial interest—and indeed the interests of the shareholders. In this, the position of the finance director has been very much strengthened by the increasing stress on maximising profit (long-term growth in earnings per share) as the company's principal objective. Here again, the competitive conditions of the post-war world (and the intensification of takeovers which is as much a symptom as the separate cause) have resulted in the traditional objective of simply keeping the company solvent converging with the objective of profit maximisation in that, under modern conditions of competition, it is only by the latter that is possible to obtain the former.

Planning

Finally in the area of policy-making there is the role of the finance director in planning. In this area his role is as much a matter of dispute as the function of planning itself. Insofar as planning is simply an extension into the longer term of the budgeting and related processes by which the company controls its shorter-term destiny, it might be expected

5

that the finance director would play a corresponding role in the process of planning.

It is certainly the case that in most companies in which the planning function is not separately represented at board level it most commonly falls within the scope of the finance director. It is in this as yet unresolved aspect of the financial director's role that it is possible to see its ultimate limitation. The sheer extent of his existing functions and the extent to which they must inevitably focus on the shorter term makes the addition of any other major responsibility impractical.

In this, as in the view that the chief executive should also be the company's long-term planner, the critical difficulty of the long-term planning function itself is posed: namely, that the managers most obviously suited to the task both from the standpoint of authority and familiarity with the short-term situation could not undertake this longer-term responsibility without major loss of effectiveness in their present roles. If this inherent weakness in the role of planning director is rectified, it is from this function that the finance director's present standing of *primus inter pares* among fellow directors below chief executive level is likely to be challenged.

Chapter 2

Profit Planning

C Townsend,
Budget Accountant, British Sugar Corporation Limited

There is nothing particularly new in the concept of planning, and indeed individuals and all corporate bodies plan to some extent as part of their normal routines. Differences lie in the degree to which this planning operation becomes a conscious part of the management of affairs and how far into the future it is projected.

Planning means the taking of decisions now which will affect the future. This chapter is concerned particularly with the long-term view, since budgetary control, which is essentially the expression of a short-term segment of the long-term plan, is dealt with in chapter 7. The purpose of this chapter is to indicate the value and importance of planning in a systematic manner and, in particular, to emphasise the primary role which profitability must play in the planning operation.

2:1 Corporate objectives and profit planning

It is not so long ago that the vast majority of British companies based their planning operations on a one-year budgeting system, supplemented by special studies such as that of the purchase of another

7

company or the problems involved in possible entry into Europe. The development and acceptance of sophisticated methods of capital project appraisal, necessitating probing well into the future, indeed over the whole expected life of a prospective asset, brought home the need for forward planning of the whole business and the realisation that long- and short-term planning should be an integral part of the management of the organisation.

Planning presupposes objectives and to be of any real use these objectives should be quite specific as to the financial performance which is aimed at; there should be an overriding statement of the sort of company or organisation that is envisaged—a basic philosophy. For example, the statement of corporate objectives of Hewlett Packard firstly states its philosophy to be:

> To recognise that profit is the best single measure of our contribution to society and the ultimate source of corporate strength. We should attempt to achieve the maximum possible profit consistent with our other objectives

Peter Drucker, in his *Practice of Management* lists eight areas in which performance objectives have to be set. They are: market standing, innovation, productivity, physical and financial resources, profitability, manager performance and development, worker performance and attitude, and public responsibility. Although profitability is put as just one of a number of key aims, the productivity of all must have an effect on profit and they are all reflected in the profitability performance, which must therefore be the ultimate measure of success in competitive business.

In arriving at the overall profitability objective a number of basic questions need to be answered about the company, for example:

1 What kind of business is it really in? Is it the ice-cream business, the food business or the leisure business?
2 What should the company be selling? Should it be selling ice-cream or a range of food?
3 Where are the company's markets and what market share does it want?
4 What growth rate is required? This should include consideration of profit, sales volume, cash flow, assets and the value of the equity of the business

2:2   Definition of profit planning

Long-range profit planning is a systematic and formalised process for purposefully directing and controlling future operations toward desired objectives for periods extending beyond one year.

2:2:1   A systematic and formalised process

Effective profit planning cannot be carried out in a casual manner and should emerge from a rigorously disciplined examination of all the aspects of the business and of alternative strategies which may present themselves. Once a plan has been hammered out it becomes the framework for piloting the affairs of the organisation so that they move towards *desired objectives*. Up to some point in time, which will depend upon the nature of the business, plans may be modified, but beyond this point decisions have to be implemented in such a manner that they can only be revoked at a cost; it is at this stage that plans have crystallised into a budget against which actual results will be compared.

A systematic approach will involve all aspects of the business resulting in an integrated plan in which areas such as selling, production and finance are balanced to produce the best level of profit having regard to the constraints within which the company is expected to have to work. In order to produce such plans with adequate consideration and in due time, strong central responsibility is needed. A systematic sequence of collection of information, communication, analysis of the situation and the synthesising of a viable and acceptable plan becomes an essential part of the operation; otherwise the plan will become merely an interesting exercise seen to have no real relevance to the company. A sense of urgency and teamwork will only be achieved with rigorous control and a rigorous timetable.

2:3   The need for long-range planning

The need for long-range profit planning arises basically from the change in business conditions which have taken place in recent years. The rate of change is accelerating and at the same time some aspects of business have become less flexible, both of which factors have increased the need for forward planning. The purpose of planning is for a business to set a

9

course which will secure the benefit of profitable opportunities and at the same time to minimise the less favourable aspects of change which intrude on its operations.

The following particular factors are at work, the full advantage of which can be taken only by looking ahead.

2:3:1   Rapid technical change

With automated machines and computer techniques the mechanisa-sation of factory and office processes proceeds apace; new processes and products are becoming more rapidly developed, with the result that many products are obsolescent when they first appear on the market—the product life cycle is contracting and today's products have to be backed up with new developments ready to take their place when they go into decline, or even before.

2:3:2   Massive capital outlays

Production is becoming more capital-intensive, which means that investment in new plant must continue to rise if profitability is to be maintained. This substantial cash outflow has significant effects on cost structure which will continue to be felt for some years. Many costs which in the past may have been variable by means of short-term decisions that could immediately affected them, now tend to become fixed and can only be significantly affected in the longer term. A further transformation from variable to fixed cost is the move away from "blue collar" to "white collar" work and with it the movement of more employees into salary grades away from wage earning.

2:3:3   Intensified competition

The symptoms of intensified competition are often reduced profit margins and the appearance of excess capacity. This is brought about in no small measure by integration and diversification, whereby the large corporations bring to bear higher marketing and selling skills.

2:3:4   The increasing complexity of business organisations

Many large companies have widely-spread manufacturing units and offices which are operated on a policy of decentralised responsibility.

In a diversified organisation a number of different and unrelated products may be involved. In order to achieve the best corporate results there must be a co-ordinated plan or framework within which each division can work.

Long-range profit planning is concerned with the strategic moves needed to bring the company where it should be in a defined period of time, probably five or ten years. Only by taking a long-range view can provision for the long-term future of the business be made; concentration on current situations, particularly in periods of expanding sales and profits, results in complacency and it is precisely in such periods that management tends to write down the potential benefits to be gained from looking forward. Adverse conditions make planning even more imperative because in this case planning may be a question of survival so that profits can be made at some later date. Looking into the distant future involves some degree of uncertainty: profit planning aims to identify the future conditions and business environment in which the organisation will be working, and allow the preparation and evaluation of alternative courses of action. From this process can emerge a rational course of action which can be followed in the knowledge that it has evolved from a realistic assessment of the future trend of events, thereby minimising the uncertainty.

2:4 Benefits of profit planning

While planning in the sense that has been discussed has the specific purpose of planning for profitability, other benefits of a less specific nature will emerge when a formalised approach is used, as much from the actual process of planning as from implementation and enforcement of the plan.

Preparation of a profit plan imposes a discipline on all levels of management both as to the quality of the work which goes into the plan and as to keeping to a rigid time-table so that the plan can be refined and approved in good time for implementation. It necessitates a high degree of co-ordination and teamwork, which in turn demand good communication within the business—profit planning will put the limelight on those areas which are deficient in these respects.

If properly organised and fully supported from the top, profit planning should have the following beneficial effects:

2:4:1   Encouragement of an atmosphere of profit and cost consciousness

Participation in development of the plan generates profit conscious-
ness and provides an encouragement and incentive to look for profit-
making or cost-saving opportunities. Further, when performance is
subject to measurement against a plan, care in day-to-day operations
will be exercised.

2:4:2   Management development

Decentralisation of responsibility can and should be a feature of
profit planning. As a result, each manager must look critically at his
own area of responsibility, which should help in developing his managerial talents.

2:4:3   Every facet of the business must be critically examined

Such a critical appraisal is bound to give rise to enquiry as to the cost
and even the necessity of the various functions of the business and the
procedures involved.

2:5   The importance of profit

Modern business has various responsibilities, all of which can only be
met in a profit situation since, certainly over the longer term, a loss-
making business will go out of existence. Responsibilities exist to:

1 *Shareholders*, who expect a return on their share of the equity of the
   business in line with other investment possibilities and commen-
   surate with the risk involved, and a growth in the value of their
   shareholding
2 *Employees*, whose security may depend upon the continued existence
   of the company and whose level of earnings may also depend upon
   its prosperity
3 *The community*. It is becoming increasingly recognised that industry
   and commerce have a responsibility to the community in which they
   operate. This can extend to environmental aspects such as the pre-

vention of pollution and the provision and support of local amenities
4 *Government*, by making a contribution to national prosperity. Taxes
   on profits provide a major source of revenue and go towards the
   various social services, defence and national investments such as
   improved communications

These responsibilities should be reflected in the objects of the organisation but they can only be sought through the medium of profit, that is,
the conversion of the resources available into goods and services on
which a return is made by selling them to customers; the efficiency with
which these resources are utilised and the effectiveness of the selling
operation will determine the profit (excess of income over costs).

Profit is, in effect, a common denominator which measures how well
a business performs, but the question arises as to what is to be regarded
as an adequate profit. While there may not be a complete answer, it can
be stated that a well organised profit planning programme will help
towards maintaining a level of profit which will ensure the continuation of the business and the fulfilment of the responsibilities referred to
earlier. Certainly, profit growth coupled with a high level of profit and
the ability to maintain reasonable profits during a period of recession
will help towards:

1 Ensuring that shareholders receive an adequate dividend
2 Preserving the asset worth of the business during an inflationary
   period by the ability to set aside out of profits a sufficient reserve to
   provide for replacement of assets at current prices
3 Generating out of profits a sufficient cash flow to provide capital for
   expansion
4 Providing funds for the search for, and development of, new and
   improved products to replace existing products before they go into
   decline

2:5:1 How much profit?

To businesses which are at this point in time fighting to remain intact,
this question may seem somewhat academic. However, the fact remains
that a business cannot survive for any length of time in a non-profit-
making situation and planning must be aimed at moving the business
into a position where it can both be profitable and remain so. This

raises the question, referred to earlier, of what an adequate profit is, and the further question of how it should be expressed so that a judgement may be formed as to its adequacy. Probably the most helpful approach to this problem is the use of ratios to show the relationship between vital financial factors of the business; such ratios assist in thinking of profitability, as a measure of the use of resources, rather than of absolute profit, which may in certain circumstances be dangerously misleading.

Since this chapter is concerned with profit planning, it deals only with those ratios which are of direct relevance, although it must be remembered that other derived ratios may be of considerable value for more detailed control.

The main, or primary, ratio to be considered is:

$$\frac{Profit}{Capital\ employed}$$

This ratio shows the rate of return on the total capital employed in the business and is comprised of two other ratios:

$$\frac{Profit}{Sales} \quad \text{and} \quad \frac{Sales}{Capital\ employed}$$
$$\text{(profit margin)} \qquad \text{(capital turnover)}$$

It will be seen from the above that an unchanged return on capital employed could result from a lower profit margin and higher rate of capital turnover; similarly a constant profit-to-sales ratio with an increased turnover of the same capital employed would result in a higher rate of return. Thus, the interacting of these two factors is one of the keys to profitability.

These ratios by themselves have some value and any profit plan must crystallise itself into a plan for a given rate of return. Their main use, however, lies as a means of both internal and external comparison.

1   *Intra-company comparisons.* These can be of value in matching the results of one unit against another within the organisation to determine relative profitability. In making such comparisons, it is important to ensure that the figures used are prepared on a consistent basis, otherwise the results may be misleading rather than helpful;

14

the benefits of uniform accounting systems and procedures will be apparent here. Further, it is important to remember that although one part of the organisation may show a lower rate of return, it may nevertheless be making a substantial contribution to the corporate profits.

2 *Inter-company comparisons.* Comparisons with other companies in the same line of business will enable management to see how the company stands up against its competitors. Obviously, the task of obtaining such information about one's rivals is not easy. Published accounts may be used but inevitably they suffer from some limitation as to the amount of information disclosed and the fact that some window-dressing may have taken place. Many trade associations have available for their members statistical information and ratios which can be extremely useful. Another most useful source of information is the Centre for Inter-firm Comparisons run by the British Institute of Management, which has made special studies of the problems involved.

Return on capital employed can be examined over a period of years in order to establish any trend which may be showing itself. If this exercise is carried out the effect of inflation must be considered; this can be taken into account by the application of an appropriate price index such as the Wholesale Price Index published in the *Monthly Digest of Statistics.*

2:6   A profit planning programme

It is emphasised at this point that planning is a comprehensive process in which all parts of a business should be involved and, as such, it must be the direct responsibility of the chief executive of the organisation. There must also be active participation by all line management. Profit planning is part of the over-all planning process and is an area in which the finance function has a major role to play.

As indicated earlier, however the plan is prepared, it must result in a projected profitability. There are two extreme ways in which the planning operation can be approached, both of which would seem to be too dogmatic, and probably the most successful way to proceed lies somewhere in between—a synthesis of both approaches:

15

1   The *active* approach gives precedence to the profitability objective over other aspects of the plan, which then have to be moulded to meet that objective
2   The *passive* approach whereby the profit objective is subordinated to other aspects of the plan in the absence of a clearly defined long-term profit goal

Clearly, the plan must be feasible as a whole; in considering a medium-to-long-term plan (in some highly fashion-oriented business two years may be long-term) most factors which in the short-term may be fixed as, for example, production capacity, do in fact become flexible and may, therefore, be receptive to modification; one can, therefore, consider examination of the profit objective as a starting point.

Mention has been made of profitability measurement by use of the ratio profit/capital employed (or return on investment) and other derived ratios. While these are useful, particularly as means of comparison or for identifying trends, they are not entirely satisfactory as a basis for setting the overall profit objective because they do not take into account the attitude of the equity shareholders, who are entitled to have their risk compensated. Shareholders can have their expectations satisfied in two ways:

1   By an appreciation in the value of their holdings on the stock market
2   By a steadily improving flow of dividends

Some indication of the rate of return which shareholders may desire over the period of the plan can be obtained by consideration of the following factors:

1   Alternative investment opportunities, that is what they could earn elsewhere from comparable equity investments
2   What the shareholders have received over the past few years
3   The effect of taxation, especially capital gains tax which, in recent years, has resulted in shareholders receiving an increasing part of their return in the form of capital growth instead of dividends

In establishing the profit objective, regard must be had to the effect of inflation, which seems now to be a part of our normal economic experience.

Consideration should also be given to the capital gearing of the business, that is, the proportion of long-term borrowing to equity capital. Gearing up will result in an increased return to the equity shareholders provided that the return on the funds borrowed will remain "significantly higher than" the cost of financing those funds. The purpose of this is to achieve a sufficient flow of net profits to allow the equity shareholders to receive a flow of earnings in the form of dividend and capital growth that will give the sort of return which has been estimated as outlined above. It is then possible, by adding back any preferential charges such as preference dividends, to arrive at a profit net of tax, which can be grossed up for estimated taxation and interest charges to determine the desirable profit before interest and taxation.

Estimation of a profitability objective on the above lines provides a guideline against which the whole profit, can be worked out. It becomes necessary to relate these earnings to the business by calculating the return required on retained earnings and new borrowings or share capital to achieve them; this then becomes the yardstick against which the capital expenditure programme of the business must be planned.

2:7 Basic considerations for the plan

Before any detailed planning can be embarked upon, environmental factors will have to be established, since decisions will be taken which involve the sinking of new capital, the effect of which, once done, cannot be undone.

2:7:1 Economic forecast

The prime consideration is the market having answered the questions posed earlier as to what business the company is really in and what share of the market it wishes to attain. General economic conditions are clearly of vital importance to investment decisions, as may be other factors perhaps having a semi-political flavour; an obvious example is the entry of the UK into the Common Market and the possibility of a larger "home" market with a common external tariff against countries outside the European Economic Community. The rate of economic growth must also be relevant. Larger companies may have their own economic departments to carry out any studies in this field, but intelligent use of material in government publications and from other sources provide a useful source of information.

2:7:2   Market forecast and analysis

A picture of the whole market for the products of a business is essential to the planning operation and information on such matters as the following is needed:

1 Who is the customer for the company's products?
2 How does the customer buy these products?
3 What changes are taking place as regards outlets?
4 How large can the market be expected to be over the planning period?
5 What changes in the structure of the market can be anticipated as a result of changes in fashion or competition?
6 What "substitute" products may be on the horizon which might usurp the company's market?
7 What consumer needs in the company's market segment are not at present being satisfied?

2:7:3   Company sales plan

Having regard to the market forecast:

1 What share of the market do we wish to take?
2 How are these sales split up by geographical area, type of customer, etc.? What new or modernised products do we need?

2:7:4   Manpower plan

For the survival of the business, plans must be made to ensure that the multiplicity of skills necessary for its operation, from the shop-floor up to top management, will continue to be available. Such aspects as the following need to be considered:

1 Training. How to develop the potential of employees, relationships with training boards and obtaining the maximum benefit from training levies

2 Recruiting. What the needs will be to cover turnover wastage and new facilities and how recruitment will be effected
3 Industrial relations. Ensuring that good lines of communication are maintained in a growing business

2:7:5 Facilities plan

Thought must be given to the location of manufacturing facilities in relation to markets and means of communication, the location of executive and selling functions, welfare facilities, and the reorganisation of existing facilities (for example, plant layouts) with a minimum of capital expenditure; these are matters lying outside the direct scope of this chapter, but they are crucial to the success of the total planning operation.

2:7:6 Divisional plan

The profitability objective having been established, it is necessary in a large business to relate it to the component parts of the organisation and to set profit objectives for these parts in terms of return on capital employed or some other appropriate yardstick. Each division or section of the business can then prepare proposals in terms of product development, capital investment and resource planning designed to achieve the corporate objective. At this stage line management becomes closely involved in the planning process and by working out proposals which are realistic and attainable it will generate a sense of purpose and responsibility which will motivate towards achievement of the objectives when the plan has been approved for action.

Looking at this from a central point of view, conflicting claims on the resources of the business will become apparent. The divisional plans may then be modified or referred back, projects being judged according to their potential; it could be that, even after review, it becomes clear that, in the short term at least, the designed profit objective is not attainable and corporate plans have to be modified accordingly. Full consultation with divisional management will help to create an atmosphere in which the final corporate profit can be strived for.

2:8   The financial plan

The importance of the involvement of all facets of the organisation in the process of planning has been stressed. It remains to consider the financial planning section of the programme and the role which the finance function has to play.

The financial plan has three major sectors:

1   The capital structure plan
2   The capital expenditure plan
3   The cash flow plan

2:8:1   Capital structure

Earlier reference has been made to the question of the gearing of capital, that is, the proportion of long-term borrowing and fixed-interest finance, such as preference-share capital, to equity capital. A high gearing means that a large proportion of earnings would be earmarked for payment of such interest and dividends; in prosperous years the equity shareholders would show substantial earnings, but in the more lean years they might find an accumulation of preference dividends which would be a prior charge on future earnings.

One of the effects of corporation tax is to encourage the raising of capital by means of debenture issues, the interest on which becomes a charge against profits for tax purposes. If capital investment is to be met by borrowing, timing will be very important as will the choice between long- and short-term borrowing.

2:8:2   Capital investment

For earnings growth, a business must be able to recognise investment opportunities and reap the benefit from them. It therefore follows that conflicting projects emanating from divisional proposals should be properly assessed and ranked. This matter is dealt with in more detail in the next chapter.

2:8:3   Cash flow plan

The flow of cash through a business is its life blood. Simply stated, cash flow is the difference between cash receipts and cash payments and the aim of cash flow planning is to ensure that sufficient cash is available to pay the debts of the business as they arise. It may involve short-term borrowing to meet a temporary cash shortage, as for example, in a seasonal industry. Since the over-all plan may involve large capital expenditure projects timed to produce a cash inflow at a certain point in time, any delay in the completion of the project, or an unexpected additional cost, can result in a cash flow crisis (profitable businesses have failed through lack of appreciation of the importance of the cash position); the plan must therefore allow for this contingency and forward plans must be made accordingly, at the same time endeavouring to ensure that excessive cash does not remain idle in the company.

2:8:4   The financial picture

The information which has been brought together in the various studies made along the foregoing lines will be presented ultimately in the form of financial figures, including the following statements projected for the period of the profit plan:

1   The estimated profit and loss position
2   The capital expenditure plan showing phasing of expenditure and claimed savings
3   The estimated balance sheet
4   A statement showing sources and uses of funds over the planning period

These statements will be supported by any statistical data relevant to the plan which will assist in its interpretation.

2:8:5   Operation of the plan

Once the plan has the approval of the board of directors, it then becomes a question of implementation and control. A reporting "pyramid" will need to be introduced, giving control information in considerable detail at divisional level with summaries at the higher levels of management. Reports to departmental and divisional management will be more frequent and will depend on the time required for action; the form of these reports will depend very much on the type of industry and organisation involved but the important point is that they should be designed to highlight areas which appear to be drifting away from the plan and which therefore demand action. Summarised reports will be prepared by operating units in a multi-divisional business and these in turn will be summarised to produce a corporate progress report; this will probably be prepared four-weekly but certain key information may be reported more frequently to maintain a tight control as, for example, changes in cash resources where top management can make optimum short-term use of the resources available.

Simple examples of formats for summarised reports are shown in figures 2:1 and 2:2.

	THIS MONTH			YEAR TO DATE			PREVIOUS YEAR TO SAME DATE
	Actual	variance from plan		Actual	variance from plan		Actual
	£000	£000	%	£000	£000	%	£000
Turnover							
Contribution							
Less fixed expenses							
Operating margin							
Other income and expense							
Net profit before tax							
Average net capital employed							
Profit per cent net capital employed							
Profit per cent sales							
Sales per cent capital employed							

Figure 2:1   Example of a format for a divisional operating report

2:8:6   Revision of the plan

The operational reporting system will be providing a feedback of information on actual performance and action will be taken where

	1970	1971	1972	1973	1974	1975
The market						
Product group A:						
Estimated total market						
Planned market share						
Product group B:						
Estimated total market						
Planned market share						
(all product groups)						

Performance data
Net turnover
Net pre-tax profit
Average net capital employed
Return on average net capital
  employed

Financial Control Data
(1) *Profit*
    Net profit before tax and
      interest
    Interest
    Net profit before tax
    Taxation
    NET PROFIT

(2) *Capital investment*
    New facilities
    Alterations
    Research and development
    Renewals and replacements
    TOTAL CAPITAL
    EXPENDITURE

(3) *Funds flow*
    Sources
    Funds generated by opera-
        tions:
      Profit
      Depreciation
      Other receipts
    TOTAL SOURCES OF
    FUNDS   (A)

    Uses
    Capital expenditure
    Investments
    Working capital
      Debtors
      Creditors
      Inventories
    TOTAL USES OF FUNDS   (B)

Surplus or shortfall (A – B)

Finance by:
  New money
  Loans
  Bank balances

Figure 2:2   Example of a format for a profit plan highlight summary possible and appropriate to bring this performance back in line with the profit plan where departures occur. For various reasons, however, the original plan may have ceased to be realistic and comparison between actual results and the plan may be meaningless. In these circumstances the plan should be revised and it should in any case be reviewed at, say, twelve-monthly intervals, "rolling" the plan for a further year; it is on the whole inadvisable to revise the plan too frequently and unless there has been some fundamental change in the premises on which the plan was based or there has been a new strategy, revision should be avoided. Revision should be systematic, involving all levels of management again, and it should follow the same general pattern as in the preparation of the original profit plan. As time progresses an accumulation of historical data collected and analysed in the form required will become available, thus making the whole operation more straightforward and less time-consuming, but the danger of allowing the operation merely to become a matter of routine must be avoided.

Revision may become necessary, as a result of, amongst other things:

1 Too optimistic a view having been taken of the performance potential from existing facilities
2 A change in the economic environment
3 A changed strategy resulting, perhaps, from a new product completing development earlier than anticipated in the original plan
4 A change in the market forcast

2:9 Limitations of profit planning

The purpose of this chapter has been to show how the development of a profit plan can be of benefit to a business. Management must not, however, fall into the error of thinking that it will provide a panacea for all the ills of the company and it is as well therefore to consider some of the possible limitations of profit planning.

2:9:1 Profit planning will not succeed in its purpose without sound business judgement and management to back it up.

The plan is the result of consideration of various alternative proposals based at some stage on management decisions. The viability of the plan will depend in no small measure on the soundness of these decisions.

2:9:2   Profit planning is not a guarantee of success

While the plan may be a blueprint whereby certain objectives may be achieved, actual performance may fall short of the standards which have been set and basic factors outside the control of the business, on which the plan was built, may change. Flexibility of response to such changes will help to mitigate the effect of these factors on the business, and the existence of alternative plans which can be brought into operation at short notice can also be advantageous.

2:9:3   The danger of over-planning

While a considerable amount of detail and consultation is always necessary to produce a viable plan, if too much attention and time is paid to detail and "tossing it around" it may never be available in time to be brought into operation.

Over-planning may also have the opposite effect to that intended and it may destroy initiative, particularly if dictated too strongly from the centre.

2:10   The accountant's role in profit planning

It will be clear that financial management has a key role to play in the planning process. Objectives have to be stated in financial terms, background historical financial data has to be provided, alternative strategies have to be evaluated and proposed courses of action have to be assessed for financial feasibility. An integrated company-wide master plan has to be prepared by the co-ordination of detailed plans. Operational controls have to be established and administered to measure actual performance against the planned objectives, and assistance must be provided to the other managerial functions in the review and revision of plans. In other words, while profit planning must be the responsibility of the chief executive of the business, co-ordination and servicing of the planning process may well fall fairly and squarely on the accountant.

2:11   The link between profit planning and
and budgetary control

The relationship between these two processes is a very close one and the two terms are sometimes used synonymously. A budget is, in fact, best regarded as a short-term segment of the profit plan against which active performance will be measured by a system of budgetary control. Budgetary control covers the whole system of operational reporting but is more specifically associated with the more detailed departmental operations and the explanation of variances. This subject is dealt with more fully in a later chapter of the book.

Budgetary control is an essential part of the feedback of information necessary for the modification of future plans on a rational basis.

2:12   Conclusion

To sum up, profit planning entails:

1   Looking into the future
2   A flexible attitude and a capacity to adapt to changes which will take place
3   A quick reaction to change and the ability to sense when the symptoms of change are present
4   The involvement of all levels of management, with new thought being devoted to the merits of decentralised control and responsibility

Chapter 3

Capital Investment Planning

Tessa V Ryder Runton, formerly Senior Financial
Analyst, Group Planning, Rio Tinto-Zinc Corporation

Some discussions of capital investment planning seem to imply that on any one date a board of decision-takers receives a list of new and evaluated opportunities. The contribution of the planner is thought to be in ranking this list like a row of schoolboys in size order. In practice this type of situation, which suggests the development of virgin territory, is rare, and the planner and the analyst are called upon to advise on the profitability of changes in and additions to the continuous processes of the organisation. Opportunities arise in irregular sets. Transactions do not have to involve the use of new capital in a new project to merit analysis, the spending of any funds on any asset with a life and a value is a capital investment, as is the signing of a long-term contract for goods, services or for a lease or hire-purchase, etc. The possibilities to be examined include plans to replace or expand current operations, suggestions for cost savings and also disinvestment, whether by sale or close-down or merger. Usually, the only real ranking that can be done is between doing nothing or deciding between several mutually exclusive ways of doing the same thing (for example, deciding the timing of the start and the duration of an operation, building a big or a small plant, using labour or automation, leasing or buying premises or choosing a site). The analysis of these types of situation is called financial *optimisation* (page 45).

Every transaction should ideally be analysed so that the optimum financial benefit can be realised. In practice of course, innumerable operations are so small that formal assessment would be a waste of resources. Some companies have gone so far as to prepare a corporate model computer program of the whole organisation, enabling their analysts to perform some theoretical experiments on possible future development plans. Various projects are "fed in" like ingredients into a soup and the effect of their various quantities and qualities on the flavour is tested.

Financial optimisation penetrates every smallest branch of a lively organisation but the initiative and responsibility necessarily stems from the chief executive. Whatever the aims of the company are, they cannot easily be fulfilled without meeting financial standards. As well as being a catalytic initiative, capital investment planning is the formal thought that precedes the most important financial decision-taking of the chief executive and his close advisers who are concerned with the future of the company. The planning cannot be centred on some remote part—and it is not sensible to authorise corporate planning merely as a kind of status symbol. In a small organisation the chief executive will personally do the capital investment planning, but in a larger company he would employ an assistant or set up a corporate planning department or engage special consultants to help. There are no reasons why the company accountant should or should not be more involved than others. Capital investment planning involves considerations of accounting, economics, knowledge of or access to knowledge of the processes of the business and, above all, good communications with *all* concerned. All are concerned in the substance of the company's future. Modern analysis techniques are available to analyse the data of projected plans. Senior management time can thereby be saved for concentration on those matters which can only be assessed in the light of experience and judgement: matters to do with politics, personnel, future technology, etc. Decisions taken after formal analysis techniques should be reviewed at a specified later date to discover why the actual outcome differed, as it always does, and whether any lessons should be learnt. Without a review discipline, analysis techniques could be manipulated. With a re-appraisal discipline success can perhaps be repeated.

3:1   Overall and specific targets and standards

Unless some thought and some guidance have been given to where the company is and wants to be going, the corporate planner is like a blind-folded man leading the blind. Many companies have set up formal strategic planning procedures and set explicit aims. It is highly desirable for all senior executives to have some idea of what is, and in particular what is not, appropriate to the company's business, whether in such matters as the spread of resources, public and financial reputation or geographical or product diversification.

Most companies would claim to be in business in the interests of their shareholders, whether private or public. Financially these interests are the maximisation of present and future profits. Not many other aims can be indulged in by unprofitable organisations. Should shareholders, corporate members or financiers become dissatisfied with the company's operations they may withdraw their support, leading to such awkward problems as strikes, loss of morale and personnel, shortage of funds, unwelcome lowering of the company's share price if it is publicly quoted or stormy annual general meetings. Any of these can lead to undesirable vulnerability resulting in a takeover, closedown, or governmental interference. The corporate planner must therefore pay attention to the proper sharing of the cake and the maintenance of the desired financial and public image. The shareholders cannot have their cake and eat (or reinvest) it.

The well-organised company sets specific targets and monitors its standards for financial performance. These, which include accounting ratios and so on, are discussed in later chapters. Capital investment planning, which always judges the present opinion of possible future events, makes use of special standards which should be completely understood by those concerned. The major standard, the *cost of capital*, is discussed below, but the corporate planner must be aware of standards specific to the business in question—he should know about the special circumstances which restrain the company's plans. Monopoly or anti-trust or other relevant laws, such as those concerning proportions of labour employed, are examples. It is sometimes desirable to avoid operations with costs which compare badly with those of competitors. The bankers will have views on matters such as the appropriate gearing (leverage) and debt service cover for the type of business in question.

Shareholders may be used to a particular pattern of annual dividend payment. Sometimes it may be necessary to make advance plans to cope with a future event, such as the company seeking a public quotation, or the inevitable retirement of the chief motive force whether it be the founder/chairman or, sometimes, the nature of the environment—for example, a new town will eventually reach its planned size, after which intensive building will slow down.

3:2   Cost of capital

This is the major standard of comparison used in modern financial analysis techniques and is a vital company statistic needing careful calculation. It in no way excludes the consideration of other standards. It is hard to think of any operation, business or way of life that does not involve the bartering of resources. Gold-mines get worked out and it is not beyond man's ingenuity to run through the largest fortune. It is therefore fundamentally true that for survival the return on one's resources of capital must equal the cost of that capital. For growth the return must exceed the cost. Those who want to ensure or influence their security need to estimate the cost of their capital by some method other than by letting their return on capital diminish until they go bankrupt. Subsidies – even of losses – are only another way of stating that zero or negative returns are acceptable in particular cases. Of course, subsidies may lead to costs in another form.

The realities of commercial life have caused the cost of capital to be a very complex subject. Any comparisons must be made between like numbers. A percentage profit before tax made on a hotel in Bermuda bears no relationship to the same figure made after tax on a farm in Scotland. A profit expressed as a percentage of capital employed should not be compared with a discounted cash flow yield. Many measures of company performance can be devised and are invaluable particularly to those who work them out, as distinct from people who, very often, are not completely familiar with the definitions involved. The comparison of discounted cash flow (DCF) yields with a carefully estimated cost of capital perhaps leads to fewer pitfalls. In particular, the time-value of money is taken into account. All the financial effects are assessed and tax and inflation are treated similarly in the calculation of the cash flow and the estimation of the cost of capital. Company cash flows are normally prepared net of corporation tax but before personal taxes due on distributions. The financial consequences of loans are built in. Because of inflation it is wise to make sure that the cash flow is either in real terms or in money terms (or approximately so), but the effects of inflation must be thought through. (See page 38.) Given such a cash flow technique the cost of capital should be estimated using similar principles.

3:2:1   The cut-off point

Most companies use capital from many sources—equity, retained earnings, grants, overdrafts and short- and long-term loans. A company operating normally has an established gearing, or leverage, between debt and equity. Since debt is cheaper than equity to service (under the present UK tax system), the company tries to raise as much outside money as possible, while lenders are concerned to keep the gearing at an acceptable level. A recognisable balance is found and it is worth noting that it is the company's gearing—not gearing caused by the special circumstances of a particular project—that is of interest here. Once the costs of all the separate sources of capital have been identified the company will normally use the cheaper money first. The cut-off point of available capital is ultimately reached when no more equity can be raised. However, as more equity is invested further loans can be raised to keep the gearing balance. It is fortunately sufficient for this purpose to assume, unrealistically, that this is a smooth process. The cost of the ultimate capital available (the capital cut-off point) is then the weighted average of the costs of new equity and long-term loans in the gearing proportions. This is known as the *marginal cost of capital*.

It can be argued that it is too conservative to use this extreme, as it were, cut-off point. It is, however, dangerous to use, for example, the weighted average of costs of funds in the proportions in which they are at any time being used because this can change. (The *average cost of capital*.) Capital investment analysis is aimed at discovering the financial truth about the plan being analysed. If it does not meet the survival standard of the organisation, that fact should be clearly stated before the discussion as to its desirability begins. In practice there are many apparently unprofitable processes that go on in any business because, in fact, they enhance the profitable processes which, of course, should outnumber them. Obvious examples are the provision of catering and other services for the work force, advertising, research and so on. It used to be thought that DCF analysis of itself led to categorial "yes" or "no" judgements on any plan, whereas in fact all it does is to marshal the financial facts for the guidance of the decision-takers. In addition, it can point to the less unprofitable alternative of two ways of tackling a loss-making but necessary job.

3:2:2   Cost of captal: risk

Adding some number to the cost of capital standard to make due allowance for risk is too easy a method. Every case will be different and should be examined to see what effect undesirable occurrences would actually have. There is a lot of difference in saying that project X, which appears to have a DCF yield of 15 per cent compared with the 10 per cent cost of capital is so risky that it is unacceptable unless it can be planned to have a 20 per cent yield, rather than "we look for 20 per cent yield projects because of risk."

3:2:3   Calculation of the cost of capital

The cost of equity capital is equal to the minimum return which the shareholder will accept. Such return is the sum of his net of tax dividend and his net of capital gains tax capital growth, whether he realises this now or later. Most multi-shareholder companies are obliged to make some assumptions when trying to put a figure on the cost of equity capital. One assumption, which is of fairly wide application, is that the equity is provided by an average shareholder paying standard-rate taxes, who holds the share in an average portfolio and on average expects to receive a return in real terms, net of tax and inflation, which is no less than the average such return earned by his portfolio over the past years. Such a return may be 7 or 8 per cent. Much has been written on this subject.[1] Although each company should assess this problem in the light of its own circumstances, it has proved desirable to cut some corners in order to arrive at a solution. The final figure used is then grossed up to what must be earned in the cash flow in order to service the required return and the taxes payable thereon. For example, if the return required is seven per cent net of inflation and of an effective rate of all personal taxes of 35 per cent, then the part of the cash flow which is financed by equity must earn approximately 11 per cent.

The long-term debt of which the cost is required can be thought of as an "average debenture" and it might bear a coupon of about 7 per cent. £7 of interest is therefore paid annually on each £100 of loan. If, however, the equity shareholders were instantaneously to take over the loan, the consequent change in the cash flow for that year would not be £7 but £7 less corporation tax. Ignoring complications of allowances, which in fact are used elsewhere, if the tax is 45 per cent, the £7 saved on interest results in an increase in the cash flow of £3.85. Looked at, as it were, from the cash flow point of view, the loan costs about 4 per cent—but this is before allowing for inflation. An assumption needs to be made of the current average annual inflation rate, say 3 per cent. Although inflation in fact diminishes the value of the principal of the loan, thereby making repayment less onerous, it is possible to allow for it as a package with the interest. The real cost of the loan is, in fact, 1 per cent after tax and inflation. The reference books expand this argument but a good average set of assumptions is shown below:

	Real terms	Money terms (assuming 3 per cent annual inflation)
Cost of new equity	11 per cent	14 per cent
Cost of long-term debt	1 per cent	4 per cent

If the debt/equity ratio of the company is 30/70, then the weighted average cost of capital is, in real terms:

$$\frac{11 \times 70}{100} + \frac{1 \times 30}{100} = 8 \text{ per cent}$$

or in money terms, 11 per cent.

It is impractical to quote a company's cost-of-capital standard except in round numbers. It is important to make sure that everyone for whom it is important knows the standard and checks the calculation should there be a drastic change in tax structure or gearing, etc. The minor day-to-day changes in the company's commercial circumstances and actual sources of capital used will seldom make a change in the cost of capital of anything like a percentage point or even a half-point.

3:2:4 Returns on projects for which debt is specially raised

The standard of comparison for the returns on such projects must still be the company's cost of capital calculated using the company's gearing. It is incorrect to re-calculate the standard if the project's gearing is markedly different. This would only be done if this project were so large or were one of a series which effectively changed the nature of the company's business and, therefore, its credit rating in the eyes of its bankers. This could occur, for example, in a diversification from speculative business into real property.

Suppose a project of significant size were to merit a special loan, perhaps from the government concerned. The company might also be able to raise a loan on the project's working capital, but if this should be realisable in the event of an early close-down or other unexpected occurrence, it is not capital at risk. The forecast cash flow will normally be calculated incorporating all the effects of the proposed loans. This is the equity cash flow and the return thereon is the return on the equity capital in the project. If this equity is considered as the company's contribution to the project's funds, the return can be judged against the cost of capital standard. An argument can be made that it should be judged against the cost of equity capital (for example, eleven per cent in real terms as described above), but this can lead to conservatism, confusion and discussions as to whether the government loan "belongs" to the project or not, and so on. It is better to calculate the return on the *capital at risk* to the company and compare that with the marginal cost of capital. If it is clearly possible that there are circumstances in which the company might have to take over an unsecured loan, then it is desirable to calculate the "total cash flow." This can be done in one of two ways: either by recasting the cash flow statement as if the unsecured loans had not existed; or by adding back to the equity cash flow the unsecured loan receipts and repayments plus the net-of-tax loan interest which is saved. If the return on the total cash flow meets the company's standards, the project can demonstrably stand on its own two feet. The capital at risk in an operation can be the equity alone or the equity plus one or more of the available loans, depending on the securities, which might include realisable working capital, mortgaged buildings, saleable machinery, etc.

3:3 Traditional techniques for testing viability

The rather natural question: "when do I get my money back?" has often been answered by the traditional technique of adding up the cumulative forecast profit from the profit-and-loss account year by year until the amount of the original capital investment is reached, thereby giving the years to *payback*. Such a calculation is inconclusive because standards are very varied, definitions of the original capital vary and there is the question of whether the profit used should be before or after tax. In addition, no account is taken of the later profits, if any, and there is no measure of whether anything is, in fact, made on the investment at all. In particular, the method ignores the *time-value of money* as well as the effects of inflation. A better payback calculation is the *discounted payback* (see pages 39 and 54).

Another traditional technique involves the use of *balance sheet ratios* for current and proposed operations. These include the ratios of profit to capital employed, of profit to sales, and many others concerning the stock, current assets and liabilities, working capital, etc. These ratios are useful for regulating smooth operating but are unhelpful in judging profitability because of definition problems and the choice of standards, but mostly because the time-value of money is not included.

One ratio used is the *return on capital* (known as "the accountant's return" or the "book rate of return," etc.). An average profit (before or after tax) is calculated on a number of years of the proposed project and this is expressed as a percentage of the capital employed. The latter is often defined as the initial investment or the average capital employed over the years, thereby allowing for further investment, depreciation, etc. This procedure suffers from the same snags as the techniques mentioned above and, in addition, smooths out the effect of irregular annual profits. Clearly, quick profits are preferable to a slow build up, but advantages or disadvantages are obscured.

3:4 Modern techniques for testing viability

The traditional techniques take no account of the time value of money. Money received today is much more valuable than the same money received after a delay. Present inflationary conditions further increase the difference. This is the principal fact which modern analysis techniques have incorporated to improve on past procedures. The work involved has increased but once an analysis discipline has been set up, decision-takers can expect that the realities of the given data for some plan will be clearly identified. They can then concentrate on the non-financial problems involved, judge whether the data is sufficient to work with and act accordingly.

3:4:1   Net present value method (NPV)

The net present value of a project is the net present value of the cash flow calculated at the company's cost of capital discount rate. A zero NPV shows that the project repays the captal invested plus the minimum acceptable return which is equal to the cost of capital rate earned on the invested capital throughout the project's life. Positive NPVs show that the return is even better. Negative NPVs show that the minimum return is not achieved.

3:4:2   Discounted cash flow yield (DCF)

This is often known as *the internal rate of return* (IRR), *the DCF return, the actuarial return*, etc. DCF and IRR are defined as the true annual rate of return earned on the capital outstanding in the project. This is *not* to say that capital released by the project also earns such a return. Re-investments, whether wise or not, should be kept separate from the analysis of a project on its own merits. The DCF or IRR is judged against the cost of capital standard.

3:4:3   Annual capital charge (ACC)

The method, which is described in the reference books, is useful for constant annual cash flows (or annual cash flows made constant by discounting and "spreading" as an annuity), which are compared with an annual capital charge. Properly applied, this method is useful but involves much more calculation and, therefore, more danger of error.

3:4:4   Net terminal value

This is not commonly used but is quoted as an example of an unhelpful technique that can be invented. Here the net value is calculated by compounding at the company's cost of capital rate to the terminal date of the project. Even if there were some certainty as to this date it seems difficult to judge a value then expressed.

3:4:5   Profitability index

There are some practitioners who, possibly mistakenly, see difficulties in the use of the DCF/IRR. They approve the calculation of the NPV but find the answer, which is of necessity expressed in currency, difficult to use. A figure such as the profitability index is then prepared, being a percentage of the NPV to the capital employed, but this suffers from problems of definition and standards of comparison. An easier way round this problem is the use of NPV and DCF simultaneously, which has the benefit of using the advantages of each method.

3:4:6   Cash flow discipline when using these techniques

The discounted cash flow techniques use as their raw material the *cash flow* resulting from some plan. Profit flow study is necessary for proper annual accounting as required by shareholders, etc., but it is the cash flow that should be studied to identify the return forecast and the finance that is required. The cash flow for a period is the difference between moneys received and moneys paid out. Provisions for depreciation, future tax, etc., are excluded, but any loan receipts or repayments and any capital expenditure are included. The cash flow of a project is a forecast of the total monetary effects computed periodically (annually or monthly, etc.) over the whole life of the project, including scrap values, etc. Such items as tax-savings achieved on other profits of the organisation because of allowances due to the new project, or any other cash effects which would not occur without the new project, for example, the cost of head office extensions or replacing an executive who would be transferred, should be included.

If a project is of infinite or indeterminate life, the cash flow should reflect this. It can be assumed, for example, that from, say, year 20 onwards the cash flow will remain constant in real terms and this can be discounted without trouble. The discount factor for an annuity to infinity is the reciprocal of the discount rate expressed as a decimal so that the 5 per cent factor is 20, the 15 per cent factor is $6\frac{2}{3}$, etc., but the discount factor would have to be adjusted for the date the annuity began. The forecast annuity from year 20 onwards would also be discounted by the nineteen-year discount factor to obtain its present value.

An attempt must then be made to decide whether the cash flow is in real terms or in money terms with respect to inflation and, if necessary, alterations must be made so that the correct cost of capital standard is used (see page 31). Tax-allowance and loan-servicing schedules are always in money terms but sales and costs figures are usually forecast in real terms. It is usual for the marketing and production departments to project schedules showing changes in sales percentages or production costs without allowing for external price changes. Very often if inflation can be judged to have the same effect on both prices and costs it is fair to take current figures and note that the gross profit forecast will be in real terms. In this case it is fair to take *all* the cash figures as real and note that the cash flow is in real terms. This, in fact, will be a conservative assumption because inflation has opposite effects on loan repayments and tax allowances. In cases of high inflation forecasts, or different effects on prices and costs, and for lengthy projects, the above assumption is not possible. In this case some estimate must be made of the inflation pattern over the life of the project, this estimate could differ for use on prices, on costs and on the overall situation which affects loans, allowances and the cost of capital. All figures are then adjusted to be in money terms.

It should go without saying that cash flows are prepared after the effects of company taxes when paid. Sometimes it is necessary to consider any likely future changes in tax structure. In this, as in treating inflation and in all problems of data uncertainties, it is important not to be over meticulous, particularly at the onset. Analysis of the most roughly prepared cash flow will show whether it is worth spending any further time attending to the details. The first question to answer is: "What is the profitability of the given set of data (warts included)?" If the answer looks promising it is then sensible to take the time to examine the given data, prepare a detailed cash flow and look at possible outcomes of the *project* as opposed to one set of data. The analysis should then examine sensitivities, risks and probabilities and the effect of the project on the organisation as a whole.

3:5   Additional techniques

There are two other techniques worth mentioning.

3:5:1   Discounted payback

This is a quick method of calculation but it is not a sufficient test of profitability. Once the NPV has been calculated, it is easy to add up the discounted cash flows cumulatively from the start of the project until the sum becomes positive. The turning point is the discounted payback of the project and is defined as the time when the invested capital has been returned together with the minimum acceptable return earned thereon. Where a project is subject to technical obsolescence, future competition, or political risks such as nationalisation, or possible disastrous events such as earthquakes, etc., the discounted payback gives a measure against which the possible or desired life of the project can be judged. (See also page 54.)

3:5:2   Decision-trees

Much of capital investment planning involves the arranging of a continuous series of actions which may be altered in the light of future events or future actual patterns of marketing, etc. It is possible to set out all likely outcomes in a map known as a decision-tree—it grows as it is extended further into the future. NPVs of each likely chain of events can be prepared and this could help the decision that must presently be taken. Very often decision-tree calculations are of the expected value of the outcome. To calculate expected values the probabilities of likely intermediate events or outcomes are incorporated. Decision-trees have been extensively described.[2] A decision-tree is shown in Figure 3:1.

Faced with the need to decide whether to install a computer the possibilities and likely events might appear as shown. The decision taken would depend, financially, on the relative NPVs or expected values of the three good possibilities. Expected values are weighted by the relevant probability—for example, if there is a sixty per cent chance of an NPV of £100 the expected value is £60.

3:6   DCF and NPV in more detail

3:6:1   The use of the concept of present value

The mathematical definition of the DCF yield is that it is the discount rate which, when used to discount the cash flow, gives a zero net present

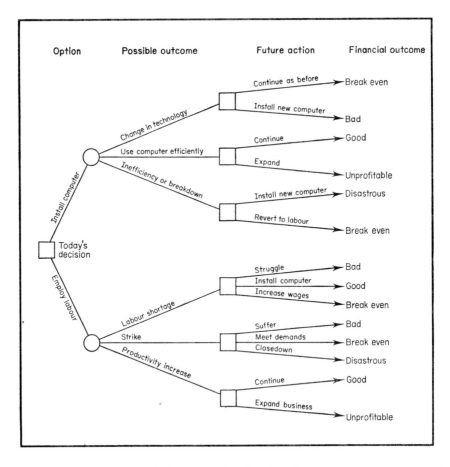

Figure 3:1   Example of a decision-tree

value for the project. The NPV (which is calculated at the cost of capital discount rate) should not be confused with the many net present values which can be calculated using other rates.

The calculation of the NPV consists in setting out the cash flow, discounting it to the present time and adding up the net total. DCF or IRR calculations necessitate trial and error. If, however, the graph shown in Figure 3:2 is borne in mind, the process need not be lengthy.

Most practitioners find it convenient to calculate the NPV first. If this shows, for example by being positive, that it is worth doing more

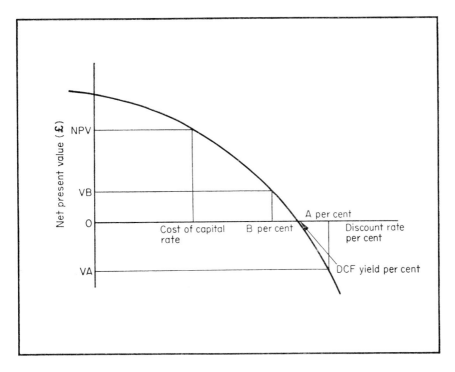

Figure 3:2   The use of trial rates to calculate DCF

sums, a guess must be made of the next trial rate. A positive NPV indicates that the DCF return will be greater than the cost of capital rate: how much greater can sometimes be guessed by the size of the NPV. Trial rate A per cent is used and will give a net present value VA on the graph. Consideration of this result might lead to trial rate B per cent and VB. Having thus both over- and under-estimated the answer, the true DCF can be found by mathematical interpolation, or by drawing a similar graph (provided, that is, that the trial rates are not more than one or two percentage points apart—if they are, the curve that represents the relationship would lead to too inaccurate a result, which should be checked by another trial and interpolation or extrapolation).

The following example shows how this procedure applies. Suppose the cost of capital is 11 per cent and an investment is being considered which costs £1500, lasts four years and has no terminal value:

41

Time in years from today	Cash flow £	Cash flow discounted at:							
		11 per cent		20 per cent		17 per cent		16 per cent	
		Discount factor	value	factor	value	factor	value	factor	value
0	(1500)	1.000	(1500)	1.000	(1500)	1.000	(1500)	1.000	(1500)
1	100	0.901	90	0.833	83	0.855	86	0.862	86
2	1000	0.812	812	0.694	694	0.731	731	0.743	743
3	1000	0.731	731	0.579	579	0.624	624	0.641	641
4	100	0.659	66	0.482	48	0.534	53	0.552	55
Net present values			199 this is the NPV		(96)		(6)		25

By interpolation between the net present values calculated at 16 per cent and 17 per cent the DCF yield is calculated to be

$$16 + \frac{25}{31} = 16.8 \text{ per cent}$$

The same result is obtained extrapolating from the 17 per cent and 20 per cent figures:

$$\text{DCF} = 17 - \frac{3 \times 6}{90} = 16.8 \text{ per cent}$$

Interpolation between the 11 per cent and 20 per cent figures, however, gives the answer

$$11 + \frac{9 \times 199}{295} = 17.1 \text{ per cent}$$

which may be too inaccurate, although in this case the return would probably be quoted as 17 per cent. These figures could also be found graphically.

Discount tables are available for all periods—weeks, quarters, years, etc.—and to various numbers of places of decimals. It is not normally helpful to calculate the cash flow in too small periods or to discount it using more than four-figure tables. It is more important to notice that the tables normally refer to points of time and the cash flows represent a total for a period. A fitting assumption is needed. It is easy if the majority of receipts and payments occur at the beginning or at the end of the periods. For flows which are continuous and irregular over the periods, the total cash flow is often assumed to arise mid-year. The calculation should therefore be refined. If only annual discount tables are available, the half-year discount factor at r per cent can be calculated from the equation:

$$\text{Discount factor} = \frac{1}{\text{square root of } (1 + r \text{ expressed as a decimal})}$$

Examples

(A) In the example suppose the investment is bought today and the operation is immediate and continuous. The NPV calculation becomes:

Time from today	Cash flow £	Present value at 11 per cent Discount factor	Present value
0	(1500)	1.000	(1500)
$\frac{1}{2}$	100	0.949	95
$1\frac{1}{2}$	1000	0.901×0.949	855
$2\frac{1}{2}$	1000	0.812×0.949	770
$3\frac{1}{2}$	100	0.731×0.949	69
			289

(B) Suppose again that the operation were to be built up and paid for over one construction year. In this case the £1500 cash flow is similarly assumed to be mid-year. The NPV can then be obtained from the first calculation, which has so far given a present value six months from today, by discounting the result by six months. NPV today = $199 \times 0.949 = £189$. The DCF yield is 17 per cent in this case, as before, because it is mathematically true that the same yield is given wherever the zero is taken. In (A) however, the DCF will need to be re-calculated to take account of the refined timing.

3:6:2 The use of present value—the multiple solution problem

Irregular cash flows which include a negative cash flow for a year following some positive cash flow pose a special problem, but not in the NPV calculation. For the DCF yield calculation the kink in the NPV/DCF relationship as shown in the graph in Figure 3:3 is eliminated by adjusting the cash flow:

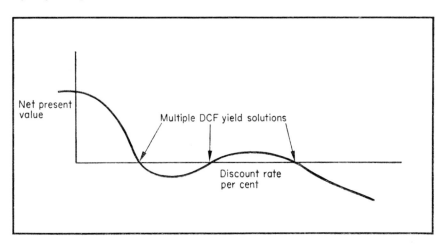

Figure 3:3   Graph showing the multiple solution situation

The most conservative assumption for a surviving organisation is that its money achieves a return no less than its cost-of-capital rate. Theoretically, money can be withheld in the company from one year's cash flow to prepare for a negative cash flow in the following year. The cash flow adjustment is therefore as follows: the negative cash amount is discounted by one year at the company's cost of capital rate and the resulting amount is deducted (put aside) from the preceding year's cash flow. Should another negative result, the process is repeated until the condition of a negative cash flow following a positive cash flow is eliminated. The adjusted cash flow is then discounted in the usual way to calculate the DCF yield. For example:

Project *cash flow*			*Adjusted* *cash flow*
⋮	negative cash flow	discounted negative	⋮
⋮	discounted at cost	cash flow deducted	⋮
⋮	of capital rate—	from previous year's	⋮
+250	10 per cent—for	cash flow	+150
−110	one year	+250−100	0
⋮	−110×0.9091	=+150	⋮
⋮	=−100		⋮

44

Negative cash flows occur during a project when expansions or replacements are made and at the end of projects to pay outstanding tax bills, for restoration of amenities, etc.

3:6:3 The use of present value—optimisation of mutually exclusive alternatives

Financial analysts are constantly being asked to advise as to which of two viable alternative investments is financially preferable. Optimisation routines of this nature can save a lot of money especially if introduced at an early enough planning stage. Optimisation can make savings on the smallest problems, such as initial designs, where choice is involved. Such choices include large long-life machinery versus cheaper short-life machinery, labour *versus* automation, the choice of site, speed of construction, shaft versus open-pit mining, air *versus* sea transport, and so on; in each case choice of one excludes the possibility of choosing the other alternative. Use of the net present value calculation is the easiest approach. Suppose that in a company with a cost of capital of eleven per cent the choice is between:

method A (which is capital intensive) showing a NPV of + £1500 and method B (with a lower capital cost) showing a NPV of + £1300

The actual question to be answered, since both methods are financially desirable, is whether the expenditure of the extra capital involved on Method A is worthwhile. The *incremental investment*, which is represented by the difference between the cash flows of the two alternatives (cash flow A and cash flow B, for each period), shows a NPV of + £200 (NPV A -- NPV B). It is therefore worth spending the extra money. Where the patterns of the alternative cash flows are very different, the incremental approach avoids problems in defining the exact difference in capital expenditure.

Use of the DCF yield approach is also straightforward but contains a snare for the unwary. The question of whether the incremental investment would be desirable is answered by finding the DCF yield on the incremental cash flow (cash flow A minus cash flow B, for each period). If the incremental DCF yield is greater than the company's cost of capital rate, then alternative A is financially preferable. When setting out the results, however, an apparent problem frequently arises. For example:

Method		11 per cent NPV	DCF yield
A	Expensive	+ £1500	14 per cent
B	Cheaper	+ £1300	16 per cent
A—B	Incremental investment	+ £200	13 per cent

It looks as though one should choose method B because the DCF yield is better than that in A. This is an illusion because the capital on which the yield is earned is different in each case. The analysis of the incremental investment points to the same answer whichever method is used. It is often argued that, perhaps, the incremental capital should be spent on some other investment which might show a better return than the 13 per cent here. This could be the case in conditions of severe capital rationing when investments yielding 13 per cent cannot be financed. In other conditions there is no conflict and both investments are desirable. Of course, more than two methods might be available, in which case several incremental investment choices would be compared.

For theoretical reasons, when mutually exclusive opportunities are being analysed, equal cash flow periods should be compared. This is often difficult but a three-year-life machine can be compared with a five-year machine by taking three years of cash flow with a scrap value added for the longer-life machine. Alternatively a fifteen-year period can be taken with five three-year machines compared with three five-year machines. The most sensible assumption will be obvious. For problems such as the quick exploitation of an opportunity compared with slow exploitation a special assumption is made to fill the gap in the project years.

Slow Operation ←————————————————→ end
Quick Operation ←————————→ end
                          ←————'gap'——→

During the period of the gap it is assumed that the company will carry on its business making a return at least equal to its cost of capital rate. Then, in the comparison, a NPV of zero can be added to the quick operation's NPV and like project lives are being effectively compared.

3:6:4   The use of the present value technique—how much is achieved?

This technique does not make decisions. What it does is to marshal the given data to show the inherent profitability and to enable comparisons to be made with helpful conclusions. In particular, the analyst or project promoters are shown whether the project is worth the expenditure of any further time on considerations such as the data uncertainties of the project risks or their likely effects on the company's business as a whole.

3:7   Computational resources

Although computers are invaluable as calculating aids for large and complex problems they should not be used indiscriminately because the cost, including the time taken to eliminate errors, can become disproportionate to the problem being analysed. Time-sharing arrangements using borrowed working programs can be invaluable. The arithmetic involved in the modern analysis techniques, except in probability analysis, is such that it can be done on simple problems using everyday calculating aids or even long multiplication.

Although practitioners usually set up double-check procedures to avoid calculating errors, it is undesirable to be too accurate, that is, to use too many places of decimals, etc., particularly in the early stages of analysis. Rounding of figures should, however, only be done on the data and on the final result. Further detail can be gone into later.

Calculation shortcuts and standard procedures for all problems are often sought in this field. If, however, they are used without understanding or without necessary adaptation to the different circumstances of each case, much more time can easily be wasted than if the problem were initially approached from first principles. Some shortcuts are available to be used with great care in problems of the replacement of machinery and tax allowances.[3]

3:8   Data

The collection and sifting of project data normally leads to far more problems than the analysis. This is no reason for allowing less than rigorous analysis techniques. If a quick look at the first set of data indicates a promising idea, it is sensible to re-examine the data before extending the analysis. Data is given, begged, borrowed or stolen, but in spite of, or because of, the uncertainties involved the best method to obtain good understanding leading to better decisions is to establish as a top priority good communications with the project initiators. Discussions "on site," as early as possible should be held so that there is no suggestion of a planning ivory tower set-up. Diplomatic approaches to the hard-worked estimators who have to grapple with impossible forecasting problems can lead to good understanding, not only of the best realistic guess at some figure, but also of the possible range in which it may lie and of the possible probabilities involved. Conversation with outsiders often helps clarification. Much the best hunches are those agreed by two or more experts. Special and outside experts should only be called in to advise on variables found by sensitivity analysis to be critical enough to merit the cost of the advice.

A special problem to be tackled is that of inflation, particularly when costs are subject to special pressures leading to price-rises greater than the general rate. The analyst will have to take a view as to when it is safe to assume that, on balance, costs and revenue will be similarly inflated, leading to cash flow forecasts in real terms, or when estimates must be made in money terms (see also page 38).

3:8:1   Missing data—reverse economics

Very often, data is simply not available for such vital factors as the achievable price for a new product, the size of the reserves in a new oilfield, the time required to obtain safety clearance or planning permission or the market or technological life period. Reserve economics is the formal technique whereby it is possible to define the achievable or viable range for the missing data. If a graph is drawn of the profitability (NPV or DCF yield) of the project against invented values for the missing data, it is possible to find what value gives the minimum acceptable result. If that value is very unrealistic, it may be possible to conclude that the new product will not be profitable, or the oilfield cannot be economically exploited under present circumstances. A decision might then be taken to stop any further expenditure on the promotion of the idea. If a project must be killed off or frozen it is far better halted early before reputations become involved.

This technique is also useful in the consideration of the merger, takeover or sale of a company, or its flotation on the public market. An attempt is made to forecast the foreseeable cash flow of the company —possibly including benefits, whether in the financing or caused by savings in the new managerial context. The present value of the forecast cash flow divided by the number of issued shares will give a measure of the acceptability of a quoted or offered price or will indicate what price to set at the beginning of negotiations. Attention should be paid to which cost of capital rate is used. For example, in considering a take-over, the buyer will use his own cost of capital rate, not the rate of the company being considered. If the takeover, merger or public flotation would cause the future organisation to have a different financing pattern, especially gearing, it may be necessary to consider what the future cost of capital may be.

3:8:2   Uncertain and erroneous data

A good approach to uncertain data is to attempt to identify in what range the answer may lie. This is sometimes done by adding to the best guess two more guesses, one of which is the most pessimistic and the other the most optimistic. In this way it may be possible to exclude too much subjcctivity on the part of the estimator, who might previously have thought that his future depended on the success of his estimates and who therefore, understandably, introduced too much conservatism. In large organisations a chain of conservatism may be introduced. In such cases the analyst must try to assess the realities and it is helpful if the motivations of the personnel are adjusted so as not to interfere. Over-estimating can be as wrong as under-estimating and can easily lead to the raising of too much finance or too early expansion.

It quite often happens that data is manipulated, either innocently or deliberately, to achieve the desired result—usually the acceptance of a scheme by head office or of a contract in a tendering competition. The results can lead to disaster, as in the case of Rolls-Royce, or at least to public embarrassment. A good review discipline can go a long way to avoiding or sorting out such problems. Having obtained three estimates for the critical data, or ranges in which they might lie, sensitivity analysis can be carried out. Alternatively, a calculation of the likely profit or, more usually, loss, should everything turn out for the worst, can help in a discussion. If the organisation simply cannot survive such a loss and the chances of it are at all great, then possible profits, if everything turns out well, may have to be foregone.

3:9 Sensitivity analysis

This technique can highlight the facts and problems caused by the risks and uncertainties of the plan under discussion. It has limitations but can be carried out with a minimum of calculating aids if necessary. The aim of this analysis is to discover the value of an uncertain variable at which the project is just profitable. Two or three calculations will give the necessary sensitivity curve.

3:9:1 Example

A project is showing a negative net present value at the company's cost of capital rate. What would need to be done to make it profitable? The sensitivity graph is drawn (Figure 3:4) and shows that the operating profit would need to be raised by ten per cent for the project to show a minimum acceptable return. All other things are assumed at first to remain constant (capital cost, speed of coming into operation, life of the project, tax, inflation, etc.).
Data which gives the desired result:

	Original estimate	Acceptable estimates				
Price per unit £	20	21	20	20	20	20	20.3
Volume/Number sold	10	10	10.5	10	10	10	10.15
Labour cost £	40	40	40	30	40	40	38
Materials cost £	50	50	50	50	40	50	47.5
Overhead cost £	10	10	10	10	10	—	9.5
OPERATING PROFIT	100	110	110	110	110	110	111.045

It is thus possible to say that the project would be acceptable if either the price could be raised by 5 per cent, or the volume sold by 5 per cent, or if the labour cost could be lowered by 25 per cent, or the materials cost by 20 per cent or the overhead cost by 100 per cent. Another possibility to explore would be if (as shown in the final column) both the price and volume sold could be raised by $1\frac{1}{2}$ per cent at the same time as all costs are lowered by 5 per cent.

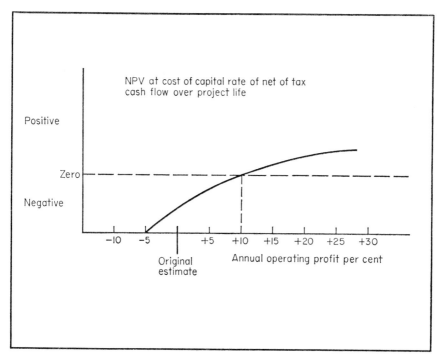

Figure 3:4   Graph sensitivity of project viability to profit variation

The graph could have been plotted using IRR and the acceptable rate as cut-off line but this involves more sums.

One more uncertainty can be explored to extend the analysis. Suppose, for example, that the market for the product is thought to last ten years but could be hit by competition in eight to twelve years time; further calculations give the graph shown in Figure 3:5. Annual operating profit is thought likely to lie between 95 and 120. Assuming the variables examined to be the most critical, the profitability "envelope" is shown by the two outer curves and the dotted connecting lines. This "envelope" is divided into two parts by the cut-off line of zero net present value. By inspection of the two areas it is possible to conclude that the project has roughly only a forty per cent chance of being viable. The worst likely outcome is also shown. The decision may then be more easily taken.

Should the whole "envelope" be above the cut-off line it would be possible to conclude that the project is profitable in spite of the

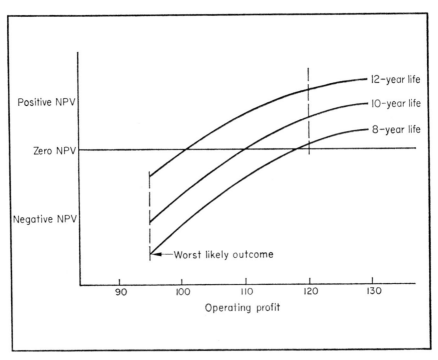

Figure 3:5   Graphical analysis sensitivity of two variables

uncertainty in the variables considered and these are then defined as uncritical. Further effort could then be concentrated on other variables.

This technique is limited to two dimensions. It is, however, of great value, even without calculating aids, because of its simplicity in demonstrating the effect of apparently daunting uncertainties.

3:10   Probability analysis

This is the ideal towards which sensitivity analysis is the first step, but the calculation is so extensive, though not difficult, as to require the help of a computer. Great efforts are being made by large organisations and consultants to prepare flexible computer programs to conduct probability analyses on a wide variety of projects.

The data required is further examined to discover the likely probabilities of each variable lying in each part of the likely range. Subjectivity is not avoided by this but the further discussion can sometimes help clarify the situation. The results could be shown for each variable in a histogram, which is a practical approach to the underlying mathematical curve. An example is shown in Figure 3:6.

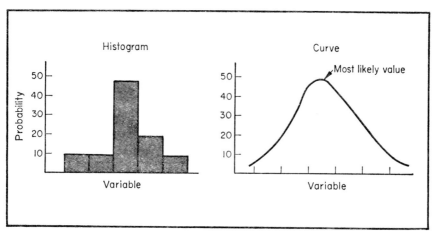

Figure 3:6   Example of a histogram

Mathematical sampling using such data for each significant variable results in the type of profitability/probability graph shown in Figure 3:7. The peak of the curve shows the most likely outcome, but there is a significant chance that the yield might be negative or that the original investment would not be recovered. The area under the curve being taken as unity, the area to the left of the cost of capital cut-off point, if measured, gives the exact probability of unprofitability.

The use of sensitivity and probability analyses does not remove uncertainty and subjectivity of data, but that is no argument for not using what is a fine aid to clarification.

3:11   Risk

Uncertainty of data is not the only unknown bedevilling projects. There are also many possible events which could have a highly significant effect. Such events include acts of God (earthquake, flood, etc.), of governments (tariffs, nationalisation, etc.), of competitors, of technological improvement. Some risks can be insured against. In every case it is helpful to define the risk and assess its possible effect ("what happens

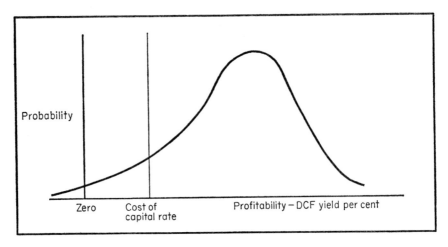

Figure 3:7   Example of a profitability/probability graph

if . . . ?"), and in particular when such an effect might occur. If the likely loss caused by the risked circumstances were to be disastrous to the company, then perhaps the venture is too risky. There are several ways in which organisations of different kinds can proceed to minimise the effect of risk. Obvious examples are diversification, both geographically and in the nature of the business, the tying of customers or suppliers to long-term contracts, and the cautious introduction of new or different scale business.

A somewhat lazy and limited method of allowing for risk is to alter the company's cut-off criterion for the purpose. If the cost of capital were nine per cent, the company might demand a minimum return of eleven per cent on a project to allow for risk. Because, however, circumstances and the chances and effects of risks continuously change, such a directive might not at all meet the realities of every case.

3:11:1   Discounted payback calculation

Unlike the traditional payback calculation, which takes no account of the usual requirement to make some return on an investment, the discounted payback calculation helps in the judgement of project risks. The period calculated is that measured from the beginning of the investment to when the capital has been recovered plus a minimum acceptable return earned on the capital used. At such a point of time the net present value of the project cash flow, discounted at the company's cost of capital rate, is just zero. Cash flows arising after this breakeven point contribute to a return on the project which is greater than the cost of capital rate. The calculation of the discounted payback period is quickly made using the existing calculation of the project's NPV, using as before, the cost-of-capital discount rate. Taking the figures from the example on page 42:

Terms in years from today	Cash flow £	Present value at 11 per cent factor	value	Cumulative net present value
0	(1500)	1.000	(1500)	(1500)
1	100	0.901	90	(1410)
2	1000	0.812	812	(598)
3	1000	0.731	731	133
4	100	0.659	66	199

The discounted payback period ends between two and three years from today. More exactly it takes

$$2 + \frac{598}{731} = 2.82$$

years to recoup the £1500 investment plus the minimum acceptable return earned thereon. Thus, if uncompensated takeover or nationalisation, or the disappearance of the market is expected within thirty-four months, the project has a high risk of never becoming profitable.

The calculation of the discounted payback period is not of itself a method of assessing profitability of the whole project.

3:12   The discussion forum for capital investment problems

Good decision-taking depends more than on anything else on good communication. The decision-takers (at the level appropriate to the size of the proposal) do well to arrange a free debate between the project sponsors, the experts, the analysts and themselves. Documentation of the proposal, the analysis, the decision and any argument or discussion are of great value to all concerned in future planning, as well as in the operation and future re-appraisal of the present project. In such an arrangement no one has anything to fear if he has nothing to hide. There is often a useful spin-off in the form of the clarification of objectives and policies. Clearly, the decision will rest on the judgement of the facts and figures of the plans in relation to the risks, uncertainties, intangibles and management problems, as well as the relevance to interrelated projects and the mapping of the organisation's future as a whole. The contribution of the techniques described in this chapter is only in assembling such facts as can be established and in highlighting the likely probabilities. This, however, is of great value in releasing management effort for the interpretation of the problems.

Most private organisations are to some extent limited as to the amount of capital available, particularly for unspectacular investments. It would be convenient if all projects turned up simultaneously and could be ranked in order of magnitude of profitability and then accepted in turn until available funds were used up. (Such a procedure is to a certain extent available to the public sector at the beginning of a budgetary period.) In practice, however, in most companies projects turn up irregularly or ideas may crystallise at uneven and unknown intervals. It is therefore highly desirable to establish and monitor a clearly understood set of criteria, normally including the company's cost of capital in real terms, against which each scheme can be measured as it arises and progresses. On average there is some chance of a good choice of investments so that, at the minimum, the return earned on the company's capital is no less than its cost and funds will be available or obtainable to finance future profitable ventures, whether new or improving on present operations.

3:12:1   Tactics

When analysis precedes or accompanies negotiations with governments, financiers, associates or opponents, it is usually helpful to make calculations to understand the opposite point of view, which might be based on different methods or criteria.

There are few organisations which can avoid differences of opinion leading to apparent or very real conflicts. The experienced decision-taker and his advisers can normally recognise the behavioural signs. Avoidance of discussion is not always for good reasons such as a real emergency. Emergencies can be contrived by skilful delays and, perhaps, decisions can be precipitated by prompted outside pressures. Decisions taken in real emergencies should be appraised and documented as soon as possible. If a decision-taker is known to be susceptible to private discussions, then project sponsors will be quick to arrange suitable lobbying. Such a situation has its obvious dangers.

A very real problem can arise in planning investments which can or should be phased. Commitments to small investments, which inescapably lead to subsequent heavy expenditure or embarrassment if the second stage is deemed unacceptable, should be recognised as chain opportunities. Appraisal of the first stage should be accompanied by a best guess of the subsequent likely history and the project should be discussed at the level relevant to the whole operation, in which case the decision will be taken after consideration of the future commitments. The decision-tree technique examined earlier can help.

When a superficially attractive proposal is financially marginal, special care must be taken. At this time criticism may be made of the company's criteria which were otherwise accepted when the proposals were better than marginal. Such criticism at this time may not always be valid. In this situation excessive subjectivity may be introduced into uncertain data; in fact, some estimators claim to be able to produce estimates which pass company tests. Wide discussions of parameters, perhaps calling in outside advice, as well as the discipline contained in the carrying out of sensitivity and probability analysis, go some way to reduce this risk. A well established routine of project monitoring, re-appraisal, review or ex-post evaluation, or whatever the subsequent comparison of forecast with actual results is called, is in this case especially valuable.

3:13   Re-appraisal: ex-post evaluation and capital expenditure reviews

It has been said that, without subsequent re-examination, formal planning appraisal techniques are largely counter-productive. Ex-ante evaluation—the prior preparation of forecast results—is very necessary in the raising of finance for a project, either internally or externally, and obtaining the desired go-ahead. There is, however, no certainty that the combined estimates and skills which resulted in the forecasts have been optimised unless a subsequent view is taken.

There are well established commercial routines whereby periodic (weekly, monthly, quarterly, annual) accounts are made of both financial and physical resources used and benefits achieved, and reports are made to relevant technical and financial monitors. Usually the results are compared with annual and three- or five-year plans for the project or the organisation as a whole. Variations are studied and adjustments are made.

There is, however, additional benefit to be derived from extending the monitoring and control routine and adding re-appraisal disciplines. This is, of course, easier for organisations conducting recognisably distinct operations which grew from a clear and, hopefully, fully-advised original decision. It is, however, not impossible to reproduce estimates of how the scheme might have looked *ab initio*, or to separate multiple operations into defined parts. It is also beneficial to conduct re-appraisals aimed at learning from experience before a project finally ends (for example, when full operation had been expected) although at that date an ex-post evaluation might also be valuable.

In the past this sort of procedure was inclined to be called a post mortem rather than a post audit or, better, a review. The atmosphere was one where there was already a "dead body" (or project) or else it seemed that the obvious sequel would be a witch-hunt followed by execution. A review, on the other hand, involves the parading of the victorious troops with the trophies highlighted. Any idea of threat must be avoided.

Basically all projects should be reviewed to answer the questions: "Where did we go *right*?", as well as "Where did we go wrong?", if we did and were not the victims of circumstances. The object of the exercise is to learn by experience.

Answers gleaned from reviews are very varied: be kind to minority shareholders: don't trust the Ruritanians: let us continue to take a second opinion on market estimates: weren't we lucky "they" put the price up: start optimisation studies before the plans are published: remember to consider building each plant double (or half) the size, or in phases: and so on. Occasionally, but less often, the conclusion is "starve the workers" or "sack the chairman."

What is a project? Anything the company plans and does plus anything else the company simply does. The two lists may not be the same and it is always possible that the unplanned actions are the best. Perhaps the planning procedures then need reviewing. For distinct and reasonable-sized projects it is a good idea to agree a reviewing date at the time the go ahead is given. Such a date could be when full production is achieved or when sales reach a certain target. A calendar date is then given to the forecast event. When that date arrives the review should start: if full production has not been achieved that is not a sufficient reason to delay; speedy action might be desirable or, if it is not, it would be nice to know that it is not.

It is unfortunately necessary to take a cynical look at projects built for less than the forecast cost, sales that noticeably exceed budget, and other such successes. If the planners' faults were not in their stars but in themselves they should remain as underlings. People have gone as far as saying that it is useless to plan at all unless one also reviews the results. But, as always, too much is as bad as too little.

It is not always clear who should best conduct re-appraisal reviews. Conflicts may be avoided if the project operators undertake the review in the normal course of their duties. It is highly desirable also to include some sort of outside view to ensure a balanced opinion as to why the resulting return exceeded or fell short of, or is being reassessed at a different rate from, that first forecast. The review should, of course, cover all the unquantifiable as well as the measurable aspects. If the organisation sets up a separate reviewing team its members may need great powers of diplomacy as well as of detection and endurance.

Reviews are discussed preferably at the same forum as are capital expenditure proposals, or, at least, the decision-takers should check that re-evaluation has taken place. Very often the lessons do not need to be driven home but have been learnt in the course of the operation.

The introduction of this routine is often problematical. As usual, opposition may be a cover. Other avoidance tactics can include radical changes of scope of a project leading, amongst other things, to a delay in the review date. Significant changes of scope should be appraised as rigorously as are new projects.

3:14   Can a company afford not to plan?

It is not only fashionable but also demonstrably valuable to use modern management techniques. More can be extracted from such an organisation than the prestige due to an apparent status symbol. Initially the introduction of capital investment planning on a formal basis, but conducted as flexibly as possible, may be difficult. Help can be obtained from consultants to prove the value and set the ball rolling. Ideally the way of thinking in present value terms using clear criteria should permeate through the whole staff so that all opportunities and alternatives are assessed according to their effect on company objectives. If such planning is not, however, conspicuous for its liveliness, then it is dead. Appraisal can illuminate the smallest problem and transform bigger ones.

3:15   References

1 For example, A J Merrett and Allen Sykes: *Capital Budgeting and Company Finance*, Chapter 4, and *The Finance and Analysis of Capital Projects*, Chapters 3, 4, 17, etc, Longmans.
2 *cf* Howard Raiffa, *Decision Analysis*, Addison-Wesley Publishing Company Incorporated, 1968.
3 For example, A J Merrett and Allen Sykes, *Capital, Budgeting and Company Finance*, pages 85 and 166, Longmans.

Chapter 4

Managing Working Capital

Geoffrey P E Clarkson, Professor of Business Finance,
Manchester Business School

Bryan J Elliott, Lecturer in Finance,
Manchester Business School

Working capital is that proportion of a company's total capital which is employed in short-term operations. It is customary to divide working capital into two categories: gross and net. Gross working capital is the sum total of all current assets, while net working capital is the difference between current assets and current liabilities. The former presents the financial problem of how to manage the individual components which comprise the list of current assets. The latter has financial significance for two reasons. The amount of net working capital represents the volume of current assets which are being financed by long-term sources. Though current assets and liabilities are turned over within relatively short periods of time, the net balance of current assets is that proportion which is permanently owned by the company. The second point is that creditors have a particular interest in the net working capital position and regard these assets as the ultimate source of funds for the repayment of their loans.

Current assets consist of all stocks, including finished goods, goods in process and raw materials; accounts receivable (debtors); short-term investments (near cash); and cash.

Current liabilities are a company's debts which must be settled within the following twelve months. They represent goods delivered, services rendered, and the remaining credit obligations of the firm. They may require early settlement, or involve an interest charge which can vary from zero in the case of net monthly accounts due, to bank charge rates on overdrafts. Current liabilities represent the total amount of short-term debt. They are the cheaper forms of debt but involve the highest insolvency risks. For current liabilities have due rates for payment and cash must be found to settle these accounts.

It is the function of financial management to fund the company debt at the lowest cost consistent with acceptable risk. This is readily evident when the net working capital position is examined. Since net working capital is the net value of current assets this balance must be totally financed from long-term sources. Thus, the management of current assets and current liabilities is an important part of financial management.

4:1 Working capital ratios

The liquidity and solvency of a firm are closely related to its working capital position. The usual way to measure a company's liquidity is to divide the current assets (gross working capital) by the current liabilities to get the current or two to one ratio:

$$current\ ratio = \frac{current\ assets}{current\ liabilities}$$

This ratio, sometimes called the working capital ratio, provides a rough measure of the safety afforded to the company's short-term creditors. For, in the event of a technical liquidation, current assets are more likely to yield a higher percentage of their real value than are fixed assets. Short-term lenders regard current assets as the ultimate source for the repayment of their loans. Consequently, the higher the current ratio the greater is their feeling of security.

The working capital ratio is frequently misleading and often has little value as a tool for financial management. To calculate the ratio, figures are taken from a balance sheet. These numbers reflect the past activities of the firm. Though it may comfort a manager to know that his current ratio was in satisfactory form two months ago, he knows nothing about its present state. Not only do balance sheets always represent the past, but they are also summary statements of the accounts. They do not include information on timing, particularly with reference to the periods within which the current liabilities become due. A company could have a current ratio of four to one at the time of its audit, but if its current assets were primarily made up of goods in process and most of its current liabilities were due at the end of the current month it might face a severe shortage of cash. On the other hand a company which acted as an agent buying and selling finished goods could have a low current ratio and be in a sound liquidity position.

One way of coping with the inadequacies of the current ratio is to consider the company's liquid assets in relation to its current liabilities. Liquid assets consist of cash; such investments and securities as can be realised without difficulty (near cash); the cash value of debtors (accounts receivable) and a realistic assessment of the cash value of raw materials, goods in process and finished goods held in stock. The cash value of debtors can be taken as the percentage of their book value that can be obtained in terms of a loan from a bank or debt factoring organisation. The immediately realisable cash value of stocks is much harder to assess since most companies have already raised an overdraft against their book value. Companies that use raw materials listed on commodity exchanges or whose finished products have an immediate and widespread market can claim a significant cash value for their stocks. Companies whose stocks must be cleared through its traditional marketing channels can claim little immediate cash value for those stocks. In many cases a conservative estimate of the cash value of stocks and debtors is given by taking debtors at 100 per cent of their book value and ascribing a zero cash value to stocks.

Dividing liquid assets by current liabilities gives the quick or liquid ratio:

$$quick\ ratio = \frac{liquid\ assets}{current\ liabilities}$$

This ratio has significance if the timing between the receipts generated by the liquid assets and payments falling due is in suitable balance. If timings are balanced, liquid assets and current liabilities should be managed so that the quick ratio is approximately equal to one. If it is less than one, liquid assets no longer cover the payments due, while if the value is much greater than one, scarce resources are being wasted by being kept idle in a needlessly liquid condition. Despite the refinement provided by the use of liquid assets, neither ratio deals with the immediate present. In addition, both ignore the flow of cash through the company's accounts, a flow which is of prime importance to its operating liquidity and solvency.

4:2 Decision-making

The management of working capital is concerned with two distinct but interwoven sets of activity: short- and long-term financial operations. The former poses the problem of managing the individual current asset balances which make up the gross working capital position. Long-term working capital management is concerned with providing the volume of net working capital required by the company's current and future activities.

It would be very convenient if it were possible to prescribe the precise amount of gross and net working capital each company needs. Unfortunately, such is not the case. Manufacturing and merchandising enterprises, to mention but two examples, will invest different proportions of their total available monetary resources in working capital. Furthermore, some businesses will buy their fixed assets such as land, buildings and machinery, while others will lease these items. Each situation creates its own working capital problems that must be decided within the constraints and plans of the individual company. The object of this chapter, therefore, is not to tell managers what working capital they require. Rather it is to present a number of analytic techniques which will identify the decisions to be made when applied to the data of any company. It is management's job to make and take decisions. All that technical analysis can do is to identify the decisions that have to be made.

The fundamental problem posed in the management of net and gross working capital can best be illustrated by examining the effects on a company of an increase in sales. To fill new orders extra units must be produced. Extra production requires additional raw materials, labour and overhead expenses. Even after the sale is effected an interval of time will elapse before payment is received. Throughout the manufacturing, selling and delivery period the company's activities have to be financed. Though the effects of this financing will eventually be reflected in the current and quick ratios, it is the pattern and timing of the expenditures and receipts that generates the company's current liquidity and solvency.

4:3 Example of working capital flows

Consider the consequences of the following sequence of events on the much simplified balance sheets of two companies, Liquidity Company Limited and Efficiency Company Limited, whose starting balances are given in Figure 4:1. Both companies receive an order for £500 000 of goods. The order itself has no effect on working capital, it merely becomes an entry in the order book. Suppose each company has sufficient productive capacity available to handle the order. It has to buy £100 000 of raw materials. These materials are purchased on terms of net cash monthly. Gross working capital grows immediately by £100 000. This increase in gross working capital is financed by the supplier who is not paid until the month's end.

Liquidity Company				
Net worth	£3500	Fixed assets		£2500
Current liabilities	500	Current assets:		
		Liquid assets	1000	
		Other assets	500	1500
Total	£4000		Total	£4000

Efficiency Company				
Net worth	£1800	Fixed assets		£1300
Current liabilities	1200	Current assets:		
		Liquid assets	1200	
		Other assets	500	1700
Total	£3000		Total	£3000

Figure 4:1   Balance sheets (all figures in £'000s)

The raw material begins its passage through the manufacturing process. In consequence a direct wage bill of £100 000 is incurred. By the time the goods are completed labour and overheads have risen to a total of £200 000. To produce orders the companies have had to find £300 000 to pay wages, overheads and suppliers' bills.

Suppose both companies borrowed these funds from their respective banks by extending their overdrafts. Current assets rise by £300 000 and current liabilities show a corresponding increase. Notice that these transactions have not affected the net working capital position. What have decreased are the current and quick ratios. This is readily seen in Figure 4:2. Both companies are now noticeably less liquid. Though the Efficiency Company was and is in the weaker financial position, the Liquidity Company has incurred a proportionately greater reduction in its current liquidity. Now consider the effects of completing the sales transactions. The order is delivered and an invoice sent out for £500 000 on terms of net cash monthly. The stock of finished goods has been turned into accounts receivable (debtors) which are valued at the sales price, assuming no bad debts. The value of liquid assets rises immediately by £200 000. Current liquidity improves when judged by the ratio test, but a cash shortage remains until the debtor's account is settled.

Liquidity Company

	Before	*After*
Liquid assets	£1000	£1000
Other assets	500	800
Current assets	1500	1800
Current liabilities	500	800
Networking capital	1000	1000
Current ratio	3 to 1	2.2 to 1
Quick ratio	2 to 1	1.25 to 1

Efficiency Company

Liquid assets	£1200	£1200
Other assets	500	800
Current assets	1700	2000
Current liabilities	1200	1500
Net working capital	500	500
Current ratio	1.4 to 1	1.3 to 1
Quick ratio	1 to 1	0.8 to 1

Figure 4:2   Working capital positions before and after completion of order

4:4 Timing of flows

The pattern of payments and receipts which are a part of all business operations depicts the occasions when financing is required. The purchase of materials generates trade accounts payable (creditors), and the manufacturing process creates labour and overhead expenses, all of which have to be paid at regular but independent times. Stocks of goods in process and finished goods have to be handled, stored and shipped. Each operation incurs additional expense that has to be paid as it becomes due. Finished goods, which have been sold, are then delivered, usually on credit terms. Credit sales generate trade accounts receivable (debtors). It is at this point that cash shortages reach their peak. Companies face a variety of cash demands, including tax payments, all with individual timings. As a rule they have only one major source of cash revenue—credit sales with yet another timing.

The management of the cash flows is crucial to the financial life of an enterprise. It may be necessary, as well as desirable, to finance such payments by short-term borrowing. Such borrowings must be planned. It is as foolish to borrow money and not use it as it is to discover a sudden need that can only be met by an immediate increase in overdraft. Banks, like other lenders, dislike lending at short notice. They also have their cash flow problems. Further, when a company needs cash urgently the risk of insolvency is at its highest and willing lenders become scarce as the risk increases. Many profitable companies have gone bankrupt because they ran out of cash. Solvency can always be maintained by holding large amounts of cash, but excessive cash implies a high level of net working capital. Net working capital is financed from long-term sources, and it is obviously expensive to finance excess cash holdings from long-term funds. A more effective manager will determine the minimum cash required, will study the pattern of receipts and payments, and will plan both his short-term borrowings and investments such that the company is neither wasting its funds nor running unnecessary risks. He will manage money and finance so that it is neither idle nor over-traded.

4:5 Flow of funds

The pattern of payments and receipts noted above is a simple instance of the flow of funds through a company's activities. These flows are usually audited on specific dates, such as the end of each month, quarter or year. Over such intervals of time, the total net flows consist of a balance of all cash transactions. Receipts from sales, for example, are balanced against the funds used in the generation of those sales. Similarly, cash borrowed during the period is offset by payments made on the debt.

Total net cash flows are calculated by comparing balance sheet entries for consecutive time-periods. Changes in assets and liabilities are important, for they identify the cash transfers that have been made. A decrease in an asset's value implies that a corresponding increase in cash has been generated from this asset. Alternatively, an increase in asset value means that additional funds were invested in it and implies a net decrease in cash. A decrease in cash can also be produced by reducing liabilities, while any increase in liabilities or net worth (shareholders' equity) means an increase in funds. These sources and uses of cash can be summarised as follows:

Sources of cash	Uses of cash
Decrease in assets	Increase in assets
Increase in liabilities	Decrease in liabilities
Increase in net worth	Decrease in net worth

Net working capital is increased by paying off current liabilities or by a net addition to current assets. It is decreased when there is a net increase in current liabilities or a decrease in current assets. In Figure 4.3 an example is provided of two companies both of which have the same net working capital position. Company A has no current liabilities at all and current assets of £20 000, while Company B has a net difference between current assets and liabilities of £20 000. If the question is asked, which firm has the better working capital position, what is the answer? Is it an advantage to have no current debt? Ought it to be a part of long-term financial planning to reduce current liabilities to a minimum?

The answers to these and other similar questions can be readily determined, but only if certain fundamental aspects of financial management are recognised and understood. Primarily, the ability to manage and cope with debt is a function of earnings not assets. Though assets are mortgaged to raise debt, and lenders are concerned about the proportion of assets to debt, debts are paid out of earnings. It is only in emergencies, the result of bad planning and control, that debts are

Company A			
Net worth	£40 000	Fixed assets	£28 000
Long-term debt	8 000	Current assets	20 000
Total	£48 000	Total	£48 000

Net working capital = £20 000

Company B			
Net worth	£40 000	Fixed assets	£28 000
Long-term debt	8 000	Current assets	30 000
Current liabilities	10 000		
Total	£58 000	Total	£58 000

Net working capital = £20 000

Figure 4:3   Example of net working capital

repaid by the forced sale of assets. If the lender's guide of a quick ratio of one to one is accepted, then the upper limit of current liabilities is given by the value of the company's liquid assets. The lower limit is to have no current debt at all. Beginning with the balances represented by Company *A* the effects on the firm of adding current liabilities can be examined.

Suppose that Company *A* is currently enjoying an annual turnover of £100 000 and is earning on these sales £18 000 before taxes. Liquid assets of £9000 are recorded as part of the £20 000 investment in current assets made by Company *A*. According to the current liquidity measure generally accepted, earnings of £18 000 can support a level of current debt determined by the following relation:

$$\frac{current\ liabilities - liquid\ assets}{cash\ earnings\ before\ tax} \times 365$$

Cash earnings before tax is defined as forecast before tax earnings plus expected depreciation less contracted capital expenditure for the period in question. In the absence of detailed management accounts, the company's reported earnings before tax can be used as a rough guide.

Dividing net current debt by earnings before tax and multiplying by

69

the number of days in the year gives the total number of days required to pay off all current debt out of earnings. If this number of days exceeds 365 then unless earnings grow, the company may not be able to meet its current obligations. If the number of days is less than this upper limit, the level of current debt is readily manageable in the absence of any sudden drop in earnings. Such is the essence of control. The financial manager has to decide on the number of days to be set as the company's standard. Suppose 280 days is chosen as the criterion by which the volume of current debt is to be judged. Then Company A could take on current liabilities of:

$$current\ liabilities = \frac{(18\ 000)(280)}{365} + 9000$$
$$= £22\ 800$$

A company does not just acquire additional debt. If a loan is generated the funds are invested in some asset. Hence, the problem is to combine the knowledge of how much debt to afford with the capacity to make effective use of these funds once they are accepted.

Suppose that management has approved the indications of the calculation and increases current liabilities to a level of £22 800. Clearly, the company's creditors may become dissatisfied if the quick ratio is consequently allowed to fall below one to one. An obvious answer is to use such additional borrowed funds to increase sales. A growth in sales can only be generated by increasing production, which in turn requires additional raw material. By negotiating trade credit to finance stock purchases, overdrafts and other short-term funds will be available to finance the sales campaign. As sales are made, the level of accounts receivable will grow. Control must be exercised to ensure that the average age of these receivables does not also increase.

After a period of time Company A will have absorbed this additional finance. Current assets will have increased by £22 800 so that total assets will now stand at £70 800. Originally, Company A generated sales of £100 000 from total assets of £48 000. In other words, the turnover of total assets in sales =

$$sales/total\ assets = 2.1\ to\ 1$$

If the firm maintains this rate of activity, the new level of assets will enable it to sell:

$$70\ 800 \times 2.1 = £148\ 000$$

of goods a year. The extra finance of £22 800 has produced additional sales capacity of £48 000. If these sales are made and the profit margin is maintained, annual sales of £148 000 will produce earnings before taxes of £26 000. These earnings can in turn be used to finance additional debt and the cycle begins again. Growth takes place.

To summarise, the position of Company *A* as described above can be considered. An increase in current debt of £22 800 has made it possible to:

1 Increase current assets by 110 per cent
2 Increase total assets by 47 per cent
3 Increase sales, if turnover ratios are maintained, by 48 per cent
4 Increase earnings before taxes, if profit margins are maintained, by 27 per cent
5 Increase its capacity to manage further current debt.

These are highly desirable results. That they can be achieved by taking on current debt as one of the more important aspects of financial management. For the primary objective is to increase a company's earnings and the growth and management of gross working capital is an essential ingredient in this endeavour.

An important point to note about the measure of liquidity is that it can be used to determine whether a company is wasting available resources by not having enough current debt. If the calculation should yield a number of days less than 200, then it is clear that additional current finance can be obtained without due risk. If earnings are rising, a number close to the limit of 365 can be safe. If earnings are steady or subject to a fall, a reserve allowance must be made. A number like 250 days might be indicated. Whatever the situation it is management's job to assess the trend of earnings and make the decision on what degree of risk to take.

4:6 Managing accounts receivable

Trade accounts receivable are a product of credit sales. If a company were to make all sales for cash it would have no accounts receivable and no need to finance its sales by the use of current debt. Most companies, particularly in manufacturing, sell on credit and it is these companies with accounts receivable balances that this section concerns.

4:6:1 Net cash value

The average collection period (or age) is an important indicator of the liquidity of receivables. The longer an invoice goes unpaid the less likely it is ever to be paid. Doubtful accounts turn into bad debts when they are left uncollected. Hence, to assess the liquidity of a given balance of receivables it is necessary to investigate the relation between the age of an account and the likelihood of its being collected. An inspection of past accounts will reveal the proportions to use. For illustrative purposes suppose the collectable percentages are as follows:

Age of account	Collectable percentages
1–30	99
31–60	98
61–90	95
91–120	70
121–	50

Applying these percentages to the receivables balance recorded at a particular time-period will produce the net cash value of those receivables. Thus a £100 000 credit sale in the age category 1–30 would have a net cash value of £99 000. The same sized sale in the 121 days plus category would have a net cash value of only £50 000. It follows that an increase in the average age of receivables means a deterioration both in liquidity and real value.

Suppose that management has decided to do something about its deteriorating receivables position. What are the possible actions it can take and what credit policy ought to be adopted? Solutions vary from leaving things as they are to the opposite extreme of withdrawing credit facilities and insisting that all future sales be contracted for cash. Every solution will generate its own pattern of cash receipts and, depending upon its stringency, will entail certain costs. Thus, an increase in cash flow can be measured against the cost of generation. The net value to the company, given by a variety of alternatives will aid management in taking a decision to adopt a particular credit policy.

It is most unlikely that a new more stringent credit policy can be effected without cost. Management will wish to determine the probable cost of persuading customers to pay their bills within a new time limit. Obviously, such cost must not exceed the benefits to be derived from the new policy. The limit to the cost is determined by calculating the discount which the company could afford to offer as an incentive leaving itself no worse off than under the old credit policy. In other words, the interest rate or discount that will equalise the present value of these two streams of income must be calculated.

4:6:2   Financing accounts receivable

Encashing receivables, like obtaining an overdraft or trade credit, is an important part of short-term working capital management. The basic objective in financing accounts receivable is to generate the maximum cash inflow at the lowest possible cost. One possible strategy was noted above: to offer a discount for prompt payment and a maximum credit period of thirty days. Although there is a large range of alternative financing policies, three important types of approach exist. The first is to sell, each month, all receivables to a commercial factor for cash. The second is to borrow against the receivables balance. The third is to develop a credit and collection department of such capability that other companies' receivables can be purchased and processed with the company's own assets to yield additional earnings.

4:6:3   Factoring accounts receivable

The factoring of accounts receivable is accomplished by offering the entire collection of receivables to a commercial factor. If a satisfactory price is negotiated and the sale is made, the factor takes on the responsibility for collecting all accounts due. As a consequence he also accepts the risk that some accounts will prove to be uncollectable. The purchase price is determined on the basis of the net cash value of the receivables balance. Though practices can differ, the purchase price is usually stated in terms of an advance payment of, say, ninety per cent of the net cash value. The balance, less service and financing charges which may amount to two or three per cent, is paid to the company on the average due date of the accounts.

For example, suppose a company has a receivables balance with a net cash value of £100 000. The average age of these receivables is thirty days. The factor offers £90 000 cash now, and the balance less service

73

and finance charges in thirty days. The amount of this balance depends upon the quality of the receivables. If the credit worthiness of these accounts is high, the factor's charge is low. It is higher in cases where the risk of bad debts is high. Suppose in this instance, that the total charge is two per cent, then the balance of £8000 will be paid at the end of the thirty days.

To collect £90 000 at the beginning and £8000 at the end of the month, this company has to be willing to pay £2000. If accounts are sold at this rate each month of the year, the annual charges would amount to £24 000 or twenty-four per cent of the average receivables balance. This may appear to be a high charge to pay. However, the company has no direct collection charges of its own. The factoring cost has to be compared with this saving. The evaluation criterion is the company's cost of its own credit and collection department for the year. Moreover, cash today is worth more than cash at the end of the month. In any assessment of the cost of factoring the fact that the company's own credit department will not produce ninety per cent of the cash value of all receivables on the first day of every month must be costed and allowed. An annual charge of twenty-four per cent of the average receivables values may well become quite an attractive proposition when the alternative costs are taken into account.

4:6:4   Borrowing on accounts receivable

An alternative method of raising money on accounts receivable is to pledge them as collateral for a loan. Many companies do not like the thought of having a factor collect from their customers. None the less, they cannot afford to tie up cash in receivables. A loan based on these receivables can be readily negotiated with commercial or merchant banks and may well provide a more acceptable financing vehicle.

With a loan of this type, the company retains the obligation to collect the receivables as well as the risk of doubtful accounts becoming bad debts. The usual practice is for the finance house to lend the company a proportion, say seventy or eighty per cent, of the net value of the receivables. Interest can be charged either on a daily basis or on the actual cash advanced. A service charge may also be included. Usually, the company will pay off the loan as receivables are collected and, as a result, the net cost to the company will be less than that charged by the factor on an outright sale. It must be noted, however, that the factor carries out credit accounting, ledger keeping and collecting as part of his services. The company is responsible for all these activities if it merely borrows money on its receivables.

4:6:5 Buying accounts receivable

Many companies are in a position where they manage and finance their own credit sales. Such companies have credit departments and managers whose task is to service their customers' accounts and collect the receipts when due. One alternative to selling or borrowing on receivables is to go into the business of collecting receivables in a serious way. If the company already has a credit department, why not put it to work in a more efficient and effective manner? A satisfactory credit department will find little difficulty in providing a collection service for receivables from other companies with similar customers. The question to answer has two parts and can be stated as follows: is it cheaper to sell receivables outright to a factor or to process them? Whatever set of reasons persuade a company not to sell its receivables, economies of scale suggest it will be cheaper, per account collected, to behave as a factor and buy other companies' receivables. Accounts receivable can be purchased just as they can be sold.

4:7 Managing stocks

Stocks of raw materials, goods in progress and finished goods pose a number of management problems. On the one hand there are the questions of warehousing and storage. Decisions on what levels of stock to keep are determined by economic order and production batch size considerations. These, in turn, help to specify the minimum and maximum stock levels required. On the other hand there is the question of how to finance these stocks and how to control the investment of funds in this type of asset.

The average age of stocks on hand can be computed. The stock balances at the beginning of the period are divided by the purchases expected during the period and multiplied by the number of days in the accounting period. This calcualtion can be made for each category of stock as well as for the total balance. For example, within the raw material stocks used in a particular company's manufacturing process there is a variety of items such a sheet steel, copper bars and metal rods which are purchased in substantial quantities. Raw materials, as far as this company is concerned, also include items which are the finished products of other companies, such as die castings, gear assemblies and many types of fittings. The manufacturing process takes some time to complete and in so doing produces a number of stages of goods in progress. Raw materials have been partially assembled into finished goods and stocks of goods in progress are normally held at a fairly high level, representing a substantial amount of invested funds. Finished goods stocks are not large and every effort is made to keep them within reasonable bounds.

Suppose the age classification of the die casting stocks are as given in Figure 4:4. It can be readily seen that over sixty per cent of these die castings have been on hand for over forty-five days. Suppose a check on the composition of these aged stocks shows that some castings are used early in the productive process while others are not employed until much later. Moreover, some of the castings are speciality items which may remain in stock for many months at a time. In short, the company really uses two classes of die castings: those which are processed within thirty days and those which may take many months to clear.

Efficient management of raw materials requires that these stocks are turned over rapidly. The longer a given item remains in stock the more difficult it becomes to collect the full cost through the sale price. In many instances, however, there are some items, such as special die castings, sub-assemblies, etc., which cannot be moved through the productive process with the desired speed. The financing of stocks can be readily geared to the ageing process, and it is this criterion which is discussed below.

Classfication (Days)	Amount	Percentage each is of total
0–15	£17 000	16.0
16–30	13 000	12.2
31–45	9 000	8.5
46–60	29 000	27.4
61+	38 000	35.9
	£106 000	100.0

Figure 4:4   Age classification of die castings

4:7:1 Types of stock finance

Stocks can be used to raise funds in a number of ways. The simplest procedure is to use these assets as collateral for a secured loan from a commercial or merchant bank. To do so the value of each item or class of items must be noted and approved. As in the case of accounts receivable, the loan will be based upon an agreed percentage of the net cash value of the stocks. As stocks are consumed in the productive process, the net cash value declines and unless the balance is maintained by new purchases the size of the loan has to be reduced by a proportionate amount. As a result, taking a secured loan on rapidly moving raw materials is a complicated process and may not be worth the effort. An analysis of the age classifications reveals those stocks which remain unused for the greatest periods of time. These are the items to use as collateral if loan financing is desired. If the average age of certain materials, say die castings or other speciality items is eighty days, this length of time is sufficient to make a collateral loan worthy of investigation.

Raw materials which are purchased in bulk and which take some time to be delivered to the company can be financed *en route* by means of a trade bill and/or warehouse receipt. In either case, the financing instrument is, in effect, a secured loan on the value of the itemised goods. Warehouse receipts are issued by the warehousing company and can be used by the company: to reclaim the goods when required; to borrow funds by pledging the receipt as collateral; or to sell the goods in question by presenting the receipt for sale on the commodity market. The trade bill is based upon the bills of lading, which represent the goods in transit from the supplier. These bills become negotiable if endorsed by a commercial house and can be sold outright or used as collateral for a loan. In both of these cases the company is delaying the investment of its own funds until such time as the goods are actually delivered to its factory for processing.

4:8 Managing accounts payable

The management of accounts payable is essentially a simple operation. As indicated earlier, it is both informative and useful to maintain control over the average age of the oustanding trade credit. The decision whether to settle accounts payable at once or later depends upon the discounts, if any, that are offered for prompt and early cash payment. If discounts are available from suppliers, then advantage should be taken of the offer. Such reductions in cost can always be compared to the value of keeping this amount of credit unpaid. In most cases it is a sound financial rule to accept cash discounts whenever possible.

Some suppliers do not offer cash discounts. In this event, they should be approached with a view to striking a bargain. The promise of prompt settlement will often produce an agreed discount even if this is not part of the company's normal sales policies. If all efforts to achieve discounts for immediate cash payment fail, there is no incentive to settle the account and every reason to delay payment until the last possible moment.

The management of accounts payable can be broken down into two parts:

1   For all accounts on which cash discounts are available, ensuring that settlement occurs before the cash due date
2   For all accounts with no discount ensuring that payment is not made until the agreed due date, but no later.

Financial management is responsible for maintaining the credit standing of the company as well as generating the necessary credit financing. To be known as a late payer does not enhance the company's reputation. To be known as a company that is aware of the value of money and insists on bargaining for its most effective use engenders respect and, in all likelihood, will lead to even higher credit rating.

The remaining current liabilities offer little scope for active financial management. PAYE withholdings are taken out of wages and salaries every time employees are paid. These withholdings do not have to be paid to the appropriate authority until certain calendar dates have been reached. Companies have free use of these funds for an average thirty to forty days. If total wage and salary payments are rising, so will the amount of credit that this free source of funds represents. Since the size of the withholdings is not under the company's control, management only has responsibility to use these funds while it can and to make sure they are paid to the tax authorities when due.

Similar comments pertain to the payment of the company's tax obligations. Though tax assessments must be paid, there is no justification for paying them in advance. Tax reserve certificates are offered for sale to tempt companies, by a small discount, to settle their obligations in advance. To buy a tax reserve certificate is to make an investment with zero liquidity, for these certificates can only be used in dealings with the Inland Revenue. All other short- or long-term investments have a degree of liquidity and many exist which also provide higher rates of return. Thus, before purchasing tax reserve certificates their rate of return should be compared with other available short-term investments. The money market can always supply an investment with a high degree of liquidity and a due date coincident with tax outlays.

Chapter 5

Forecasting Financial Requirements

R L Mansbridge, Controller,
IMS International Inc

Management performance is judged by the financial press and city analysts by earnings per share growth, profit and turnover growth and by the maintenance or improvement of the profit to turnover ratio. One side of the company's performance very rarely mentioned is the management of financial resources. Rarely mentioned, that is, until there is an abrupt announcement that the company cannot pay its creditors and that it is going into liquidation. It is amazing how many companies with otherwise good management make this error. Partly this is due to management equating profits to cash in the bank; partly to management leaving anything to do with finance to the accountant because it is too complex for the non-financial man; and partly to making the accountant responsible but not giving him the authority to do anything about it.

The subject is, of course, complex if one includes the raising of capital, international movement of money, optimum financing of projects and tax implications. But this is not the area where most companies operate. This chapter therefore concentrates on how to plan and control that very necessary resource in every company—money.

5:1   Timing of cash plans

There are essentially three time-spans which a good financial manager must cover in his cash planning. The planning is mentioned first at this stage as it comes first in time, but equally important is the control.

Plans are of no use unless there is a good control mechanism to highlight when, where and how events are off plan. This probably applies more in cash planning than in profit planning. If a company makes an unplanned loss one month or one year, this does not usually have such a devastating effect as if the company cannot pay its wages one Friday.

The three time spans are:

1   Monthly cash forecasts for, say, the next three months
2   Short term cash forecasts of, say, one or two years, probably by month
3   Long-term cash forecasts for five to ten years, usually by year

The day-to-day planning and control of cash is omitted here as this is purely the arithmetic and checking of bank statements.

The timings of the cash plans are dictated mainly by the budgeting or planning cycle of the operation. It is essential that the cash plans lock into profit and balance sheet planning.

5:2   Monthly cash forecast and control

Assuming that the company's planning and reporting system runs by calendar month, this forecast should be produced as near the beginning of the month as possible. It shows:

1   Actuals for the last month, over/under plan and over/under last month's forecast
2   Forecast for next month, over/under plan
3   Forecast for month two, etc., over/under plan

A diagram of this is shown in Figure 5:1. This is very simply a statement of money received and paid, showing how last month compared to the plan and prior forecast. It shows forecasts for months one, two, three etc., again against the plan. The length of the forecast is determined by the urgency of the cash position. Thus, if the overdraft is right up to the limit in a tight money situation and there are large seasonal payments, the forecast will go further than three months to cover this.

The plan column mentioned will be the short-term forecast showing the month-by-month movement of cash which links in with the budget of profits.

The forecast for next month will be those figures which the financial manager is planning to pay and receive next month. To do this he will use the following sources of information:

1   Calendarised profit and cash plan
2   Short-term profit outlook for next month (if this is done month by month)
3   Debtors and creditors ledger
4   Information on taxes, loans, etc.
5   Capital expenditure authorisations
6   Last month's actuals

Thus, the short-term forecast should accurately give the money movements picture for the next two or three months. It will also be closely locked in with the activities of the company, that is, production, sales costs, etc.

The variance from plan will be analysed in conjunction with the profit and cost variance statement. Variances will highlight some of the questions itemised below:

1   *Trade debtors*

Is this due to lower turnover or late payment by debtors?
Is the number of days outstanding on the debtors ledger increasing?
Is this seasonal or is a trend developing which may need more financing in future?

2   *Investment income*

Does the company still own the investments as planned?
Should future income be adjusted?

	LAST MONTH			MONTH 1		MONTH 2		MONTH 3, ETC.	
	Actual	o/u Plan	o/u Fore-cast	Fore-cast	o/u Plan	Fore-cast	o/u Plan	Fore-cast	o/u Plan
Receipts									
Trade debtors									
Investment income									
Receipts from									
Overseas sub-									
sidiaries									
Loans or financing									
received									
Other									
Total Receipts									
Payments									
Stock purchases									
Salaries and costs of									
employment									
Other overheads									
Capital expenditure									
Interest									
Tax									
Payment to									
Overseas sub-									
sidiaries									
Repayments of loans									
Other									
Total payments									
Surplus (deficit)									
Opening cash/ (overdraft)									
Closing cash/ (overdraft)									
Overdraft facility									

Figure 5:1   Monthly cash forecast

3 *Receipts/payments—overseas subsidiaries.*

Is this lower business activity or are international money trans-actions being blocked or restricted?

4 *Loans or financing received.*

Is this due to a change in capital spending?
Are planned loans not forthcoming?

5 *Purchases, salaries and overheads.*

Is this due to operating volume, price variations or late payment of creditors?

6 *Capital expenditure.*

Is planned spending cancelled or delayed?
Are costs different from plan due to price only or has there been any change in specification?

7 *Interest.*

Is the rate of interest different from the plan or is the overdraft size different?

8 *Tax.*

Is this due to a change in rates or in taxable profits?

The purpose of showing over/under forecast is to see:

1 How good a forecast was done one month prior to events
2 What changes have happened in one month which could not have been forecast

Point one above is not wholly to see whether the financial manager is good at his job, although over a series of forecasts an opinion can be formed, but also to make a judgement on how accurate the next few months' forecasts are likely to be.

Total receipts less total payments equals surplus or (deficit) each month. Hence the running balance for the next three months is forecast.

Specific decisions which should be made are:

1 If there is a cash balance, should this be invested? For what period can this be done (thirty days, ninety days, etc.)?

2   If there is an overdraft, what items of payment can be delayed?
Can the overdraft facility be increased?

5:3   Short-term cash forecast

This forecast links in with the budget or operating plan for the next
financial year. Its timing should be on the same basis; thus, if the plan
is by month, then the cash forecast will be monthly. Many companies
now plan two years ahead in their short-term planning cycle, the
second year in less detail and without such a commitment as the first.
This avoids the cliff-hanging situation in which, at the close of the
company's fiscal year, the world stops on one day and starts again on
the next.

Cash is simply one of the resources which go to make the budget
work. Within the budget all resources must be planned—manning,
facilities and money.

The main objective of the short-term cash forecast is to see how the
cash balances move, if the company does what it is planning to do.
This forecast must highlight, on a phased basis, the need for any short-
term borrowing. This is particularily relevant in a seasonal business,
even if high profits are being made. Long-term borrowing should be
decided from the figures in the long-term forecast (see later in this
chapter).

It is obviously better to plan in advance for any overdraft requirements than to borrow on an emergency basis. Whenever a request to
borrow is made, a profit budget and cash forecast is always required
by a potential lender.

Cash forecasts can be produced either by converting the profit
budget into receipts and payments or from the budgeted balance sheets.
The latter method is probably more appropriate for longer-term forecasts. Basically the end result is the same in that the movement of the
cash balance from one balance sheet to the next is shown.

As already indicated, the cash forecast must lock into the company's
profit plan. The first cycle is to agree a marketing/sales plan and
production plan. This is merged with the overhead plan to produce a
profit plan. This and the capital expenditure plan are the necessary
tools for the cash forecast.

Because all the work in producing a budget must be done before the financial year commences, an up-to-date forecast for the current year must also be calculated. The cash forecast must obviously start from a factual balance, progress to the year-end and then be calculated for the next year. This means that not only does the cash balance have to be known at the last month-end or quarter-date, but a balance sheet must be prepared also so that the outstandings are correctly brought into account.

Assuming that there is a profit forecast for the current year and that the profit and capital budgets for the next two years are agreed, the cash forecast using the receipts and payments method would show similar headings to Figure 5:2.

If the balance sheet forecast method is used, a source and application of funds statement would be produced as shown later in the chapter. This statement traces the items in the profit statement and any extraneous items which cause a cash movement for both receipts and payments. In this way a quick eyeball check of the numbers against the profit budget can be made. This is specifically relevant on the payments side where items such as salary costs and overheads are specifically identifiable.

The opening balance each month (or quarter) plus the surplus (or minus the deficit) gives the closing balance before any borrowings or loans which have not yet been agreed. This immediately shows whether loans are required. By studying the phasing it can be seen whether this is a seasonal dip or whether it looks like a permanent borrowing requirement. The correct overdraft facility is the amount up to which the bank has agreed to pass cheques.

Each heading on the cash forecast shown in Figure 5:2 could be calculated on the basis set out below.

5:3:1   Receipts from debtors

By reference to the debt collection department, the forecast of number of days outstanding for the average debtor will be made for the next year. Receipts from debtors will be calculated on the basis of the current situation and the budgeted turnover. The financial manager should specifically question how debt collection will be speeded up. This is a good objective, but as the cash forecast is always very sensitive to changes in this number, it must not be over-optimistic. With most

Quarter/Month	1	2	3	4, etc.	Total
Receipts					
Trade debtors					
Investment income					
Loans/financing arranged					
Other					
Total Receipts					
Payments					
Stock purchases					
Salaries and costs of employment					
Other overheads					
Capital expenditure					
Interest					
Tax					
Repayment of loans					
Dividends					
Other					
Total payments					
Surplus/(deficit)					
Opening cash/(deficit)					
Closing cash/(deficit)					
Current overdraft facility					

Figure 5:2   Short-term cash forecast

companies this is the only receipt of any size, so there is no compensation if an error in forecasting is made.

5:3:2   Investment income

The investment income credited to the phased profit statement will be used after allowing for the receipt of cash.

5:3:3   Loans/financing arranged

This heading will only include financing which has been arranged prior to the budget. It does not include overdraft facilities as these will be shown at the bottom of the forecast. The object of the forecast is to see how the cash deficit measures against the current overdraft facility. The types of financing entered on this line will be mortgage money which will be received against capital expenditure, or a fixed loan or debenture of which the proceeds have not yet been received.

5:3:4   Other receipts

These receipts are essentially non-trading cash receipts and would include items such as the sale of fixed assets. These are sometimes accounted for by reducing the capital expenditure but unless a simultaneous purchase and trade-in (as with motor vehicles) is involved it is better to separate the receipt from the payment.

5:3:5   Stock purchases

The payments side of the forecast follows the logic of splitting expenditure as it appears in the profit budget. Thus, in a trading company, stock purchases equals the charge in the profit budget plus opening creditors less closing creditors.

To determine the closing creditors, an assumption will be made as to whether the company wishes to, or has to, pay creditors more quickly or slowly than at present. Stock purchases in many companies represent a large portion of total payments and can be a useful form of financing. The ethics of this must be carefully weighed up, especially for large companies which have a monopolistic buying power over small suppliers. The problem for a small company trying to finance itself out of creditors is (short of being sued) whether it obtains a name for being a bad payer and whether this affects business.

5:3:6   Salaries and costs of employment

Net salaries and wages in the profit budget are usually phased in line with the cash payments. The only items to be allowed for would be commissions or bonuses which are paid at a later date. Deducted tax and costs of employment as charged to the profit statement should be adjusted for creditors at the beginning and end of the period, as for stock purchases.

5:3:7   Other overheads

These consist of all items of cost (other than purchases and salary costs) between turnover and profit before depreciation. On the working papers it is easiest to run through the calculation from the charge by item to the profit budget, adding beginning creditors and deducting beginning prepayments. With expenses which are the normal invoice and payment type, the same logic applies as for stock purchases. With cash items such as travelling, etc., the profit charge needs no adjustment for the cash budget. Items such as rent and rates are usually paid in advance on specific days and this determines the phasing of the cash budget.

5:3:8   Capital expenditure

The capital plan must be produced alongside the profit plan, which in turn incorporates the production and sales plans. Plant to produce the end product is as much a plannable item as the purchase of raw material. Usually, it is more important to plan capital, especially facilities which have a long lead-time. For each item of capital expenditure in the plan the phases of management approval, commitment and cash spending should be specified, with dates and amounts. In the smaller business, management approval is basically when the owner says that a certain asset must be purchased. In many companies commitment is synomymous with approval. This date is important, however, as once a commitment is made it will cost the company money if it reverses its decision.

At the time of a capital budget the dates of the cash spending should be forecast. This forecast would be based on experience. With capital items having long lead-times from order to delivery (for instance a factory or specially designed machine tools), the capital requisition and management approval have probably happened before the budget. In this case the cash budget is dictated by the pre-calculated figures. For short lead-time items, the capital budget should operate from when the asset is required. It must be determined whether payment will be made on the delivery invoice or by stage payments.

5:3:9   Interest

The interest charge in the profit budget is itself calculated from the result of the cash forecast. This apparent problem of putting the cart before the horse can be resolved in one of two ways: either by calculating all items in the cash forecast (except interest), finalising this before completing the profit budget; or by using the last cash forecast with a rough adjustment for known large changes to produce the interest charge (the same logic applies to interest receivable) in the profit budget. The latter would appear easier in most cases.

Payment of interest on fixed loans and mortgages would be determined by the agreements.

5:3:10   Tax

Many companies end their formal planning at the profit before tax level, on the premise that as tax is unavoidable and uncontrollable it is not worth planning. This thinking is erroneous because the payment of tax is a significant item in a profitable company.

Tax planning is essential for a company based in the United Kingdom. It is even more vital if the company has overseas investments.

The payment of tax in the cash forecast is based on the rates and rules current at the time of the budget. The only deviation from this would be when a government has made a firm commitment to change the rates of corporation tax or capital allowances.

5:3:11   Repayment of loans

This item will include those repayments to which the company is committed. It is an item easily overlooked and could lead the company into serious legal problems if it is unable to repay loans or mortgages on time. Before completing the cash forecast the finance manager should check the last balance sheet published and any loans received since with the loan agreements to ensure that he is planning repayment at the correct time.

5:3:12   Dividends

These payments will consist of the final dividend on the current year's trading and probably an interim based on the first half of the budget year's trading. The amount of the dividend on preference shares is predetermined. The ordinary dividend would be forecast based on the company's dividend policy.

Dates of payment would be similar to the prior year unless circumstances have changed.

5:3:13   Other payments

This covers any payments not itemised above. These would include non-trading or extraneous loss items and would be shown in the cash forecast as circumstances might dictate.

5:4   Source and application of funds

This statement requires the prior production of the profit budget and forecast balance sheets. There must be a balance sheet at the end of each period for which the cash forecast is required.

Many companies budget profit on a monthly basis but balance sheets are only budgeted quarterly or annually. This makes a monthly source and application of funds statement more difficult to produce.

Figure 5:3 gives a possible layout for the source and application of funds statement.

This statement links into the profit figure then adds back all the items in the profit budget which are non-cash. This is mainly depreciation, but "other" would include provisions for bad debts, stock, etc., and the writing off of patents, etc. The total of these line items represents the cash inflow due to trading.

The outflow of cash is shown by balance sheet heading. The gross increase in fixed and current assets is deducted. This is calculated by reference to the balance sheets at the beginning and end of the forecast period.

The cash movement section will show tax and dividend payments. These figures will be opening creditor plus profit charge less closing creditor.

Loans received will be only those loans which have been arranged prior to the budget being prepared. Loan repayments will be repayments of existing loans.

The net movement in cash will, accordingly, be the change between opening and closing cash balances.

Quarter/Month	1	2	3	4, etc.	Total
Profit before tax Depreciation Other non-cash items in profit statement					

Increase/decrease in:
   Fixed assets
   Stocks
   Debtors
   Creditors
 	
Tax payment
Dividends paid
Loans received
Loans repaid					

Net movement in cash					

Opening cash surplus/
   (deficit)
Closing cash surplus/
   (deficit)					

Current overdraft facility					

Figure 5:3   Source and application of funds statement

5:5 Short-term cash control

Most companies segregate their cash control away from the profit performance control. Concentration is nearly always on the latter until cash problems arise. The statement that a company has "got to make money" is heard frequently, but money in this sense is profit and not specifically cash. Many businessmen equate profit with cash, but unless the two are linked it does not always happen that one follows the other.

The reporting of cash to central management should be at least as often as the profit reporting and could be on formats similar to Figures 5:2 or 5:3. The line narrative would be the same as the plans and the headings could be:

93

This month
Actual | Plan | Over/under plan

Year to date
Actual | Plan | Over/under plan

A facing page would explain variances which would correlate with the profit variance statement.

In this way there would be two types of variances—those related to profit performance, that is, volume or cost variances on production, sales or overheads, and those related to cash management. These would include items such as:

1 Improvement in debtor collection
2 Delay in payment of creditors
3 Early repayment of loans
4 Changes in tax or dividend payment

Control of the accuracy of forecasts is exercised by the comparison of actuals to budget. But the effect of any variance is as important as knowing what the variances are. If a variance is caused by a large payment being made one day late, and therefore in the next month's figures, this must be highlighted so that the short-term forecast, which gives a picture of the cash for the next two or three months, can pick it up.

5:6 Long-term cash forecasts

The basic principles of forecasting over a period longer than two years are essentially the same as for the short-term but the process and style of approach are different. The figures tend to be less accurate, of course, and the interest lies more in long-term trends than short-term fluctuations.

5:6:1 Objective

The objective of a long-term cash forecast is to see the cash flows which will be generated by the company's long-term profit plan and to assess the capital expenditure needed to attain that plan. The borrowing requirements of the company will be seen from the cash flows and decisions will be made as to how the finance can be raised. Alternatively, if cash surpluses build up, decisions can be made whether to increase dividends, or invest the cash outside the company, or invest within the company in the form of more revenue-earning assets.

If the forecast shows up a short-term requirement for finance, this could be covered by borrowing from the bank. A decision could alternatively be made to slow down or delay expansion.

A long-term requirement for cash would initiate a study into how that cash should be raised—by share capital increase, debenture issue or mortgage of property. This would depend on a lot of factors but quite a number of these could be decided by figures in the long-term forecast. The balance sheets would show the fixed asset movements, the un-mortgaged fixed assets, the debt/equity ratio, and the current asset situation. Outside factors, such as the general business climate and likely movement of interest rates, would be part of the basic assumptions behind the long-range plan.

5:6:2 Format

The format of the long-term cash forecast could be almost identical to the short-term source and application of funds. As a balance sheet would be produced (probably yearly) for the long-range forecast, this document would be used to produce the cash forecast; the cash forecast really becomes an integral part of the creation of the long-range plan, and is produced at the same time as the balance sheets.

The cash forecast in the short-term is a fairly self-contained exercise, but the long-range cash forecast covers a lot of corporate activities.

The profit before tax will be calculate from the profit forecast. This is determined by the forecast of new products, the costs and volumes, the marketing policy and the trend of overheads.

Depreciation will be based on the current policy with respect to the assets as forecast in the capital plan. This creates a problem as the capital plan is based on the facilities required to manufacture and sell the forecast products. One way to get round this is to assume a certain depreciation content in the unit manufacturing cost and the overheads.

The fixed assets increase is calculated from a facilities plan. This plan, basically, starts from the production and marketing plan to determine what facilities in terms of factories, offices and training centres are required, from this the space requirement is calculated. This is then costed and plant, vehicles and furniture are added to produce the forecast of capital expenditure. As this is one of the major long-term decisions made in any company it is a vital part of the long-term plan.

The stock levels would be based on historical trends of the ratio to cost of sales, updated by the marketing strategy which could specify a stock build-up just prior to launch of a new product.

Debtors and creditors would also be based on trends. Debtors have a direct relationship to turnover and creditors to purchases and overheads.

The tax payment will be based on the profits after calculating capital allowances. Normally, the current rates and timings of tax would be used, unless there is firm evidence that these would change.

The dividend payment requires a corporate decision as to what the company's dividend policy will be. Failing a policy, the current rate as a percentage of distributable profit would be used.

It is unlikely that any loans arranged at the present time would be received more than two years ahead, that is, after the period covered by the short-term cash forecast. But the repayment of existing loans must be covered.

From this it will be seen that overlapping decisions and calculations are required for the balance sheets and cash forecasts.

In the same way as the long-range profit forecast locks into each yearly balance sheet and shows the performance of the business as planned in terms of turnover and costs, so also does the long-range forecast in terms of where the money comes from and where it goes.

By definition, all forecasts are inaccurate as they are calculated from what the company planners think at one point in time. Tomorrow the strategy could be completely different. The cash forecaster has two problems here: first, how uncertain is the profit statement, and second, how uncertain are the other assumptions concerning cash?

Many companies now use a computer to produce the profit effect of various strategies, and having thus homed in on a politically acceptable profit figure, proceed to calculate the cash forecast in a deterministic way with just one set of rules. It is just as important to see a best and worst case for cash as it is on the profit side—in fact, more so if the company is in a capital-restricted situation. The calculations discussed earlier should therefore each be examined to see what chances there are of the situation being better or worse. Areas of specific flexibility would be:

1 The length of credit affecting debtors and creditors
2 Any significant change in interest rates
3 Changes in the tax laws affecting the rate of tax, calculations of capital allowances, tax on interest and dividends or the time of payment
4 Changes in national dividend policies
5 Changes in the international situation affecting remittances, blocked currencies, overseas borrowings and exchange rates

Without a computer program it would be impossible to flex the above without vast manual calculations. Obviously, it would be impossible ever to finish a forecast if every contingency were to be thought of and evaluated. But it is important to look at the risks and opportunities as far as they can be foreseen at the present time. This determines the areas of the company's operation which should be more closely analysed. Very often the original policies which were used at the start of the long-range cash forecast have to be changed.

5:7 Inflation

There is much argument as to whether inflation should be brought into long-range plans and, therefore, long-range cash forecasts.

The arguments for leaving inflation out of long-range plans are:

1 The long-term marketing strategy of the company can be evaluated more correctly
2 Sales prices can be inflated as costs inflate so that profit margins are not eroded
3 The rate of inflation cannot easily be forecast and decisions could be erroneous if based on an incorrect rate
4 If every figure is inflated by a fixed percentage each year, why bother?
5 Trends are more easily identified if based on the current year's value of money

Against this are the arguments for inflating long-term forecasts:

1 Costs do inflate automatically, there is nothing management can do about this, but sales prices only go up on the basis of a management decision

2   Future requirements of cash will be in that year's value of money and not today's

3   As inflation is here to stay it should be taken into account

The net result of this is that the inclusion of inflation will depend on what the forecast is to be used for.

The problem can be solved by running two or three cases of each long-range strategy:

1   Without inflation to look at the profitability of the marketing strategy and trends of sales, costs and profits

2   With costs inflated to determine how much prices will have to be increased to maintain margins

3   With costs inflated and sales prices increased to determine future cash requirements

The long-term cash forecast must show each year, in that year's money, what cash will be generated and on what it will be spent.

Many capital projects are spread over a number of years in terms of completion and payback. Financing is often raised at the beginning and must be planned to cover the inflated costs through the project. This can be shown in a very simple graph, as in Figure 5:4. The example assumes a capital project costing £10m (price fixed) which takes one year to build. During years two to six, sales from this plant are forecast at £4m per annum with costs of £1m in present money. There is no residual value after year six. In uninflated terms the cash inflow of the project would be:

		£m
	5 years sales at £4m p.a.	20
Less	5 years sales at £1m p.a.	(5)
	Capital spending	(10)
	Profit	5

In inflated terms, the running costs (assuming 10 per cent inflation per annum) would be: year two, £1.1m, year three, £1.21m, etc. totalling £6.7m to year six. Profit would then total £3.3m, assuming sales prices

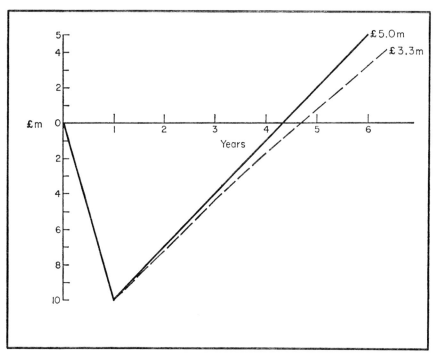

Figure 5:4   Cumulative cash flow graph

were not increased. This would then prompt a decision as to whether prices could be increased. But unless they were, profit would be significantly reduced.

5:8   Dynamic aspect

The actual cash movements change from plan in the same way as the actual profits. It is therefore essential to update forecasts continuously.

In the long-term the frequency with which forecasts are updated should be the same as for profit. This would be determined by the frequency of changed strategies and markets, and the effect of these on the resources of the company.

In the short-term the cash situation of the company and the significance of changes from the year's plan should dictate the frequency of reviews of the cash forecast. It is useless to update a no-change cash forecast where there is plenty of cash available. However, where cash is the restraining item in the company's policies, reviews more frequent than a month may be required. It is most important to differentiate between trends and daily ups and downs.

5:9   International aspects

An international company's objective for cash does not necessarily correlate exactly with the policy for profits. Whereas the profit objective could be to maximise after-tax profit so that on consolidation the group shows the best earnings per share situation, cash does not necessarily show this.

The cash policy should be determined by what the cash is to be used for. This is usually a mixture of paying the dividend of the holding company and ploughing back for internally financed expansion.

The methods of getting cash into the holding company from overseas subsidiaries are:

1   Dividends
2   Repayment of loans or share capital
3   Payment for goods exported by the holding company to a subsidiary
4   Payment by a subsidiary of management fees, fees for technological know how or royalties

All these cash transactions are subject to the roles of each country's national bank. They change frequently and are designed to guard the balance of payments positions. This is often in contradiction with a company's policy of trying to reduce its exposure to parity changes. That is, money is borrowed in a country likely to devalue and held in a country likely to revalue. Against this, of course, interest rates tend to be high in the former countries and low in the latter. This produces a compensating effect.

A financial manager's responsibilities are to safeguard company assets and take reasonable precautions against currency risks; his job is not to play the money market.

PART TWO

Costing and Budgetary Control

Chapter 6

Standard Costing and Marginal Costing

H W Calvert, formerly Principal Lecturer in Management Accountancy, North East London Polytechnic

I : Standard costing

Standard costing has much in common with budgetary control, which is considered in the next chapter. They are both methods of business control, but whereas budgetary control can be applied to almost any business and, indeed, to a person's domestic financial affairs, standard costing is generally restricted to industrial activities where there are products or processes of a repetitive nature. The accent in the case of standard costing is on products and processes, not, as in budgetary control, on the responsibility of executives.

In the early days of its development costing was directed towards providing a basis for price fixing, but the tendency is now to direct it towards control. This involves the provision of information which results in *management action* where necessary; standard cost control provides this information.

In costing, all the items of cost are divided into three main categories or elements: *materials*; *labour*; and *expenses*; but for the purposes of standard costing the main analysis is into *direct materials*; *direct labour*; and *overheads*.

6:1   Fixing a standard

Standard costing, being a technique of comparisons—the *actual* with the *standard*—the first problem is to fix the standard. There are three types of standard generally considered.

6:1:1   Historical

This is based on costs previously achieved and may easily be ascertained, but it has two principal defects. Standard costing will be of major value when applied to an industrial unit where control has been inadequate. In such an organisation the past performance may provide a weak standard which could be easily attained and so give little incentive to management and factory supervision. Also, if standard costs based on such a foundation are used as a guide to price fixing, then either prices may be fixed at an uncompetitive level or the sales department may consider that many lines cannot be remunerative.

6:1:2   Ideal

This is based on the assumptions that plant will always work at full available capacity; there will be no unavoidable loss of material; the highest grade of labour will be available and there will be no lost time. Such a standard would present a target which the most energetic supervisor would not attempt to attain and a cost which could never be achieved in practice. The result might be that the sales department would be tempted to offer products at unremunerative prices.

6:1:3   Normal or expected

This is based, probably after work study, on agreement between the management functions concerned—production, personnel, purchasing and costing on the levels which could be attained under normal working conditions. For most purposes this type of standard is to be preferred.

6:1:4   Revision of standards

Ideally a standard, once established, should not be altered, but the continued effect of wage and price increases in recent years tends to make a standard unrealistic from the financial point of view unless it is reviewed at regular intervals. A revision on more than an annual basis is not to be recommended.

From the point of view of technical efficiency an alteration of the quantitative aspect should *not* be made unless there has been a significant change in the techniques of the process.

6:1:5   Direct materials

The standard cost of direct materials will depend on the standard *quantity* of material to be used per unit produced and the standard *price* of that material. The quantity will be based on the specification of the product and the process losses and rejects which are agreed as the standard between production management and the cost department. The standard price will be based on the average price which should be paid over the period under consideration, taking into account that a material may have to be purchased from several suppliers.

6:1:6   Direct labour

Where possible the standard cost of direct labour should be based on a work study of the operations involved. This will fix the standard times for each process and, where an incentive scheme is in operation, the standard hourly rate will be that which would be payable at the standard efficiency.

6:1:7   Overheads

For the purpose of standard costing it is advisable that overheads be divided into *variable* and *fixed* items (the essential differences of this sub-division are dealt with in the section on marginal costing).

Variable overheads are generally the smallest part of the standard cost of production: they may include the power and lighting of individual machines, running maintenance and the cost of bringing materials to the work place and removing the finished production. A standard cost per unit produced can be assessed by technical advice regarding the materials used and by work study with respect to labour.

The fixing of the standard cost of the above mentioned items has been based on the production of a single unit during a given period. However the item *fixed overheads* is a cost which refers primarily to the length of the *period* and not to the quantity produced. To arrive at a standard unit cost of production for fixed overheads it is necessary to assess the standard activity for a period and the fixed overhead expenditure which should be incurred at that level.

Fixed overheads includes those items of expenses which do not vary in *direct proportion* to the production. These costs tend to change by steps at certain points in the expansion or reduction in the activity of a production unit. Certain items will be definitely fixed in respect of a production unit; rates, building insurance, general lighting, security and the maintenance of buildings and roadways are costs which will not vary over wide differences in the use of the production facilities. The fixed overhead per unit will be the budgeted expenditure for the period (preferably a year to allow for seasonal variations on certain items) divided by the relevant standard units of production.

A standard cost for each process of the production unit has now been reached, and from these process standards the standard cost per unit of each of the saleable products can be built up. This information may assist in fixing the selling price of the products, but even if sales prices are restricted by competition it will show the margin which will be obtained from the different products if the standard conditions are followed.

As explained later, in the section on marginal costing, there are other considerations apart from the standard profit which have to be taken into account when preparing a sales policy.

6:2   Cost control through variance analysis

The most important service which standard costing can give to management is information for the control of costs through *variance analysis*. The difference of the valuation of the production for a period at standard cost and the actual cost for that period is of great use to management, but even greater is the consideration of changes in this variance from one period to another. This shows how efficiency is moving.

The standard cost of the production of each section for the period under consideration will first be calculated. This will be the quantity of each item *actually* produced, multiplied by its standard cost in that process. This amount represents the cost which should have been incurred under standard conditions. The actual cost incurred will be available from the records kept in the financial and cost accounting departments. Actual material costs will be available from the stores issues and invoices for materials charged direct to individual jobs. The direct and indirect labour costs will be available from the wages analysis. Other items of overheads can be obtained from suppliers' invoices and from the apportionment of whole items of expense to the various production cost centres. The latter will apply to service charges, electricity, insurance, rates, etc., which are not allocated in the original charge.

6:2:1   Direct materials

The analysis of direct material costs can be obtained in the following manner. If the standard for producing one unit of product XYZ is, say, 10 lb of material AB at a standard price of 20p per lb that is, £2.00 per unit, and if the production in week eight is 2000 units, the standard cost of material for the week will be:

$$£2.00 \times 2000 = £4000$$

If the actual consumption of material has been 20 500 lb which has cost £4260, there will have been an *adverse direct material cost variance* of £260 (A). This information is useful to management as it is a significant amount which must be investigated. The variance may be due to a number of factors which must be isolated. The most important are the *price* and *usage* variances into which the direct material cost variance is usually analysed.

The direct material price variance is the difference between what the material used should have cost and what it actually cost. In this case the material used should have cost

$$£0.20 \times 20\ 500 = £4100$$

As the actual cost was £4260, the direct material price variance is £160 (A).

The quantity of material which should have been used was

$$2000 \times 10lb = 20\ 000\ lb$$

so there is an *excess* usage of 500 lb which at the *standard price* of 20p, costs £100. This is the direct material usage variance which, again, is adverse. Note that the price and usage variances together make up the total direct material cost variance, that is,

$$£160\ (A) + £100\ (A) = £260\ (A)$$

Where more than one material is used in making a product the price variance is generally shown in respect of each material. The usage variance can be calculated for each material, but in cases where the proportions of certain materials may vary, if there is a difference in the price of the materials, a cost variance will arise from any variation in the composition of the mixture.

If an alloy is made of 70 per cent of "A" and 30 per cent of "B" which cost, at standard prices, £200 per ton and £300 per ton respectively, and a batch of metal is made up from 600 tons of "A" and 400 tons of "B", there will be a materials mixture variance. At *standard prices* the 1000 tons should have cost

$$£(700 \times 200) + (300 \times 300) = £230\ 000$$

whereas it cost

$$£(600 \times 200) + (400 \times 300) = £240\ 000$$

giving a material mixture variance of £100 (A).

The material mixture variance is always calculated on the *standard* prices after the price variance has been taken on the *actual* material used. The fact that the proportions of the materials in a mixture are not as standard is no guarantee that a mixture variance presents reliable information. The use of an excess of one or more of the materials may be due to process technicalities.

The direct material usage variance is defined as that portion of the direct materials cost variance which is due to the difference between the standard quantity specified and the actual quantity used. Where there is a mixture variance, the difference from standard due to the total quantity of materials used is referred to as the direct materials *yield* variance. The mixture and yield variances will together equal the usage variance so that where there is no mixture variance shown, the usage variance and the yield variance will be the same.

6:2:2 Labour

The analysis of cost variances for labour is similar to that of materials, except that the major sub-variances are referred to as *rate* and *efficiency* instead of price and usage. Each production manager will require a further analysis of the efficiency variance according to the techniques of the operations and the relative significance of the individual variances.

If, in the above mentioned case, the labour cost had been set at a standard of a production of five units per labour hour with an hourly wage rate at this level of productivity of 60p per hour, that is, 12p per unit, and the wages cost of production in week eight had been 420 hours, which cost £246, there would be a direct wages variance of £6 (A) because the standard wages cost was

$$£2000 \times £0.12 = £240$$

The analysis of this variance would be direct wages rate variance

$$£420 \times £0.60 - 246 = £6 \text{ (F)}$$

The variance is *favourable* (F) because the actual cost was less than the hours worked at the standard rate.

The direct labour efficiency variance will be

$$£(420 - 400) \times £0.60 = £12 \text{ (A)}$$

—adverse because the actual hours worked exceeded the standard hours for the actual production.

Where a financial incentive scheme is in operation, it is generally found that an adverse efficiency variance will result in a favourable rate variance owing to the average rate earned being less than the standard. Conversely, if there is a favourable efficiency variance, the bonus will be high and there will be an adverse rate variance.

6:2:3 Overheads

For the purpose of variance analysis it is advisable to have the overheads divided into *variable* and *fixed* costs. A standard having been agreed for the variable overhead, the variable overhead variance can be calculated by multiplying the production for the period by this unit standard cost and comparing the result with the actual expenditure on account of the relative indirect costs. These items can be obtained from the stores requisitions, wages analysis, etc. A more detailed analysis of the variable overhead variance may not be justified on account of the expense, but, if required, that part which is due to prices can be calculated, as also can variances in the quantities of the items utilised.

As mentioned earlier *fixed overheads* are a "period" cost so that the unit cost must be compiled from the expenditure, production and working hours budgeted for the same period. In the case of product XYZ, assuming that the budget for the year is a production of 110 000 units to be produced in fifty working weeks of 440 hours each at a fixed overhead cost of £5500, the unit cost of fixed overheads will thus be 5p, and the rate per hour worked 25p. If the actual fixed overhead is recorded as £122 for week eight, the standard cost of the production is

$$£2000 \times £0.05 = £100$$

so the *fixed overhead cost variance* is £22 (A). This variance arises from two factors: the difference between the actual expenditure (£122) and the budget amount allowed for the period (£110) which gives a *fixed overhead expenditure variance* of £12 (A), and the difference between the actual production for the week (2000 units) and the budgeted production (2200 units) which gives the *overhead volume variance*

$$(2200 - 2000) \times £0.05 = £10 \text{ (A)}$$

Again, the expenditure variance and the volume variance add up to the fixed overhead cost variance.

$$£12 \text{ (A)} + 10 \text{ (A)} = £22 \text{ (A)}$$

The expenditure variance arises from the prices of the items included in the fixed overhead and the utilisation of the factors employed—higher wattage lamps being used in corridors, extra security staff being required. The volume variance is due to the production being above or below the budgeted figure, the result of the number of hours worked being above or below the budget, and the labour efficiency being favourable or adverse.

The *capacity usage variance* is favourable if *more* hours than the budgeted number have been worked. This can cause some difficulty unless it is remembered that the more hours worked, the more should be produced, other things being equal. In week eight, 420 hours were worked against a budget of 440, so there was a loss of twenty working hours which, at the fixed overhead cost of 25p per hour, is a variance of £5 (A).

The *volume efficiency variance* is related to the labour efficiency variance if the former has been based on labour hours. In some cases it may be based on machine hours. As the production is equal to 400 standard hours there is again a loss;

$$£(420 - 400) \times .25 = £5 \text{ (A)}$$

The capacity usage variance and the volume efficiency variance are together equal to the volume variance.

Where the fixed overhead is budgeted on a monthly basis and the number of working days in the month varies, the volume variance may include a *calendar variance*. This will be favourable when the number of working days in a month exceeds the average, and adverse when it is less. The greater the number of days in the month, the higher the production

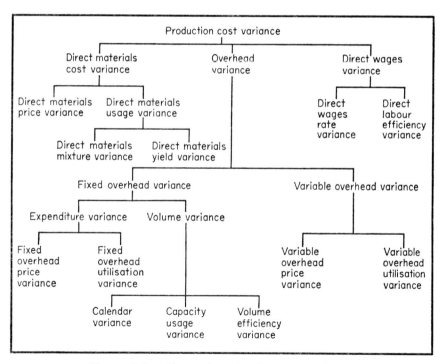

Figure 6:1   Chart of production cost variance

DEPARTMENT X   OPERATION X12A   PRODUCT XYZ

Report for week no. 8, ending 2 May 19.. Standard cost per unit: £2.22

	Budget	Standard	Actual	Variance	Analysis
Production units	2200		2000	200 (A)	
Materials lb.	22 000	20 000	20 500	500 (A)	
Labour hours	440	400	420	20 (A)	
Costs					
Direct materials £	4400	4000	4260	260 (A)	
Price					160 (A)
Usage					100 (A)
Direct labour	264	240	246	6 (A)	
Rate					6 (F)
Efficiency					12 (A)
Overhead variable	110	100	106	6 (A)	
Price					8 (A)
Utilisation					2 (F)
Overhead fixed	110	100	122	22 (A)	
Price					10 (A)
Utilisation					2 (A)
= Expenditure					12 (A)
Calendar					—
Capacity usage					5 (A)
Volume efficiency					5 (A)
= Volume					10 (A)
Totals £	4884	4440	4734	294 (A)	

Note: The standard cost for the period will bear the same ratio to the budgeted cost as the *actual* production bears to the budgeted production.

Figure 6:2   Example of a cost report

should be, thus tending to improve the volume variance. The sum of the calendar variance for the year will always be *nil*.

It has been shown how the total production cost variance can be analysed so as to show more accurate information regarding the cause of cost excesses and savings. A chart of this analysis, such as that shown in Figure 6:1, may be useful. It is not exhaustive and further analysis can be made to suit individual requirements.

6:2:4   Presentation

The presentation of the analysis of the cost variances is very important; it should be prepared so as to show the maximum of information
in the minimum of space and with economy of figures. A cost report on
week eight from the figures previously quoted might appear as shown
in Figure 6:2.

II : Marginal costing

Profit is the net receipts from the sales of the products or services which the business sells less the total costs of providing those products or services. Assuming in the first place that selling prices do not vary, profit will depend on:

1 The volume of sales
2 The cost of those sales

Every manager appreciates that the greater the excess of the selling price over the unit cost of production, administration and selling, the greater will be the profit. The question to be considered at this stage is: "What is this excess or margin?" The shopkeeper who buys all his wares from a wholesaler at the listed retail price less a trade discount of twenty-five per cent knows that a quarter of his takings, after allowing for the overheads of the business, is his profit.

In a small shop these latter items can be segregated from the cost of the produce which he sells, without much difficulty. The rent, rates, electricity, water, insurance and depreciation on the fittings will be the same whether his sales reach £400 per week, or only £40. If his business expands he may eventually have to obtain extra assistance in the shop and even acquire more equipment, scales, show-cases and counters, but with small variations in the volume of his business these items will vary little. The cost of the merchandise will, of course, vary with the quantity that he sells, subject to any special discounts for large purchases.

For the manufacturer, however, the problem is not so simple. The cost of the raw materials and components which he buys tends to vary directly with the volume of his production, but in addition to the items mentioned above there are many others which do not vary in proportion to the activity of the business and are described as *fixed*.

The classification of some items of cost between fixed and variable can be difficult. The direct labour employed for converting raw materials into a saleable product used to be considered a variable cost because, if trade was slack, workers were discharged or stood off without pay.

The cost of training labour, the difficulty in obtaining even the untrained labour and the economic consequences of the guaranteed working week have resulted in labour costs tending to become a fixed expense which only changes with large and prolonged variations in the volume of production.

The growth in the cost of the capital per head employed, with its inherent depreciation and interest charges, is continually increasing the proportion of the fixed costs in the total cost which has to be absorbed in the selling price before a profit is earned. The result has been that a school of thought has arisen which considers that the absorption of fixed costs into the costs of individual products is of little value for control purposes because it must be on an arbitrary basis which may produce an unrealistic picture of the profitability of different products. As there are at least four popular methods of absorbing overheads into product costs the variations can be significant.

The *marginal costing* advocates consider that only the variable or *marginal* costs should be absorbed into the product costs and that the excess of the receipts from sales over the marginal cost is the important factor to be considered for control purposes. This excess of selling price over the marginal cost is called the *contribution* in this country. In the USA the terms *contributory margin* and *marginal profit* are often used.

The marginal cost may be defined as:

The amount at any given volume of output by which aggregate costs are changed if the volume of output is increased or decreased by one unit.

The marginal cost being less than the total cost of a product, it follows that a selling price which would show a loss compared with the total cost might offer a fair profit compared with the marginal cost. Why, then, is the marginal cost not used as a basis for fixing all selling prices? The answer is that the contribution from all sales must first meet the cost of the fixed expenses before any net profit is made. The first application of marginal costing was as a technique for use in times of trade recession when plant was under-utilised and business could not be obtained at prices which would cover the total unit cost. A simple example will illustrate such a situation:

Plant capacity	100 000 units
Cost of 100 000 units	
Direct materials	£300 000
Direct labour	100 000
Variable production overhead	10 000
Fixed production overhead	150 000
Administration expenses	80 000
Variable selling expenses	10 000
Fixed selling expenses	50 000
	£700 000 = £7 per unit

At a sales price of £8 per unit a profit of £100 000 will be made, and this may be a fair return on the capital employed in the business. However, if the plant is working at only eighty per cent of capacity the variable cost will be eighty per cent of £420 000 or £336 000. The fixed expenses will remain at £280 000, a total cost of £616 000. The sales at £8 per unit will be £640 000 giving a net profit of only £24 000. The sales department is unable to obtain any further business at £8 to fill the vacant capacity, but a customer can be found for 10 000 units at £6.50. This business appears to be unremunerative as the total cost is £7.00 per unit. However on a marginal cost basis the unit cost is £4.20, so that the price of £6.50 will show a contribution of £2.30 per unit and this will increase the net profit by £23 000, nearly doubling that important figure.

Useful as the marginal costing technique is, there are certain precautions which must be observed when using it and there are certain restrictions on its use. The most significant of these are:

1   Business at such cut prices must not be taken on long-term contracts where there is a chance that before the contract is completed trade may improve and orders at more remunerative prices could be booked
2   Business must not be taken on a marginal cost basis in the same market where more normal prices are being obtained. This policy might offend established customers and, in the case of overseas business, care must be taken that the low price exports do not come back into this country in competition with the company's own sales in the home market

6:3   Break-even graphs

The graphical presentation of marginal costing information can be of special use to management in the form of a break-even graph or profit chart. Assuming that the fixed expenses are stable throughout the probable range of sales, the marginal cost aspect can be presented in the following manner. A graph is drawn taking the horizontal axis as the amount of the sales, either in quantity or in value; if there are a number of items sold the total figure must be expressed in value. The sales figure will start at zero and cover the maximum range of the sales. The vertical axis will represent the receipts from sales and the expenses incurred, both fixed and variable.

Having estimated the fixed expenses for the period under review this point is located on the vertical axis and from it a line is drawn parallel to the horizontal axis. From the production cost budget and the selling cost budget the marginal cost of the budgeted sales can be ascertained. A line can now be drawn from the point on the vertical axis from which the fixed cost line started so as to show at the budgeted sales the total expenses of the organisation for that level of sales. In the graph in Figure 6:3 the fixed expenses have been taken as £280 000 per annum, and the variable costs of 100 000 units as £420 000.

The receipt from sales line can now be drawn, commencing from the origin where the vertical and horizontal axes meet to show sales of £800 000 for 100 000 units. Assuming that there is a contribution, that is, that the sales price exceeds the marginal cost, this line will cut the line of total cost at a point where the receipt from sales equals the total cost. This junction is called the *break-even point*, the level of activity at which there is neither profit nor loss. The distance of the receipt from sales line above or below the total cost line will show the net profit at the relative level of sales.

6:3:1   The profit/volume (P/V) ratio

The break-even graph will show at a glance the sales which must be achieved to obtain any required net profit, and also the effect on the profit potential of variations in the fixed expenses and the *profit volume ratio*. The P/V ratio is an important factor in planning the profitability of an enterprise; it is the relation of the *contribution* to the *net sales* expressed as a percentage. A trading concern will aim at concentrating its business on the products which offer the highest P/V ratio, subject to factors which will be considered later.

The greater the P/V ratio the wider will be the angle at which the receipt from sales line cuts the line of total cost. This angle is known as the *angle of incidence* and it should be watched carefully.

Another important feature of the break-even graph is the excess of the sales for any period over the sales for the same period at the break-even point. This difference which is known as the *margin of safety*, should also be watched carefully as it indicates the amount by which the sales can fall before the profit made will be reduced to zero and losses will start to be incurred.

In drawing a break-even graph it must be remembered that in practice the fixed expenses are not constant for all levels of activity; they tend to increase in stages as the activity rises, but they do not fall so quickly when there is a recession in trade. Account must also be taken of the tendency for sales prices to fall if sales are pushed beyond a certain point. This may be due to larger trade discounts being granted. Variable costs may be reduced by bulk-buying when trade expands, but higher rates may have to be paid for skilled labour if the demand increases. These factors must be considered when the line of total cost is drawn; in practice it will not be straight but may curve upwards or downwards.

The break-even graph may be used for other purposes as well as showing the effect of varying levels of sales on the net profit. Other applications include the evaluation of different methods of distribution. Should the company run its own van or send its goods by carrier? Here the comparison is that of a fixed cost per article or per ton mile (the total cost depending on the quantity carried) with the fixed cost of a van (tax, insurance, depreciation, garage and driver's costs) plus a running cost per mile or ton mile. The break-even graph may be used to show the amount of traffic which must be handled to make the introduction of the van an economic project.

The graph in Figure 6:3 shows an orthodox break-even graph based on the figures given earlier. The graph in Figure 6:4 shows the shape which the graph might take in practice.

6:3:2 The "profit" or "contribution" chart

The break-even graph is fairly well known in industry, but for most purposes the profit chart will present the same information in a simpler

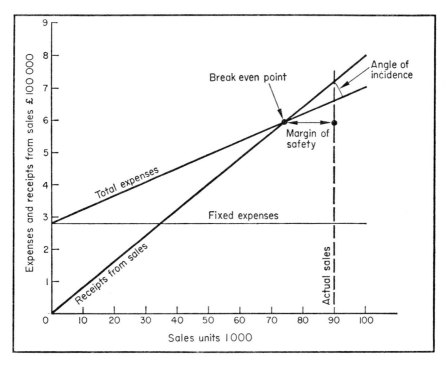

Figure 6:3   Example of an orthodox break-even graph

manner, with less probability of errors in drafting, and in a way which often displays the effect of a policy more clearly. In the profit chart the horizontal axis can be drawn as for the break-even graph, but to obtain the best effect the positioning of this on the page is most important. The vertical axis will be drawn below, as well as above, the horizontal axis. It will be graded in values but, instead of showing costs and receipts from sales, it will show profits above the horizontal axis and losses below the horizontal axis .

Taking the case previously quoted, if there were no sales there would be a loss equal to the amount of the fixed expenses (£280 000). This fixes one point on the profit line, zero on the sales line and −£280 on the profit axis. As there is a contribution of £3.80 per unit sold the profit line will start from this point and rise £3.80 per unit until, at sales of 100 000 units, the loss of £280 000 is converted into a profit of £100 000.

The graph thus drawn is that not of cost and sales but of the contribution. This line will cut the horizontal axis at the break-even point; the

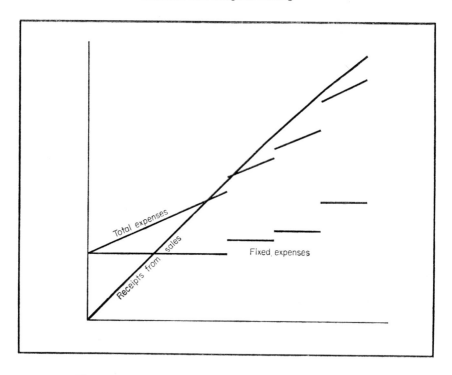

Figure 6:4   Example of a modified break-even graph

horizontal axis is therefore sometimes called the break-even line. To obtain the best use of the page an estimate should be made of the highest figure which the fixed expenses are likely to reach and also the net profit. The break-even line can then be placed so that a scale can be used which will make full use of the page. The chart in Figure 6:5 shows the information used for the graph in Figure 6:2 in the form of a profit chart.

6:3:3   The limiting factor

The P/V ratio is of great value to management, but the product which shows the highest P/V ratio may not always provide the maximum profit. Some factor limits the activity of every business; it may be sales, finance, or one of the factors of production, plant capacity, labour or materials. Shortage of one item of material or one grade of labour may

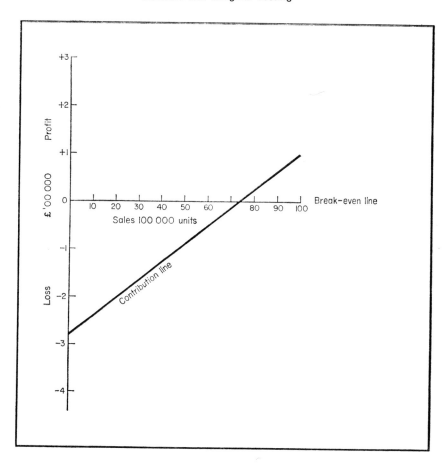

Figure 6:5   Example of a profit or contribution chart

be the limiting factor. If the plant is not fully occupied and there is no shortage of the labour and materials required, then provided that the company has the financial resources, sales will be the limiting factor. The sales department will push the sales of the items with the highest P/V ratios.

Where, however, the plant can be fully employed, the use of restricted facilities must be taken into consideration. In the following illustration it is assumed that the sales department has ample orders to employ the factory at the prices quoted:

Product	A	B
Units produced per hour	10	20
	£	£
Direct materials	4.00	8.00
Direct labour	0.08	0.04
Variable production overhead	0.16	0.08
Variable selling overhead	0.40	0.60
Total marginal cost	4.64	8.72
Selling price	5.80	10.17
Contribution	£1.16	1.45
P/V ratio per cent	20	14

Although the P/V ratio of A is much higher than B, the contribution per unit of B is greater than for A, and the contribution per hour will be £29 for B against £11.60 for product A, because twice as many units of B can be produced as units of A. Where products have to pass through several processes, the planning of production and sales to obtain the optimum product mixture is most important. It is not always best to concentrate on the products which show the highest P/V ratio or even the highest contribution per unit. Sometimes a product mixture which leaves certain units of the plant under-employed will yield the highest contribution, and *profit*.

This example shows the danger of a sales department fixing selling prices on the basis of costs, total or marginal, without understanding the implication of limiting factors which may operate with regard to certain processes.

6:4 Make or to buy?

An important decision may often face the management when the plant is fully occupied and components are required which could be made in the factory or purchased from outside sources. Apart from considerations of quality, reliability of delivery and credit terms, the profit position can be assessed by the application of marginal costing. The following simple example will demonstrate the basis of a management decision.

Component	X	Z	
Production per hour	20	30	units
Direct labour	£0.05	0.033	
Direct materials	4.00	3.00	
Other variable costs	0.45	0.167	
Total marginal cost	4.50	3.20	
Purchase price outside	5.50	4.00	
Saving per unit if made in the factory	1.00	0.80	
Saving per hour if made in the factory	20.00	24.00	

If there is not sufficient plant capacity to produce the requirements of both components, it will pay to make Z and buy X, for although the saving on Z is only £0.80 per unit as compared with £1.00 per unit for X, the saving per machine hour is £24 for Z against £20 for X. Assuming that the fixed overhead on the machine will be the same in each case, an apportionment of this cost to the two components is unnecessary and has therefore been ignored.

The application of marginal costing may highlight important factors when a decision has to be made as to which of two or more factories should be closed because of the existence of capacity surplus to needs.

Chapter 7

Budgets and Budgetary Control

Alan R Leaper, Financial Controller,
Hoover Limited—Export

All businesses have some form of budgetary control in existence whether or not they recognise it or call it by that name. Someone in the organisation co-ordinates the resources of the business in some degree to achieve some sort of plan, but whether they examine alternative plans, ideal criterion and harmony of objectives is possibly another question.

There are many benefits to be derived from the introduction of a formalised budgetary control system amongst which are:

1 It defines the objectives of an organisation as a whole and in financial terms
2 It provides yardsticks by which to measure efficiency for various parts of the organisation
3 It reveals the extent by which actual results have varied from the defined objective
4 It provides a guide for corrective action
5 It facilitates centralised control with delegated responsibility

The disadvantages of a formalised procedure are by no means so readily identifiable; in general terms they usually concern the following:

1 The additional costs/personnel necessary to perform the function
2 The suspicions aroused by its introduction that it is merely another vehicle to implement cost reduction programmes
3 The complacency of paper work becoming routine with the eventual possibility that little notice or action is taken

Immediate benefits should not be expected from the introduction of a budget procedure; it may take a year or two to educate those concerned in the proper compilation of the data required and in the proper application of the data subsequently made available.

7:1 What is a budget?

A budget is a predetermined plan, expressed in financial terms, covering all phases of a business. It should state quite specifically what is expected of the company in terms of profitability and how the plan is to be achieved. It is not a forecast, a prediction or a "guesstimate," but a well conceived plan which shows the desired level of profitability allied to all the resources available to a business.

Many alternative plans may be considered before the final one showing the most practical profit is chosen. Executives and other responsible officials from all functions of the company must contribute towards the plan. Data in the unit terms of each of the functions concerned must be collected and translated into monetary terms. For example, the sales manager is primarily concerned with units of the finished article or service and would therefore contribute the volume and models to be included in the plan. The production manager talks in standard hours and efficiencies. The personnel manager will be responsible for the levels of wage rates, absenteeism factors, welfare schemes, etc. The chief executive must be fully convinced of the benefits to be derived from the plan and really believe in it.

Budgetary control is the process of managing these facets—planning and co-ordinating all functions so that they work in harmony and control performances and costs. It establishes the responsibility, throughout the corporate structure, of all managers for achieving the company's budgeted objectives. It entails measuring at suitable intervals how the plan is actually progressing and, if divergencies are occurring, taking the necessary corrective action to ensure that the company gets back on course again.

By having a budget built up in this manner it is possible to fix responsibility at every level of the organisation—and this is important.

7:2 Compiling a budget

There is really no established order in which budgets should be prepared provided all parts are geared into a common factor. This is generally the principal limiting or bottleneck factor which varies for each individual company.

Most companies tend to establish a sales target determined on market potential and their share of the market as the basis of their budgets. Many others prefer to establish their production capacity and plan a budget to ensure the full utilisation of available equipment. The ideal, of course, is to achieve a harmony of both of these important items. However, there are many other factors which may determine the level of activity to be budgeted, amongst which are insufficient cash to finance expansion, a scarce raw material, and, possibly, the non-availability of skilled labour.

Having established the basis for compiling the budget all known external factors which could have a bearing on its fulfilment must be examined—national wage awards, sales taxes, credit squeezes, the movement of purchase prices, etc.

In larger organisations a budget committee is usually formed to review these items and determine, as best it can, the likely effect they will have on business during the period to be used in the budget. Having determined these external factors, the budget accountant/committee would advise functional and departmental managers of their effects and provide guidelines for the compilation of the subsidiary departmental budgets, the main examples of which are considered below.

7:2:1 Sales budget

The sales budget should show total sales in quantity and value. It may be analysed further by product, by area, by customer and, of course, by seasonal pattern of expected sales.

The main problems arise in the determination of quantities and the calculation of standard prices.

The budget should be compiled by the sales manager, who will seek the opinions of his salesmen and use any statistical forecasting techniques arising from market research. Other considerations include general business and economic conditions, company policies regarding advertising, new products, supplies, product demand and plant capacity.

A special pricing study is usually helpful at this stage and should show the complete product range, the sector of the market to be competed in, competitive models or products (both pricing and features available), in'roduction dates, discount structures and advertising strategy.

In some cases, when jobbing production is involved, budgets must be made in terms of the expected sales value only.

7:2:2   Production budget

The production budget is a statement of the output by product and is generally expressed in standard hours. It should take into consideration the sales budget, plant capacity, whether stocks are to be increased or decreased and outside purchases.

The form the budget would take depends upon circumstances. Usually the quantities are shown for each department (known as budget centres) and information is taken from machine loading charts, material specifications, time schedules and other production or time-study records.

The production budget will be prepared by the plant manager in close co-operation and collaboration with accountants, production engineers, work study engineers and other key personnel.

At this stage, the sales and production budgets should be compared to ensure the maximum utilisation of capacity aligned to satisfactory sales growth. If the sales budget exceeds the production capacity, decisions on capital expenditure and new plant may be required before proceeding further. If significant under-utilisation of existing capacity is denoted, decisions on how best to use this spare capacity must be undertaken to determine, for instance, if sub-contract work is profitable, if a revised pricing structure could increase volume or if plant should be declared redundant and scrapped, etc.

7:2:3 Production costs budget

This supplementary budget should determine the "cost of sales" allied to the required production.

Generally, by far the largest element in cost terms is direct material. This part should be compiled by the chief buyer in conjunction with the production manager. Using the sales and production budgets, it will determine the requirements of raw material and piece-parts, period by period, to meet the output, and will be evaluated in cash cost terms. Considerations should take into account bulk buying, delivery periods, stock holding, suppliers credit terms and trade discounts, as well as recognising any changes in material specifications, new model introductions, etc. In timing the purchase of raw materials, piece-parts, etc., consideration must be given to the necessity to keep inventory levels to the very minimum and thereby not tie up valuable capital. Special competitive pricing exercises should be undertaken from potential suppliers to ensure that costs are strictly controlled and keen.

Direct labour is another most important element of production costs. The work study department should be called upon to establish standard times for individual units. These may then be evaluated by the required volumes and converted into direct labour requirements. The degree of labour efficiency must be determined, as must the type of employee necessary, that is, male/female; skilled/semi-skilled/unskilled.

Direct expense budgets covering warehousing, transportation, warranty and special tools should be determined by the appropriate managers responsible for incurring or approving the respective expenses.

Factory overhead costs (burden) should be established by departmental foremen and consolidated by the production manager. Expenses of all types should be considered and some assistance may be necessary from the finance department in determining depreciation, insurance and other expenses possibly beyond the control of the local foremen.

7:2:4 Personnel budgets

This is a headcount schedule of the total labour requirements necessary to carry out the sales and production budgets and, in fact, run the whole business from managing director to office boy and production worker to office cleaner. It should be prepared by the personnel department in conjunction with all other functional departmental heads.

The schedule will show the number of personnel required, the hours to be worked, wage rates, salaries, etc., and should be built up by departments. The respective costs should, of course, be incorporated in the applicable departmental budgets. The recruitment and training policies of the company will be incorporated in the budget and cognisance should be taken of all labour-related costs, for example, national insurance, and pension schemes.

7:2:5   Operating and service department budgets

The type of department falling into this category may be administration, finance, selling, advertising and service, and might also include warehousing and shipping.

The departmental head of each of these functions will be responsible for compiling his individual budgets. The data included will cover personnel requirements by number grade and be cost-determined in conjunction with the personnel manager; departmental running costs detailed by account, namely, utilities, operating expenses, depreciation, insurance, rates, etc.

Special note should be taken of competitors' activity in determining the size and use of the advertising budget.

If raw material or bulk purchases are necessary, the usage and cost of these will be planned with the purchasing agent or chief buyer.

The basis of determining costs included in these budgets invariably depends on the actual trend in previous years adjusted, of course, for known changes. It should also be remembered that historical costs will include inefficiencies and these must be identified and determined if likely to continue. The considered effects of volume and activity should also be borne in mind.

7:2:6   Capital expenditure budget

This supplementary budget is usually compiled by senior management in conjunction with engineering and technical services.

The budget will show details of the capital expenditure proposals in the period of the master budget and will probably be prepared for a number of years because of its longer-term implications. Items included will be distinguished by the various types of assets—land, buildings,

equipment, furniture, etc., and should also state the reasons for proposals—replacement, new methods, capacity, etc.

Back-up data should also accompany the proposals to justify the
expenditures, and will take the usual forms of capital evaluations, such
as return on investment and discounted cash flow analysis. The strain
on cash resources should also be considered when compiling this budget.

7:2:7   Cash budget

This budget, although a supplementary one, is generally compiled
after the master budget has been consolidated initially, although not
necessarily approved or accepted.

The financial controller, with the assistance of all other management,
should determine the timing by period, usually monthly, of production,
sales, etc., and then prepare the effects on the cash balance. The reason
for this budget is to determine by period where additional cash may be
required or where surplus cash may be available for short-term investments.

The income side is built up from the sales and debtors budget plus any
other miscellaneous receipts, such as loans, new capital, sale of assets,
grants, interest, etc. On the expenditure side will be the incurred expenses
of the production and service department budgets, purchasing and
capital expenditure budgets plus other payments relating to the distribution of profits, such as dividends and income taxes.

7:2:8   Profit and loss account

The main part of the master budget is the profit and loss account. This
budget will summarise the effects of all the relevant data contained in the
supplementary operating and service department budgets, sales,
purchasing, personnel and capital expenditure (depreciation, salvage
receipts) budgets. It will be prepared in months or other chosen periods
and be compiled by the financial controller. A sample profit and loss
statement incorporating provisions for budget and standards is shown
in Figure 7:1

7:2:9   Balance sheet

The other part of the master budget is the balance sheet which will
show the net effect of the budgets on the financial position and worth

	BUDGET	%	STANDARD	%	ACTUAL	%	VARIANCE
CURRENT MONTH							
Gross Sales							
Less: Deductions from sales							
Total Net Sales							
Manufacturing Standard Costs							
Material							
Labour							
Burden							
Direct expense							
Total Standard Costs							
Standard Manufacturing Gross Profit							
Budget and Volume Variances							
Actual Manufacturing Gross Profit							
Expenses							
Selling							
Advertising							
Administrative							
Engineering							
Total Expenses							
Operating Profit							
Other Income and Deductions							
Net Profit Before Taxes							
Income Tax Provision							
Net Profit							

Figure 7:1   Example of a profit and loss statement

of the company. Again, being compiled by the financial controller, it will consider information contained in the budgeted profit and loss account, capital expenditures and cash and the related movement of the working capital and financing.

Management must examine these results of the profit and loss and balance sheet master budgets that result from the consolidation of the subsidiary budgets and determine if they are acceptable. Do they show the most practical overall profit to be accepted as a plan for the ensuing year or period to be budgeted? If the answer is negative then the problem areas should be determined and the departments concerned advised specifically of their shortcomings. As all the budgets are mainly inter-related, such a change generally means the resubmission of all the subsidiary budgets. Whilst this exercise may appear to be rather long-winded and even time-wasting, it is one of the real values of preparing budgets in this manner in that the consideration, discussion and communication of the short-term profit objective of the company is involving all levels of management in its achievement, and by this process is most likely to reveal the maximum practical profit objective for the company.

In practice, a lot of companies tend to take either sales or production in isolation and agree independently what the level of activity should be in these fields; once decided on, they proceed to build all the other budgets around them. If the resultant profit is in excess of the outlook for the current year, they are happy to leave it as such. However, assuming that the job is to be tackled properly, it is at this stage of review that any attempts at over-budgeting or, worse still, conservative budgeting, should be weeded out. The level of responsibility for perform-ance of the plan from each manager should be agreed upon, so that he fully commits himself to its attainment.

When the master budgets have been finally agreed upon and accepted, they should be adopted formally by management as its policy and plan for the forthcoming year or period and thereby provide a budget against which performance or achievement will be measured.

7:3 Controlling the plan

As indicated, the budgets are built up by responsibility. It follows, therefore, that operating statements will be prepared for each of the budget centres involved. These should form part of the management information system used to control actual performance against the budget plan.

Good budgetary control follows the management theory of "management by exception." Whilst management is provided with full details of expenditure, sales, production, etc., under its functional control, reports and information should be focused on matters that are adverse, or that show an unusual favourable variance, so that its energy is concentrated in the right direction and its effort is not being diluted with a lot of information which merely indicates that things are going as planned.

There are differing schools of thought on the amount of detail that should be provided to management. Some management accountants prefer to provide only data over which managers have some degree of control. For instance, if depreciation policy is decided by the board, there is no point in giving an operational manager a depreciation charge for, say, the machine shop. He has no control over what that charge will be; according to this theory, this information is unnecessary and does not help him to perform his part of the plan under normal conditions. This theory does not give management the full picture and lacks the important benefit of enabling management to see the overall effect and contribution of its department to the business as a whole. The statement may be broken down into two sections labelled "controllable" and "uncontrollable." Just what is controllable or uncontrollable can be surprising. For example, a shop foreman shown a list of fixed assets in his area on which there is a depreciation charge may well indicate items of equipment which are surplus to his requirements but for which he has not bothered to raise a disposal request. These items can then be removed from the department, sold with good salvage values being obtained, valuable floor space being released, routine maintenance checks ceasing and administration time and effort being saved in searching for and identifying equipment at physical inventory time.

7:3:1 Timing of feedback

When considering the subject of control the question of timing is of great importance. When should the measurement of control be effected and over what period? Having decided the period the budget is to cover, which is most usually annual, the budget itself will be set on a twelve-monthly or a thirteen four-weekly basis for the subject year, but this, of course, will depend entirely on the type of business. In addition to the detailed annual budget, most companies have some form of long-range plans for a number of years ahead covering, for instance, the profit and loss account, balance sheet, cash flow and probably capital expenditures.

This longer-term planning concerns itself primarily with determining whether or not the internal fund flow of the business will cover its commitments and capital expenditure programme, etc., but of course the longer-term plans will not be prepared in anything like the same detail as the yearly short-term operating budget. It is a matter of individual company requirements to determine which data is best controlled on a quarterly, monthly, weekly or even daily basis.

An organisation must generally have a fairly sophisticated accounting system to generate and disseminate information on a daily basis and this type of data is generally confined to production data. Standard hours produced, finished units, efficiencies, absenteeism, etc., all lend themselves to daily control. Billings in terms of unit sales and value would best be reviewed on a weekly basis, although for local consumption this, again, may be preferred on a rough daily basis.

All other profit and loss data would be embodied in a monthly financial statement and a balance sheet could be prepared on a quarterly basis.

Whatever is right for a business must be determined by the constraints within which it works and what is needed to control the situation. Normally, data of a daily and weekly nature is restricted to middle management to facilitate operational control and is not fed through the pyramid of top management unless a special situation demands such close control. As a general rule, the lower down the management line one goes, the sooner information should be in management's hands. The foreman should have his output in standard hours measured against budget and his material usage for his batch of machines during the following morning so that he can take the necessary corrective action to correct any deviation from his target.

Thus it has been said that this first-line information is the life blood of the business, and the accounting results which follow at the end of the month confirm and quantify an already known situation.

7:4   Flexible budgets

One criticism of budgetary control which is sometimes raised is its rigidity, where actual results may be the outcome of circumstances changed from those on which the budget was originally prepared.

Budgets, when set and agreed upon, can only take into consideration one set of circumstances. As actual conditions seldom equate with budgeted conditions, the difference between actual costs and budgeted costs must be demonstrated. Information should, therefore, be available to suggest the appropriate level of expenses, generally known as budget standards which fluctuate at varying levels of production activity or sales volume.

In order to achieve control of this situation, flexible budgetary control was introduced—as opposed to fixed budgets. Flexible budgeting is applied in businesses where it is impossible to make a firm forecast of the future conditions. Fixed budgeting should be satisfactory for the more stable industries; however, these are very few and far between and flexible budgeting is more widely used.

Flexible budgeting is designed to provide a more realistic picture of the variance between actual expenses and budgeted expenses. One expects to be able to distinguish that part of the variance which is due to volume and for which a manager will not have control, and that part of the variance over which the manager should have control. To achieve this, one must be in a position to calculate budget standards at varying levels of activity.

The application of this calculation is demonstrated below by considering first a report on the basis of fixed budgeting and then showing a similar report calculated on a flexible budgeting basis. Before looking at these reports, it must be clear that costs are classified for flexible budgeting purposes. This in itself is a most difficult task and one that may be tackled in many ways which cannot be amplified in this chapter. However, for the purpose of this exercise, the following broad categories are used:

1   Fixed costs. Costs which do not vary in the short-term with volume
2   Variable costs. Costs which do so vary
3   Semi-variable. Costs which will vary with volume but not in direct relationship

The previous chapter on costing provided detailed examples of these types of expenses; of course, if standard costing is already applied in the company, the setting of a flexible budget is rendered considerably easier. If standard costs are not available, the technique of marginal costing will need to be applied in dealing with individual costs to determine the degree of variability. Scatter graphs or the regression theory may be used. Figure 7:2 is based on fixed budgeting and demonstrates how much the actual is off target. This type of measurement is an improvement on, say, measuring against last year's performance when circumstances may have been different. The report provides some conception of the amount by which actual experience varies from budgeted plans.

Expense type	Budget £	Actual £	Variance £
Material	10 000	12 500	+ 2500
Labour	5000	5900	+ 900
Rent	3000	3000	—
Salaries	1000	1100	+ 100
	19 000	22 500	+ 3500

Figure 7:2   Example of fixed budgeting

However, if one is to adhere to one of the basic principles of budgetary control, that people should only be responsible for costs over which they have control, this report may not provide the solution.

Figure 7:3 applies similar information but is calculated on the basis of flexible budgeting. Thus, clearly, the advantages of flexible budgeting are demonstrated by the second report. It shows in reality that instead of the manager being responsible for an adverse variance of £3500 as he was in the first report, he is, in fact, only responsible for the adverse variance of £500, the remaining £3000 being due to increased volume in production which may be the result of conservative sales forecasting, or some other factor which must be taken up with some other department in the organisation.

Flexible budgeting is thus extremely useful for getting behind the causes of variances, particularly if quantities, as well as costs, have been budgeted, with sales variances, for example, one can determine whether

	BUDGET			ACTUAL	VARIANCE ANALYSIS	
	Standard per unit	Fixed budget	Flexed budget		Control-lable	Volume
Output in units		10 000	12 000	12 000	—	+2000
% of original budget		100%	120%	120%	—	+20%
		£	£	£	£	£
Variable Costs						
Material	£1.00	10 000	12 000	12 500	+500	+2000
Labour	£0.50	5000	6000	5900	−100	+1000
Fixed Costs						
Rent		3000	3000	3000	—	—
Salaries		1000	1000	1100	+100	—
TOTAL		19 000	22 000	22 500	+500	+3000

Figure 7:3   Example of flexible budgeting

the variance is due to prices, volume, outlet mixture, product mixture or a combination of them all.

Later chapters provide further examples of budgetary control techniques employed in controlling marketing, distribution, production, research and development and overheads.

7:5   Installing the system

The organisational chart should be examined with a view to determining where the responsibility for sales, costs and profits really lies. Revisions, where appropriate, may be considered at this time. The organisation structure should be so developed as to fix responsibility right down the line. There must be an organisation chart which clearly defines the levels of responsibility and the chain of command, setting out who is responsible for what and to whom. It is desirable to support each functional position with a job description defining the function, duty and responsibility. Tradition must be ignored, responsibility and control being given to those who are responsible for taking the decisions, but care must be taken to preserve the "business flair" of an organisation, and those given the responsibility should be placed where their individual resources can be best used.

The key factors should then be determined before designing the system most suitable to the company's needs. The system design should cover flow-diagrams of the information generated, collection data necessary for budget preparation and control reports to be subsequently prepared. During this period consideration should be given to the level of sophistication of the existing information system, whether the proposed system will provide an improvement and also the level of human resources with which one has to work the new system.

Having obtained a positive reaction to these considerations, the next step is to test the initial design with various personnel at all levels in order to determine its suitability to meet their requirements for management information.

Once initial design is finalised, the next step is to prepare a series of seminars and teach-ins to explain the thinking behind the purpose and operation of the system. Questions, constructive criticisms and improvements should be invited so that all are involved and communicate at all levels.

A timetable for installation of the programme should be established. A critical path analysis is the ideal basis for identifying the order in which the budget data should be collected and which information is to be cross-referred to two or more departments.

Now is the time for the collection of information for the "first budget." Considerable time, assistance and guidance should be made available to staff at this stage, and perseverance on behalf of those taking responsibility for the installation of the system will be required. It is vital that all levels of management go through the discipline of thinking through and preparing their portion of the budgets. Miracles should not be expected from the first results. It is not unusual for a company to take two or three years to get a control system of this nature fully operational. However, at each stage one should expect to produce some results which are usable even in the first year. What these results will be may differ from company to company but initially they usually provide a good insight to sales and cash flow data. An important by-product is management education and awareness of what the business is all about.

7:5:1   The budget centre

Efficient control requires that it is accepted that costs are best controlled at the point where they are incurred. The transport manager should therefore control the transport departments costs. The span of control of any one person should not be unduly large however.

The area controlled by an individual is known as a budget centre. The Institute of Cost and Management Accountants has defined a budget centre as:

A section of the organisation of the undertaking defined for the purposes of budgetary control

Within the budget centre, for example, the transport department, there may be other smaller areas to which costs are attributable and for which it is deemed desirable to control a particular group of trucks. This smaller area is defined as a cost centre.

The Institute of Cost and Management Accountants has defined a cost centre as being:

A location, person or item of equipment, or a group of these, in or connected with an undertaking in relation to which costs may be ascertained and used for purposes of cost control

One person only should be responsible for incurring costs within the defined budget centre and the ultimate responsibility for budgetary control lies with the chief executive.

7:5:2   Budget period

There is no general rule governing the selection of a period of time for a budget. This will be decided by the particular circumstances of the business. For instance the fashion industry must, of necessity, have a very short budget period, sometimes of three or four months duration, whereas in the shipbuilding industry a budget may range over three or four years. For most businesses, however, the calendar year is normally the accepted period: it is broken down into twelve monthly periods and the information is complementary to the published accounts.

However, if there is a strong seasonal influence affecting sales, it is sometimes prudent to have a "model year" upon which to base the budget and this usually starts just ahead of the main selling period. Businesses which rely mainly on the summer or Christmas trade may well justify a model year. Model years, as the name implies, usually commence with the introduction of new models. A car manufacturer, for example, may run its model year from September to the following August in order to have a good start to the year following the autumn motor shows and new year car registrations. The motive behind this is that if business has not gone as well as expected there is still sufficient time before the end of the model year to curtail activity, restrict costs and reconsider expansion programmes or introduce special promotions in order to keep profits in line with, or better than, budget.

7:5:3   Budget manual

It is helpful to have such a document available within the company so that there is no ambiguity about what is required of each individual in relation to budgets. The type of information one might expect the budget manual to contain is a brief explanation of the purposes of budgetary control as practised within the company and organisation charts and job descriptions showing quite specifically the budget responsibilities for each function; routing of budgetary control forms for collection and control documentation; timetables or programmes for completion of budgets and control data feedback; budget periods; samples of reports and statements to be employed and accounts classification and coding data.

7:5:4   Budget committees

The question of who should control the preparation of the budgets and who should review these controls is one that each organisation arrives at during some stage of the budget preparation.

There are various views held on this point. If operating managements are made responsible for profits, then one of the objectives of budgetary control, that is, the proper co-ordination of the organisation, is achieved.

The same processes should be involved as with the control aspect. What an organisation should attempt to achieve is the total commitment of all levels of management to the plan. Each level of management should review its plans and performances through the usual management committees, be they formal or informal groupings, right up to the chief executive, and the overall objective should be clear and unambiguous at each stage.

However, one person will be responsible for pulling together the various parts of the master budget. This job usually falls on the chief accountant or financial controller or his department. Larger companies employ a budget manager and, of course, this co-ordinating exercise naturally falls into his lap. He may be called upon to undertake a number of exercises to determine what the various results thrown up mean within the overall company objectives, but it must be emphasised that his role is one of support. The responsibility is fixed upon the persons committing and accepting stewardship over resources.

The budget organisation can be regarded as analogous to a telephone company operating an important communications system; it is responsible for the speed, accuracy and clarity with which the messages flow through the system, but not for the content of the messages themselves.

7:5:5 Information codes

Budgetary control has extended control information beyond the more traditional accounting information to broader aspects of control, setting out data in terms of hours worked, output of production in standard hours, information on market share, quality of product, etc. This is all necessary for the achievement of the plan. However, looking at the pure accounting contribution to budgetary control, a suitable system of accounts coding should be designed so that the information is collected and analysed within the budget and cost centres.

The accounting code should be what is commonly called a subjective/ objective system. The subjective part of the code should qualify information into its primary or traditional classification, that is, the nature of the expense, for example wages, fuel, rent, etc. The objective part of the code will be used to analyse the expenditure to the cost and burden centres, that is, machine X in the machine shop.

It is important to give considerable thought to the design of the coding system, as it should not only allow for coping with existing needs for information, but also have the flexibility to be expanded to meet future demands. A system of this sort should enable a company, using the subjective code, to produce information necessary for the preparation of the traditional statutory accounts. And by going through the objective section of the code, the information required for budgetary control and management accounting can be produced which should be made available to those drawing up the budgets as appropriate.

7:6 Conclusions

Budgetary control often strikes apprehension or fear into non-financial people. People tend to be sceptical or untrusting of having their performances measured against a standard. This is a human and understandable response. Most people, at some time during their careers, have had budgetary control used against them as a cost reduction tool.

It is up to finance managers, to clarify and emphasise that budget flexing and control is an essential and deliberate need of modern day management. It is a management tool designed as a *fair* basis upon which to measure performance against a predetermined plan, and conduct business in the most efficient manner possible, thereby improving profitability.

Chapter 8

Financial Reporting Systems and Responsibilities

R M S Wilson, Group Chief Accountant,
R & G Cuthbert Limited

8:1 Systems design

8:1:1 The cycle of control

The object of systems design for financial reporting and responsibilities is to enable management to take decisions in the light of their impact on the *whole* organisation, rather than merely within a particular department.

The necessary company-wide perspective for establishing financial reporting systems and responsibilities is given by the cycle of control. Diagrammatically, this can be shown as in Figure 8:1. Reporting systems should be designed to include procedures for carrying out each of the steps within the cycle. This requires:

1 Means of communicating the objectives that the system is to serve (step 1)
2 Means of adding the additional detail to complete the planning phases (steps 2, 3, 4 and 5)

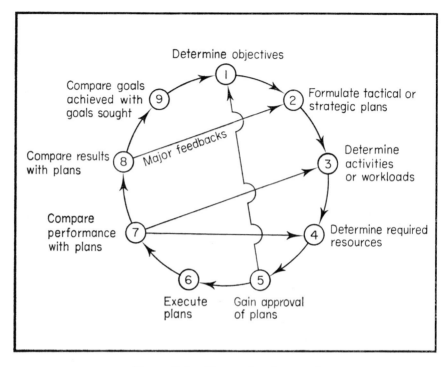

Figure 8:1   The cycle of control

3   Means of communicating with the performance group (step 7)
4   Methods of reporting accomplishments (step 8)
5   Methods of comparing performance with the plan and identifying significant variations (step 8)
6   Identification of the various corrective actions which may be taken and the means of taking them (steps 8 and 9)

In these terms, the system is designed with the overall purpose of facilitating the achievement of the company's objectives.

Characteristically, any system has inputs and outputs, and its elements are identified as constituting a system because they possess coherence, pattern and purpose. However, a company is composed of many integrated and overlapping sub-systems and these in turn are part of much larger environmental sub-systems. Consequently, it is helpful to adopt the *total systems concept*. This, simply, is an approach to information systems design that conceives the business enterprise as an entity composed of inter-dependent systems and sub-systems, and attempts to provide timely and accurate management information that will permit optimum decision-making.

8:1:2   Operating principles of systems design

Information flows are the primary centres of attention for systems designers and the actual design of systems must concentrate on the arrangement of people within the organisation.

Initially, however, the systems designer must know:

1   What the system is required to achieve
2   How well it is to do it
3   How its performance is to be evaluated

The requirements can then be expressed in terms of outputs that it *must* produce; inputs that it *must* accept; operations that it *must* perform; and resources that it *must* use.

Its performance may then be measured in terms of whichever criteria are appropriate. For example, relevant criteria will usually include some of the following:

1	Cost	6	Quality
2	Timeliness	7	Flexibility
3	Accuracy	8	Capacity
4	Reliability	9	Efficiency
5	Security	10	Acceptability

System boundaries must not be drawn to conform with organisational structure merely because of that structure. If the system is to be effective, its boundaries must not ignore *any* vital feedback channels.

Proper systems design often requires the inclusion of the effects of intangibles, especially the role of decision-makers, who are part of the total system and must be treated carefully. This shows the need for systems to be planned and programmed at the right level in the company by people who have total systems perspective and the authority to achieve broad systems integration.

Accepting that the successful operation of a financial reporting system depends more upon the principles of psychology than on generally accepted accounting principles, the basic steps in designing a new system are to:

1 Develop a basic system design
2 Analyse the interactions of multiple activities within the system
3 Specify the resource allocations
4 Prepare a preliminary plan for system implementation
5 Determine the impact of the design on profitability (or other objectives or constraints)
6 Document the new system design

The chief accountant must ensure that he has the authority of management to implement the system once it has been designed.

Any system should be tailored to the existing organisation, rather than making the organisation fit the system. However, such factors as the degree of departmentalisation, the sequence of operations, the scope of each department's activities and the basis of assigning costs, must be known in advance. Changes suggested in a systems study should only be adopted after considering their impact on the total organisation.

Whilst a full knowledge of existing accounting records and controls is the starting point, all forms, statements and controls must be reviewed. Usefulness and simplicity are the relevant criteria; this applies equally to establishing a coding system.

The installation of a new accounting system involves recruiting new staff, re-training existing staff, re-allocating duties, etc. As a result, job classifications, job specifications and the proper division of labour must be carefully considered. If the system is large, phased implementation is preferable to a single complete change, due to the latter's sheer complexity.

It is emphasised that every system should possess sufficient flexibility to allow for a constantly changing environment. (For example, within an account coding system, sufficient free classifications should be built in to allow subsequent expansion to be accommodated). Furthermore, a system producing too much information can obscure that which is relevant, whilst a system producing too little information does not favour good decision-making. Balance and flexibility are thus prerequisites to success.

If an existing system is to be improved, four basic steps should be followed; it is necessary to:

1 Identify the critical aspects that need to be planned and controlled
2 Determine what specific information is required, and amend the system by adding omitted data-flows and deleting unnecessary data-flows
3 Motivate and train line-management to use the revised system
4 Determine the best method of improving the required information within prescribed time limits

This highlights the need for a systematic approach.

8:1:3 Control as the perspective for financial systems

If progress towards goals is to be supervised, it must be observed and measured: there must be some assessment of where the organisation is compared to where it ought to be. This is acheived through control.

Control involves the use of a reliable, readily understood and sensitive system of information and standards as a basis for the management decisions that have to be taken. In this respect, the task of the accountant is to aid in establishing, co-ordinating and administering (as an integral part of management) an adequate plan for the control of all operations.

Although the company consists of the sub-systems of production, marketing, R and D, personnel, administration, etc., the accountant, by the very nature of his duties, is able to see the total spectrum of corporate activities in an integrated manner. In the final analysis, money becomes the only common yardstick for planning and gauging performance: this is the accountant's domain. By emphasising his service (as opposed to stewardship) function and by having a complete grasp of his company's activities, the accountant is able to develop the appropriate information and control systems. In fact, he can only adequately discharge his responsibility if he appreciates the type of decisions made and the nature of the activities to be controlled.

Perhaps the accountant is in the best position to consider the economics of control. The aim should be to provide an information system that facilitates control in such a way that the value is maximised for a given cost, (or alternatively, cost is minimised for a given mixture of control information).

The essential elements of control are information and action. Information without action is curiosity, not control.

The basic purpose of accounting for control is to supply data feedbacks to enable management to see, from time to time, where the company stands relative to its objectives. This demands uniformity and consistency in the approach adopted, giving the advantage that reported variances from plan provide the input for:

1 Self-appraisal by lower management
2 Subordinate appraisal by top management
3 Activity appraisal by top management (to evaluate the performance of the various company activities).

In the capacity of controller, the accountant will be responsible for:

1 Selecting the key factors and control points
2 Segregating the non-controllable factors so that the picture of the controllable aspects is not confused
3 Relating the plans and controls to individual accountability at the various levels
4 Ensuring that the setting of standards meets the needs of the control system and can be built into departmental plans
5 Co-ordinating the building up of the overall plan from subsidiary plans; and
6 Designing the reporting system for effective display of required feedback data, bearing in mind the need to integrate control data with the requirements of financial accounting and the stewardship function, which requires careful planning in grouping and classifying accounts. It is desirable that quantified objectives should be compatible with the existing information systems within the firm, otherwise the situation may arise in which there are both the traditional accounting methods of measuring performance, and a new information system designed to indicate whether or not objectives are being met

8:2   Accounting systems for control

8:2:1   Distinctions

In the context of reporting systems for budgetary purposes, it is necessary to distinguish the various types of accounting, namely: financial, cost, management, and control accounting.

Financial accounting systems report to the outside world *on* management, rather than *to* management. The traditionally aggregated figures must meet the criterion of objectivity, but this often conflicts with the more important control criterion of usefulness. Whilst financial accounting reports focus on the whole business, they must be compiled in accordance with statutory requirements and are historical in perspective. It will be evident, therefore, that financial accounting is of little value in exercising control.

In contrast, cost accounting is concerned with specific segments of the company, relating costs and revenues (and, hence, profits) to products, processes and divisions. Operational control is made effective through variances from standard, but, essentially, cost accounting is concerned with planning and controlling costs in great detail.

Management accounting aims to provide information that is useful to management, with the objectivity criterion of financial accounting being largely irrelevant, and its approach differing from that of cost accounting in that it is problem-oriented and geared to management control.

The purpose of control accounting is to indicate how successful the company is in its goal-striving behaviour. It permits the inclusion of goals other than profit (or cost reduction), and pays special attention (through the planning phase) to securing consistency amongst the objectives of the company as a whole and the objectives of its constituent parts.

Inevitably, these four broad types of accounting overlap considerably, but the demands of a variety of primary and secondary goals within the budgetary process require that control accounting, supplemented by the other forms as appropriate, be the focus of attention.

8:2:2   Financial systems considered

Given the purpose of accounting for control, several accounting systems can successfully supplement the budgetary control system.

Internal control is the process and means of safeguarding assets, checking the reliability of accounting data, promoting operational efficiency and encouraging adherence to managerial policies with which the accountant is normally associated. However, in its broadest sense, internal control embraces every type of accounting technique, and even extends beyond internal audit to the rigorous management audit. Since any system of controls requires human application, internal control exists, essentially, to ensure that the human factor acts in accordance with instructions, plans and policies.

Conventional cost accounting can be usefully supplemented by distribution cost analysis, thereby bringing marketing activities under the same micro-control as production activities.

Flexible budgeting is helped to a large extent by cost-volume-profit (or break-even) analysis in clearly portraying the outcomes of alternative courses of action in the planning phase. In addition, ratio analysis permits the efficiency of operations to be determined either before (in planning) or after (in assessing) the event.

It must be borne in mind that any accounting technique has limitations; for example, cost allocations may be arbitrary, ratios may hide compensating factors or trends, and cost-volume-profit analysis is essentially a static technique.

One means of allowing for a dynamic environment and the high likelihood of many alternative outcomes in a world of uncertainties is to build financial models.

Mathematical models are sets of equations or other expressions stating the significant factors in a particular system, and indicating the relationships between them. Although most models are simple, they do facilitate conceptions of reality, and allow the effects of alternative actions to be readily anticipated and measured.

Linear programming and simulation, along with networking techniques (such as PERT and critical path analysis), are the most favoured techniques of management science, on account of their generality of application.

8:2:3 Different costs for different purposes

Every cost-incurring activity involves sacrifice, but cost itself is not a homogeneous concept. Psychic costs are far beyond the accountant's measuring ability, but physical costs can be defined and measured in many ways—opportunity cost, direct cost, indirect cost, overhead cost, fixed cost, variable cost, marginal cost, incremental (or differential) cost, semi-fixed cost, semi-variable cost, average cost, full (or absorption) cost, common cost, joint cost, separable cost, sunk cost, avoidable cost, unavoidable cost, imputed cost, controllable cost, uncontrollable cost, replacement cost, capacity cost, standard cost, and so on.

Clearly, the accountant must carefully consider (in conjunction with those who will use his reports) the types of costs to include in any financial system. His role will be both provider of information and educator on how to use it.

8:3   The keys to control

8:3:1   What to measure

The first, and, perhaps, the most obvious requirement, is that measurement must be designed to aid interpretation.

Many companies tend to measure only material factors that are readily expressed in production or financial terms, such as time, quantity and quality. However, it is important that certain non-material factors should be measured, especially those indicating the performance of responsible individuals throughout the company.

8:3:2   Interpretation

This is the essential link between measurement and decision-making. The demands on top management are such that it is important that reports present *and* interpret the exception, in order both to conserve the manager's time and aid him in decision-making. Where practicable, trends should be displayed graphically, as, for instance, the behaviour of overhead cost incurrence in relation to the level of productive activity.

A policy decision must be made in designing control systems to determine the extent to which interpretation and decisions are to be either computable, or susceptible to routine procedures.

8:3:3   Selectivity

Control can break down because management attempts to control too

153

much and the really important issues become submerged in a mass of irrelevancies. In any series of elements to be controlled, a small fraction (in terms of elements) will always account for a large fraction in terms of effects. (This is Pareto's Law, an example being the frequently-met 18/20 rule, in which 80 per cent of a company's sales are accounted for by 20 per cent of its customers.) The key factors for control must, accordingly, be carefully selected.

In practice, most managements attempt to control many factors which, in a control sense, are unimportant because their behaviour pattern will follow that of other more essential factors.

8:3:4   Accountability and controllability

It is essential to the success of any financial control system that an individual is only held responsible for results when the following conditions prevail:

1   That he knows what he is expected to achieve
2   That he knows what he is actually achieving
3   That it is within his power to regulate what is happening

When all these conditions do not exist simultaneously, it may be unjust and ineffective to hold an individual responsible and the desired control will become impossible to achieve.

8:4   Accountability planning

8:4:1   Responsibility accounting

A financial reporting system is a means of bringing information to each level of management in order that responsibilities to the organisation may be fulfilled.

It follows that accounting figures should be compiled so that the results may be considered attributable to one person's performance. This requirement causes accounting to cross the threshold into behavioural science (especially the areas of motivation and human relations), which forms the basis for budgetary control.

Each responsible individual should prepare his budgets on the basis of controllable costs at that level of authority. Essentially, the *responsibility centre* is a personalised concept, whereas *cost centres* are frequently impersonal. (For example, a machine-shop in an engineering company will be composed of several cost centres—milling machines, turret lathes, auto-robots, etc., but it is the *whole* shop that is under the authority of the foreman. This is *his* responsibility centre.)

Responsibility accounting changes the emphasis of cost accounting from traditional product costing to vigorous planning and cost control through the budgetary process.

Cost classification is a vital area of responsibility accounting, the aim being to assign costs to the individuals who are responsible for their incurrence. However, charging individuals with only those costs subject to their control has many attendant practical problems, comparable with the problems of joint cost allocations when facilities are shared. The general rule is to charge the person who can bring the greatest influence to bear on cost incurrence with responsibility for that cost, rather than making some meaningless apportionment.

8:4:2 Responsibility centres as a basis for reporting

Reports should be fitted to the various areas of responsibility, and as one moves further up the managerial hierarchy, more cost items will be reported at each level, since more costs are controllable as the scope of managerial responsibility enlarges. Top management will therefore receive a summary of *all* costs, made up of controllable costs at each subordinate level, plus those relevant to the top level.

Such reports can do little to rectify previous mistakes, but by indicating exceptions to plan they ensure that the investigation of causes helps to prevent future mistakes. The orientation is clearly towards the future rather than the past.

A common weakness in many companies is an over-emphasis on current profit performance. For example, return on capital by division, plant, or product-line helps to explain changes in the rate of return for the company as a whole, as well as assisting in appraising the performance of individual managers. But two principal dangers exist in this approach. Firstly, both profits and the capital base must be clearly defined to avoid misunderstanding, (for example, whether before tax or after depreciation, etc.). Secondly, sub-optimisation through departmental-orientation rather than corporate-orientation on the part of individual managers can result from emphasising the department to the exclusion of the company as a whole. In addition, the more general problems of arbitrary cost allocations and the holding of individuals as being responsible for non-controllable costs exist.

The adoption of a systems approach should ensure the highest degree of consistency between departmental and corporate goals. However, divisional responsibilities must be specific, since control must be specific. Should an individual manager's budget be modified, it is imperative that he be informed not only of the modification but also of the reasoning behind it. If this practice is not followed, the manager may lose confidence in the attainability of the budget (no matter how specific it may be) and fail to see how his budget fits into the overall corporate pattern. (The guiding principle is that those charged with responsibility should be consulted on all matters relevant to it.)

In summary, anyone fixing responsibility and implementing the control related to it should:

1   Define clearly the organisational structure, and delegate responsibility so that each person knows his role
2   Determine the extent and limits of functional control
3   Ensure that responsible individuals are fully involved in preparing budget estimates, since they will be held liable for deviations
4   Provide those responsible with means of exercising control, in the form of regular "relevant cost" statements
5   Organise ways and means by which subordinates may report to superiors on significant variances and corrective action taken (or to be taken)
6   By the above procedure, confirm that every item of expense is the responsibility of some person within the organisation and also that every responsible individual knows for what expenditures he must account, and to whom

The ability to delegate is one sign of a good manager, and the budgeting process enables control of expenditure to be delegated. Specifically charging managers with responsibilities is an important way of ensuring they are performed satisfactorily, since few people will reduce costs unless control has been specifically delegated to them.

8:5 Motivation

8:5:1 The impact of control on individuals

For control (as distinct from planning) purposes, the use of accurate calculations and their transmission (in the form of results) to others may be beneficial, harmful, or neutral, depending upon:

The kind of persons and tasks involved
The setting in which operations are conducted
The vehicle, time sequence, etc., used for information transmittal

It becomes apparent, therefore, that the effect of control on individuals can play a large part in the effective control of the company.

Budgets have been known to unite employees against management where reports show results rather than reasons, or are excessively historical in relation to future goals, or are prepared by inflexible and narrow-minded accountants.

One vital study in this area, C. Argyris, *Personality and Organisation* (New York: Harper Brothers 1957), quotes the following statements from supervisory management:

I'm violently against the figures. I keep away from showing them to the workers. I know the boys are doing a good job They're trying to do their best. If I give them the heat with this stuff they'll blow their top.

You can't use budgets on people. Just can't do anything like that. People have to be handled carefully and in our plant carefully doesn't mean with budgets. Besides, I don't think my people are lazy.

As a result of the pressure, tension and general mistrust of management controls, the above-mentioned tendency of employees to unite against management may result. Such controls as budgets tend to make employees feel dependent and passive, which emphasises their subordination to management—not only are they told *what* to do, but also *how* to do it. Consequently, great care must be taken in administering management controls to ensure that employees do not experience such factors as pressure, inter-departmental strife, barriers to communication, or inclinations to be department-centred rather than organisation-centred. Such care will involve:

1 Reporting both results *and* (insofar as possible) reasons
2 Emphasising both past *and* present performance
3 Maintaining flexibility
4 Stressing the established goals

The problem of directing activities towards goals is one of motivation, which is often overlooked by conventional budgeting methods. The budget is *not* the goal, it is the plan that should aim to motivate goal-attainment. As such, it should be based on realistic expectations, which demands effective communications between the different operating levels of the company.

Good attitudes must provide the key to successful budgeting. This is facilitated by satisfactory relationships between subordinates and superiors, which rests on the existence of clear-cut organisational lines and the disposition to delegate authority along with responsibility. Budgets should not be used as pressure devices, since this will prohibit the development of team spirit in striving to achieve planned goals. A budget should be seen as a yardstick—not an instrument of pressure.

By helping to clarify targets and by demonstrating the interpendence of the different sections of the business, budgets form a powerful means of motivation. If the budgetary process does not aid in motivating people in the right direction, then serious thought should be given to discontinuing or thoroughly revising the procedures practised. The ideal situation is that in which a control system is so designed that it leads people to take actions that are not only in their own best interests but also in the best interests of the company.

It becomes necessary, therefore, to consider the *aspiration levels* of different individuals. This requires the incorporating of sufficient flexibility within the budgetary system to improve motivation by the upwards or downwards movement of targets in order to achieve continuous improvements in goal-attainment.

8:6 Management information and reporting systems

8:6:1 Management information needs

How effective a manager is in his job will depend upon how much, how relevant and how good his information is, and how well he interprets and acts upon it.

Nevertheless, one hears frequent complaints from managers that information is too late, of the wrong type, unverified or even suppressed. It is evident, therefore, that if information is to be of value, it must be clear, detailed, timely, accurate and complete—not merely some vague figures thrown out by an unplanned system. Management information and its presentation must observe the important concepts of control, namely: accountability, controllability and selectivity. In addition, data should be checked for the four important qualities of impartiality, validity, reliability and internal consistency.

Basically, the manager needs information to:

1   Assist him in decision-making
2   Indicate performance and achievement
3   Help him in making plans and setting standards

As frequently happens, the manager may not know the precise information he needs (or, alternatively, what information is available.) The accountant can help by observing the types of decisions made, testing the adequacy of existing information, suggesting alternate data-flows, determining what information is available and indicating the means (and costs) of collecting it.

The process of collecting, analysing and using information is essentially the same in any size of business, whether for routine purposes or for special projects, such as long-range planning. What does vary is the method of collection and analysis. The difference is in the relative employment of manual as opposed to mechanical systems. The increasing adoption of electronic data-processing should ensure that fewer managers will have cause to complain about insufficient, inaccurate or delayed information.

In aiming to provide the right information to the right people at the right time and at the lower cost, the financial reporting systems should

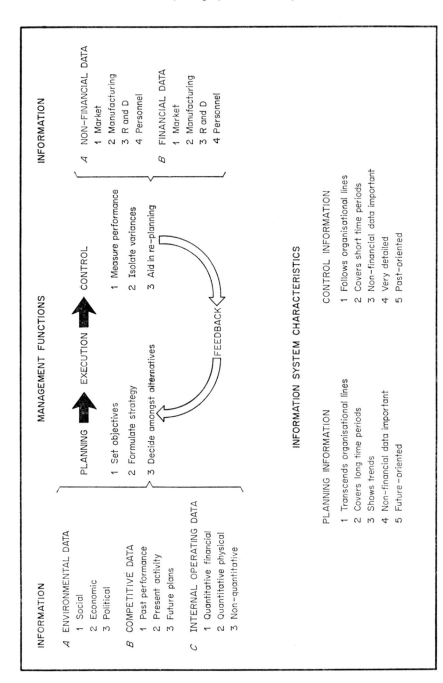

Figure 8:2   Anatomy of management information

be incorporated into a total systems framework such as that portrayed in Figure 8:2.

8:6:2   Uses of financial information

A great deal of information, whilst useful for planning and control, is primarily raised for some other purpose that is only tangentially related to the planning and control purpose.

The accounting routine provides the bulk of data in many companies derived from:

1   Payroll procedures
2   The order-processing cycle, beginning with the receipt of an order and ending with the collection of accounts receivable
3   The procurement and accounts payable cycle

Since so much information is within the accounting sphere, the accountant must play a most important role in reporting on accomplishments.

Financial reports are essentially statistical tables, the brevity, arrangement and content of which should all be subject to the prime test of *usefulness*. However, accounting statements generally describe what *has* happened within the company, and omit such items as:

1   Information about the future
2   Data expressed in non-financial terms, such as that concerning market share, productivity, quality levels and adequacy of customer service, etc.
3   Information dealing with external conditions as they might bear on a particular company's operations

Whilst all these elements are essential to the intelligent management of a business, the key to the development of a dynamic and usable system of management information is to move beyond the limits of conventional accounting reports and to conceive of information as it relates to the vital areas of planning and control.

The organisational structure of a company and its information requirements are, therefore, inextricably linked. In order to translate a statement of his duties into action a manager must receive and *use* relevant information. This involves using all the data and intelligence—financial and non-financial—available, rather than relying wholly on the accounting system and the reports it produces, in satisfying a particular manager's information requirements.

8:6:3   A structured approach to reporting

To achieve his aim of successfully communicating the essential facts about the business to the managers, the accountant must have a clear conception of the purposes, possibilities and limitations of the many different types of statements and reports, and also understand the problems and viewpoints of their users to ensure that they, in turn, appreciate the true meaning, as well as the limitations, of the reports that he prepares for them.

At each level of management, and especially at lower levels of the hierarchy, the accountant should pose two questions:

1   What are the necessary and controllable factors pertinent to the level of authority in question?
2   In what form are they best presented to aid in decision-making at this level?

At this stage, the two complementary forms of controlling corporate activities must also be considered. They are:

1   Control against long-range objectives or plans
2   Control against standards, representing short-term goals or targets

Both forms are essential to effective overall control, but top management is more interested in the former, and supervisory management in the latter, for obvious reasons.

A structured approach to reporting by areas of responsibility will enable top management to view the results and efficiencies of individual departments in the light of their contribution to overall objectives. If corrective action is required from the top, this may well be an indication of the failure to achieve control at a lower level.

Similarly, the existence of a time-lag between actual events and the reporting of these events, through the top management control system, may create the need for corrective action that is more drastic than if such

162

action had been instituted at a lower level of control which could be more closely associated with the actual events.

This requires that the interface of top management with subordinate management control systems should provide a rapid feedback of financial data to the former. Without this rapid feedback, when top management is obliged to instigate corrective action, it is often found that this action is delayed, that it becomes more complex and that more people become involved. This is not the most favourable setting for effective control.

Within the control framework, the characteristics of good reports are that they should:

1 Be oriented towards the user, considering both his level and function
2 Give as much information as possible in *quantitative* terms and flow both ways in the organisation
3 Be based on a flexible system that allows quick changes to meet new conditions

On a tangible plane, succinctness is a great virtue in reporting, whilst on an intangible plane, a major contribution of an adequate reporting system is that the mere act of reporting requires a manager to pause and think.

8:7   Management control

8:7:1   Definition and distinctions

Management control can be defined as the use of a reliable, readily understood and sensitive system of information and standards which ensures that resources are obtained and used effectively and efficiently in the accomplishment of the company's objectives.

Clear distinctions should be drawn between:

1 Strategic planning, which is concerned with overall policies and objectives
2 Management control (as defined above)
3 Operational control (relating to day-to-day tasks)

The setting of financial policies is a strategic planning activity, whereas planning and reporting on working capital requirements is a management control matter. At a more detailed level, the controlling of credit extensions is within the sphere of operational control.

Management control should be the focus of attention in financial reporting systems and has the following characteristics:

1 It is complex because it is concerned with the total organisation
2 The information within it tends to be accurate, integrated, and developed within a prescribed set of procedures
3 Although communication is difficult, it aims to lead to desired results by catering for the needs of many personnel, especially line and top management
4 It has its roots in social psychology and the mental activities involved are those of persuasion and motivation over a relatively short time-span

Accounting systems themselves cannot be the starting-point in constructing an overall system, since it is management control rather than pure accounting that deals with the on-going operation of the whole enterprise. The management control system will, at times, run alongside the financial accounting system, but in the rare case of conflict, it is the former that should predominate. However, since management control is the system around which others should be constructed, this system must be financial. Only in this way can it encompass all the parts of the company in common terms so as to assist management in determining that the parts *are* in balance.

8:7:2   Types and phases of management control

Three phases of control can be distinguished: pre-action control (involving co-ordination of factors involved in the operation); during-action control (which consists of directing or supervising the actual work); and after-action analysis or control (involving the appraisal of performance). All three must be experienced for control to be effective.

It frequently happens that only one phase is applied, in which case the following forms of control emerge:

1 Historical control, which is exercised by comparing performance in

at one point in tune with performance in previous periods. This is a highly subjective approach, and rarely takes reasons into account.

2 Current control, where records consist of actual results only, which means that control data for comparison is missing, making it necessary for management to attempt to control activities by hunches.

Foward planning and control, related to standards and forecasts is an approach based on the premise that control can only be exercised by positive action. It manifests itself in four major ways:

1 Control by planning or decision-making, which selects the desired pattern of resource-use following a deliberate comparison of alternatives. This is part of the budgetary process underlying all subsequent control.

2 Control by scheduling, direction and supervision. This is a narrower concept, concerned with establishing time-tables for the performance of tasks and ensuring that men, materials, etc., are available to carry out the plan. It attempts to minimise unfavourable variances from plan, and without it no control system can be expected to be effective.

3 Control by follow-up response to feedback comparisons. This consists of measuring and analysing deviations from the predetermined standards. A rational response is only possible if the basic causal patterns can be identified.

4 Control by manipulation, working through influences on planning. This consists of varying the weights assigned to each variable subject to subordinate management's control or influence. This induces a pattern of behaviour at this level which directs corporate resources towards the attainment of corporate objectives, as determined by top management.

Having considered the nature of management control, it must now be considered further within a systems framework.

8:8 Management control systems

8:8:1 Definition

In terms of management control, a suitable system may be defined as:

a set of policies, procedures, and associated information processing designed to give direction to corporate activities. This direction results from a knowledge of the objectives sought, the progress made towards them and the need for corrective action (if any).

Whilst a control system is able to exercise a positive influence on events, the system alone cannot control, it can only help the manager to achieve control. This must be done by applying scientific principles to an integrated human group activity with related physical facilities, bearing in mind that control itself is a behavioural matter based on interpersonal relationships.

8:8:2 Feedback and effective systems

The information link between output and input (or, strictly, revised input) is the feedback channel. For control to be effective, information must pass along this channel rapidly. In a dynamic environment, the time interval between deviation and correction must be at a minimum.

In the psychology field, and especially in learning theory, it has been shown that motivation is maintained at a high level when the time-lag between action and knowledge of results is minimised. This emphasises the need for a system to supply feedback information as rapidly as possible. Furthermore, it must be designed to report to those responsible for taking corrective action and not to intermediaries in the information networks of the company.

The danger exists that feedback carrying messages of failure may tempt the recipient to attack the control system rather than take corrective action. The concept of individual aspiration levels is especially relevant in this context. Furthermore it may happen that feedback shows that objectives are unattainable in terms of *corporate*, as distinct from *individual*, aspiration levels, in which case corrective action should take the form of a search for alternative objectives that *are* attainable.

It should always be recognised that systems and feedback seldom operate perfectly. In addition, people and equipment (as facilitating agents) are usually far from being perfect and, even when constrained by a system, frequently produce peculiar problems and situations.

8:8:3 Characteristics of cybernetic systems

When the input-output model of a system is fully developed with feedback loops, one enters the domain of self-regulating or cybernetic models.

Such systems are closed rather than open—they operate independently of the human factor once established. The best example is, perhaps, a simple thermostat. The computer (suitably programmed with decision-rules) is the analogous business example.

Complexity characterises cybernetic systems, with the proliferation of variety characterising the control problem. ("Variety" in this context relates to the number of distinguishable elements in the business situation).

Cybernetics, described as the science of control and communication in the animal and the machine by the man who coined the term, specifically sets out to recognise, describe and handle (through feedback principles) the complexities of the real world. By considering "viable" systems (that is, those that exist beyond a certain complexity barrier), it never errs by treating systems in an over-simplified way.

8:9   Organisation

The organisational implications of the systems approach are not such as to require wholesale changes in the organisational structure, or in administrative behaviour. Whilst some would suggest significant (and commendable) changes, from the financial point of view it is mainly necessary to ensure that accountants take a company-wide view in discharging their duties.

8:9:1   The accounting department

The size of the company will determine the degree of specialisation and exact staffing requirements. However, the starting point will be the statement of objectives, from which the organisational plan can be derived by:

1   Preparing an organisational chart with job specifications for all posts
2   Appointing suitably qualified people to these posts
3   Instituting effective methods of controlling these persons once in post

In a company of any size, the dichotomy between reporting on stewardship and to management will be recognised by the appointment of a financial accountant with responsibility for the former, and a management accountant with responsibility for the latter.

Together with the duties of the internal auditor, these functions will be co-ordinated by the chief accountant (or financial controller). In a similar manner, the management accountant will co-ordinate the duties of the budget officer, cost accountant and their staff, whilst the financial accountant will co-ordinate the payroll, bought ledger, sales ledger, cashiers and general sections of his department.

8:9:2   The budget committee

The budget committee is responsible, on a consultative basis, for overseeing the preparation of budgets. It usually consists of several members of the top managment group, preferably chaired by the budget officer.

This committee establishes the general guidelines to be followed in budget preparation, and subsequently exists to:

1   Resolve inter-departmental differences
2   Offer general advice
3   Co-ordinate budgetary activities
4   Scrutinise budget reports, comparing results with the plan and submitting appropriate recommendations upwards or downwards as the situation demands

It is emphasised that decisions about budgets should be made by the line organisation (subject to modification and approval from above), with the budget committee being purely an advisory group responsible for the speed and accuracy of the budgetary process, rather than for the content of the budget (that is, the figures themselves).

8:9:3   Management control/systems committee

The establishment of a management control committee, composed of senior executives from all functions, should increase the probability of success in adopting systematic control procedures.

As with the budget committee, it should *not* be responsible for design-

168

ing or imposing systems upon the organisation, but should play a role of guidance, leadership and co-ordination. Its particular aims may be:

1 Welding the whole company into a team, working continually towards systems improvement
2 Aiding this team by providing technical assistance
3 Both controlling and evaluating the results of system development from a managerial point of view

8:10   Conclusion

8:10:1   Weaknesses of budgetary control

Four major problem areas are frequently encountered in the use of budget systems:

1 They can grow to be so complex, detailed, cumbersome, meaningless and expensive that they become dangerous
2 Budgetary goals may come to supersede organisational goals, requiring care in using budgets as a *means* and not an *end*
3 Budgets may tend to hide inefficiencies by continuing initial expenditures in succeeding periods without proper evaluation. The budgetary system must contain provisions for re-examination of standards and other bases of planning, by which policies are translated into numerical terms
4 The use of budgets as pressure devices defeats their basic purpose

8:10:2   Flexibility

To allow for different levels of activity, and the inherent inaccuracies of forecasting in an uncertain world, budgets must be flexible.

The inability to forecast accurately does not nullify the value of the budget as a managerial tool. It does mean, however, that the budget must not be a static device that is insensitive to changing conditions. Flexibility is an obvious necessity in providing meaningful standards for guiding operations and judging performance.

Although cost-volume-profit analysis is a useful adjunct to effective budgeting, it must be accepted as a relatively inflexible tool that hinders the comparison of alternatives on account of its static nature. In more detail, it fails to take account of:

1 The dynamic nature of industrial activity
2 The efficiency of management
3 The efficiency of labour
4 Technological progress
5 The size of plant and resource limitations
6 Price changes
7 Varying product/sales mix
8 Objectives other than profit (derived from specified cost and sales levels) such as the degree of consumer satisfaction to be achieved

8:10:3 Tolerances

Even when budgets have been prepared, based on accurate, currently attainable and internally-derived standards, the financial reporting system should have tolerance levels built into it.

It cannot be expected that standards will be met perfectly, thereby requiring some measure of the significance of results vis-à-vis plans to be developed—results beyond this tolerance limit being the subject of control action, and results within this limit being accepted as random variations.

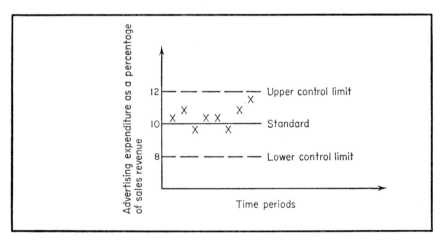

Figure 8:3 Statistical control chart

The tolerance range should not be so broad as to excuse all levels of performance, nor so narrow as to cause control action and investigation to be applied too frequently.

The statistical control chart in Figure 8:3 allows successive levels of performance for a particular factor to be observed in relation to standards, and tolerance limits set accordingly.

The aim of this chapter has been to indicate how the accountant should design and develop his reporting procedures under the total systems concept, by adopting a control perspective. An effective system must be based on personalised organisational centres of responsibility, and be sufficiently flexible to maintain a high level of motivation. Within this framework, the overriding consideration must always be *usefulness*.

Chapter 9

Control of Marketing and Distribution

M T Wilson, Managing Director, Marketing Improvements Limited

Most standard definitions of marketing clearly specify marketing's role in creating profit for the company. The Institute of Marketing, for example, defines marketing as follows:

> Marketing is the management function which organises and directs all those business activities involved in assessing and converting customer purchasing power into effective demand for a specific product or service and in moving the product or service to the final consumer or user so as to achieve the profit target or other objectives set by a company

9:1 Development of financial techniques in marketing

The application of financial techniques seems to have progressed more slowly in marketing than in other major business functions. There appear to be three major reasons why this is so.

9:1:1   Sales-orientation of marketing

First, most marketing men have risen to their present positions through the sales side of the organisation and most marketing functions evolved from sales departments. Typically, the financial goals of sales personnel and sales organisations have been limited, usually to simple revenue targets. Thus, although the nomenclatures may have changed, the basic operating methods often have not. It is not uncommon to find marketing organisations which claim to be profit-orientated. Because of the limited experience of the personnel, lack of information and ignorance of financial techniques they are, in fact, simply chasing sales volume. In such companies the first step that must be taken is to identify clearly those elements of the profit mechanism that should be under the control of marketing. Only then can it be seen whether sufficient data and techniques exist to exercise proper control.

9:1:2   Difficulty of predicting results

Second, marketing, by its nature, is involved largely with events outside the company and thus beyond its direct control. In theory, marketing is concerned with the arrangement of cause–effect relationships whereby certain inputs will create desired outputs; for example, the input of advertising and sales effort is aimed at creating a certain volume of consumer demand. Although most of the inputs can be accurately quantified in financial terms, it is often difficult, and sometimes impossible, to calculate the interrelationship between what is being spent and what is being earned. Marketing men tend therefore to rely far more on qualitative judgement than many of their colleagues. A production executive, for instance, can fairly easily produce a quantified case for new plant based on its cost and its output, supported by sophisticated DCF calculations, etc. The marketing manager will find it infinitely more difficult to produce a similar case to support, for example, a corporate advertising campaign in which, though the expenditure is known, the effect on the market-place is extremely difficult to predict or evaluate. The role of financial techniques in marketing must be inevitably more limited than in other more controllable environments. Unfortunately, however, perfection has too often been made the enemy of the good, and because exact evaluation is impossible, no measurement has been attempted. If marketing is to progress as a discipline more attempts must be made to apply financial methods whilst accepting the constraints of the situation.

9:3:1   Contrast between marketing and financial executive

Third, the career patterns of many marketing men and the apparent unpredictability of marketing results have created an unfortunate impression amongst other company executives. In terms of personality, training and experience, the marketing man and the financial executive are usually totally different. This has resulted, in many companies, in a failure of communication between the two. Again, this limits the development of financial techniques in marketing to such a degree that many marketing men think that budgetary control is simply a financial method which does not really affect them, and in extreme cases it is left to the accountants to prepare and operate the marketing budget.

If a company wishes to improve its financial control in the marketing area, it must understand why progress has been relatively slow. It must realise that there are constraints such as:

1 Lack of financial experience amongst marketing executives
2 Lack of clear definition of the marketing contribution to profit-making
3 Difficulty of prediction of marketing results
4 Lack of communication between marketing and finance

Attempts have been made in recent years to overcome some of these difficulties. Unfortunately, too often what has happened has been the application of a sophisticated veneer over the basic problems. Changes in terminology have far outrun changes in practice. For example, many companies claim to have established managerial profit responsibility. Thus a brand or product manager is charged with the profitability of the lines that he handles. Analysis soon reveals that he has little authority over many of the elements that affect profitability, such as production cost or even sales force expenditure. The danger is that senior management is lulled into a sense of false security, fondly believing that profit responsibility has been truly delegated.

9:2 Improving financial control in marketing

The improvement of financial control in marketing must begin with a clear identification of the elements for which marketing is responsible. Assuming that the company is primarily interested in making a return on the capital employed in the business, the profit mechanism can be represented thus:

$$\frac{Return}{Capital\ Employed} = \frac{Return}{Sales} \times \frac{Sales}{Capital\ Employed}$$

Return on sales will be influenced by answers to the following questions:

1 What is to be sold?
2 At what price?
3 In what quantities?
4 At what cost?

Most of these decisions will be for the marketing department to make, apart from some of the cost elements, such as production costs, etc. Sales on capital employed will be affected by how much money is involved in the various asset areas such as

1 Debtors
2 Stock
3 Work in progress
4 Land and buildings
5 Plant and machinery

The responsibility for these elements is usually far less clearly determined. Marketing must be involved because, for example, credit facilities and stock availability will have a major impact upon demand and the company's ability to satisfy it.

In the longer term the size and location of factories will depend, to a degree at least, upon the prediction of the likely trends in the marketplace. It is not suggested that all these decisions are marketing ones, simply that marketing is inevitably involved. The nature and degree of that involvement must be defined if the appropriate financial controls are to be operated, otherwise confusion and conflict can so easily arise. For example, in companies where it is unclear which function is responsible for finished stock, the production manager will tend to keep stocks to a minimum to save the costs of warehousing and tying up capital. The marketing man will attempt to increase stocks as it is usually easier to gain sales when the product is immediately available.

Having determined marketing's role in the profit mechanism, it is easier to define which financial techniques are relevant and what training is needed to operate them. Often it will be found that marketing men themselves are confused about the limits of their responsibilities. Only a small percentage of marketing men understand balance sheets and profit-and-loss accounts and this inevitably limits their perception of the profit mechanism. It is important that this lack of knowledge should be rectified as it influences many areas of marketing. For example, in marketing planning, an understanding of the function of capital turnover broadens the view of the available profit opportunities. Figure 9:1 shows how the basic profit equation can be used as a simple model to simulate alternative approaches to corporate profit goals. It widens the search from a simple examination of how sales or margins can be increased to a study of the impact made on the capital employed in the business.

Within this broader understanding of marketing's role in making profit, other financial techniques can be more effectively operated. Methods such as budgetary control become far more meaningful when the true responsibilities of marketing are recognised.

9:3 Constructing the revenue budget

The revenue budget is the financial expression of the first part of the marketing plan. Basically it lists:

1 What is to be sold? (the product range)
2 At what price? (the pricing structure)
3 In what volume? (the sales forecasts)

9:3:1 The product range

Decisions concerning which products to market tend to be extremely complex and depend upon market research and assessment, competitive

1 Assume 1970 $\dfrac{\text{R }100}{\text{CE }1000} = \dfrac{\text{R }100}{\text{S }2000} \times \dfrac{\text{S }2000}{\text{CE }1000}$

$\qquad\qquad\qquad = 10\% \quad = 5\% \quad \times 2$

2 Assume 1971 objectives—to increase profit by 10%

$\qquad\qquad\qquad\qquad$—to hold capital employed at same level as 1969

$\qquad\qquad\qquad\qquad$—to increase $\dfrac{\text{P}}{\text{CE}}$ to 11%

3 Alternative A $\dfrac{\text{R }110}{\text{CE }1000} = \dfrac{\text{R }110}{\text{S }2000} \times \dfrac{\text{S }2000}{\text{CE }1000}$

To achieve this, either—price increase without relative volume drop

$\qquad\qquad\qquad$ and/or—cost reduction to increase gross margin

$\qquad\qquad\qquad$ and/or—product mix change

Note no change in sales or capital turnover

Alternative B $\dfrac{\text{R }110}{\text{CE }1000} \times \dfrac{\text{R }110}{\text{S }2200} \times \dfrac{\text{S }2200}{\text{CE }1000}$

To achieve this—sales increase at same margins as 1969

$\qquad\qquad\qquad$—increased capital turnover rate on higher volume (e.g. shortened length of debt on increased revenue)

Note no change in % profit on sales

4 Knowing the particular market conditions decisions can now be more readily made.

Which is most likely to succeed:

$\qquad$ increased prices?

$\qquad$ reduced costs?

$\qquad$ change product mix?

$\qquad$ use capital more effectively (shorten credit, cut stock holding, etc.)

and moreover by understanding this mechanism the implications of such changes can be simulated

Figure 9:1 Using ratios in marketing planning

evaluation, production capability, promotional strength, etc. The role of financial techniques is not to pre-empt such decisions but rather to quantify more clearly the basis on which they will be made.

The development of methods such as marginal costing and value analysis enable broader views to be taken of whether a product is or can be made worthwhile. For example, a product which seems unprofitable on a standard cost basis may still be worthwhile if it is making a contribution to overheads, particularly if the capacity could not be used n any more profitable way. Similarly, variety reduction techniques and product range analysis can help to decide whether products should be simplified or removed and what the likely effect on sales and profitability will be. For instance, it is often the case that the product range exhibits the 80/20 rule, eighty per cent of the turnover with profit often coming from twenty per cent of the products. There may seem to be good rationalisations for maintaining some of the low profit or even loss-making lines on the basis that they complete the range or are demanded by particular customers. In practice, most companies find that they can reduce, often dramatically, the number of products (or sizes, colours, etc.) without affecting total sales volume but significantly increasing profitability.

New products being considered for development and introduction should be subjected to analysis by discounted cash flow techniques and other methods suitable for gauging the effects of cash in-flows and out-flows over a lengthy time period.

9:3:2   Pricing strategy and tactics

Pricing is still more of an art than a science because of the difficulties of quantifying the likely effects of price changes. Nevertheless, pricing is a key variable in the marketing mixture and there are some quantitative techniques that can guide decision-making. Basically, there are four approaches which should be used in conjunction in attempting to set the pricing structure.

The cost approach. Prices based on standard cost plus a margin are still very common. Such a simplistic approach suffers from the traditional problems of standard costing, such as overhead allocation. Even when these are circumvented by techniques such as marginal costing, cost-based pricing still has the major drawback of being unrelated to the market-place. However, cost considerations are obviously important, particularly for indicating minimum price levels below which is it not worthwhile marketing the product.

The demand approach. Price is the interface between demand and supply and, in a competitive market, it is the customer who will ultimately decide the appropriate price level. For example, customers appeared to value the Jaguar XJ6 motor car more highly than did the actual manufacturer of the car, as they were willing to pay a higher price for a used model than the company charged for a new vehicle. The problem of the demand approach, however, is estimating in advance the likely price/demand relationships. In some markets, such as those related to commodities, price will fluctuate day by day according to demand. Most producers of manufactured goods aim to maintain a higher degree of price stability and some do attempt to draw up price/demand schedules in order to position their products accurately. At least the company should have a view about the basic mechanisms of its markets. Are they sensitive to price change? Is demand likely to be elastic, whereby a change in price will create a more than relative change in demand? There are still some companies who are naïve enough to believe that a cut in price would gain them no more business but a rise in price would cause most of their customers to desert them.

Competitive considerations. Together with cost-plus, the most common method of pricing is to keep in line with competition. Although it is obviously sensible in competitive markets to monitor competitive pricing structures, this approach can lead to an undervaluing of the product and ultimately to a downward price spiral as each company attempts to place its price just below the competitor's. A more sophisticated approach to competitive evaluation is to list the major product features and weight them in terms of their importance to the customer. Both the company's and the competitive products are then rated against the scale, preferably by market research, and the resulting difference in scores is used as a basis for calculating price differentials.

Marketing considerations. There are many different marketing considerations to be taken into account when setting prices. The type of distribution channel and the margins expected, the image of the product, the values conferred and the costs incurred beyond the product itself such as after-sales service, the psychological price barriers that occur in some markets, as well as the physical price limitations imposed, for example, by automatic vending will all have to be weighed. Perhaps most important and certainly very difficult to assess is the marketing power of the company. Is the advertising and the sales force persuasive enough to achieve sales at the desired price?

It is worthwhile noting that it is seldom the cheapest product which is the market leader and that even marginal increases in price can dramatically improve profitability, particularly if fixed costs are high. Moreover, if a product is worth a high price, the initial purchase is soon forgotten as its value continues to be exhibited. Selling on low price usually means there is little money available for building up marketing skills and product value and there is no build-up of customer loyalty.

9:3:3 Forecasting sales volume

Having decided what products to sell at what price, the revenue budget is constructed by assessing in what volume the products will be sold. It is usually wise to approach forecasting in two stages. First, assuming all the variables in the marketing situation remain the same, next year's sales will be a statistical extrapolation of past performance. There are many statistical techniques of time-series analysis which enable such an extrapolation to be made, basically by extending the trend of the figures and applying seasonal corrections. Obviously, some variables will change and therefore the second stage is to identify them and assess their likely effect on the statistical extrapolation. There may be changes in external factors, such as the market, competitive activity and government legislation, as well as modifications of internal variables like promotional support, pricing structures or new product introductions. This second phase is usually a qualitative judgement, although the growing science of econometrics is enabling some companies to quantify such economic changes.

9:4 Controlling performance against revenue budget

The prime objective of establishing any budget is to provide a series of criteria against which actual performance can be measured, variances identified and corrective action taken.

To enable this control procedure to be operated more practically, some companies find it worthwhile constructing allowable variances within which no managerial action need be taken. For example, if it is known from past performance that the sales forecasts have never been more accurate than plus or minus five per cent, it is unrealistic to spend time and effort to correct a minus one per cent variance which is probably due to simple forecasting error. Figure 9:2 shows how such a concept of tolerance is built into the budgetary system.

Other ways of taking out the inevitable random variations that occur are to average variances or judge them on a cumulative basis. Whatever the system of gauging variances, there will still be differences to be investigated and corrected.

The major problem of variance analysis in revenue budgeting is

Month.................

	Budget	Actual	Budget Variance	Actual Variance	Budget Cumu-lative	Actual Cumu-lative	Cumu-lative Variance
Revenue budget							
Product A × price × sales forecast							
Product B × price × sales forecast							
Product C × price × sales forecast							
Product D × price × sales forecast							
Total revenue							
Expenditure							
Variable costs—e.g.,							
Product cost							
Distributive discounts							
Salesmen's commission							
Total variable cost							
Contribution							
Fixed costs—e.g.,							
Office rent and rates							
Light and heat							
Management salaries							
Salesmen salaries							
Admin. staff salaries							
Advertising and sales promotion							
Total fixed costs							
Profit or loss (+ or −)							

Notes
1 The Revenue budget is usually constructed on invoiced sales. There may be times however particuarly when demand exceeds supply that the order intake should be monitored as well. On such occasions the invoiced sales tend to equal production capacity not market demand.
2 Expenses have been divided into fixed and variable to allow for the application of marginal costing.
3 Variance analysis and control is maintained in two ways. First the presenting of "tolerances" (budget variance column), second the use of accumulated figures to give a year-to-date position.
4 Further comparisons can be provided by adding columns for previous years' results and future years' forecasts.

Figure 9:2   The marketing budget

identifying how much variation is due to each element of volume, price and mixture. Figure 9:3 shows how such calculations can be made.

Budget			Actual		
A	40 × £10	£400	50 × £9	£450	
B	20 × £5	100	15 × £10	150	
C	10 × £7	70	12 × £8	96	
70		£570		£696	

Total variance = + £126

1 Volume variance
   Assuming budget prices and mix had been achieved
   then a 10 per cent sales increase   = £627
                                   ∴ *volume variance* =   +£57

2 Mix variance
   Assuming actual volume and mix but at budget
   prices
	A	50 × 10	£500
	B	15 × 5	75
	C	12 × 7	84

   £659
   Sales revenue under 1 would have been £627
                                   ∴ *mixture variance* =   +£32

3 Price variance
   Assuming actual volumes and mixture but actual
   prices, revenue £696
   Sales revenue under 2 would have been £659
                                   ∴ *price variance* =   +£37
                                   Total variance = +£126

Figure 9:3   Budget variance analysis

This analysis is most important as it is only too easy to fail to recognise the nature of the changes, and so often product mix variations in particular go unchecked as long as sales volume is maintained. Because of the varying profitability of different products, a change in mix can significantly affect the profits of the company.

9:5 Budgeting and controlling marketing and distribution costs

The computation of the marketing expenditure budget must be considered in the light of the revenue budget. As marketing is concerned with arranging a series of causes to produce certain desired effects, the revenue and expenditure budgets are inextricably linked. Both, of course, are the quantification of the marketing plans which in turn depend upon the corporate and profit objectives of the company.

This concept needs emphasising because too many companies still appear to regard each element as a self-contained entity. This is reflected by the way in which some managements change the revenue budget without reference to the expense budget and *vice versa*. Most marketing men have had the experience of revenue targets being increased and promotional expenses frozen, or alternatively sales volumes accepted and marketing expenditure drastically cut. Moreover, there seems to be a continuous search for one of the Holy Grails of marketing, the "right" sales/expense ratio. As this ratio depends upon a complex series of decisions regarding market share and volume goals, distribution channels and promotion costs, it is not surprising that the range of ratios, even amongst successful companies, is vast. Furthermore, unless great care is taken, emphasis laid on fixed figures of sales/expense ratios can lead to a reversal of the causal relationships. Instead of the level of marketing expenditure being a determinant of the level of revenue and profit, the projected volume becomes the arbiter of how much can be spent. Thus, in companies which believe that the "right" figure is, for example, ten per cent, as volume rises automatically more is spent, whether or not it is needed to produce that volume. Conversely, when there is a tightening up of the market, perhaps due to competitive pressure, and revenue falls, less money is available for promotion just at the time that more effort is in fact required.

It is within a clear framework of the nature of marketing expenditure that the budgeting can proceed. There are three major areas that account for the majority of marketing expenses:

1 Distribution
2 Sales force
3 Promotion

9:5:1   Distribution costs analysis

This area has attracted increasing interest in recent years as more companies have realised how much of the final price has been accounted for by distribution costs. Even ignoring for the moment "costs" such as trade margins, it is estimated that physical distribution alone, which includes such items as warehousing, stock financing, transport, insurance and administration, can cost up to twenty per cent of the final price.

Another major reason why so much scrutiny has been devoted to this area recently is that in most companies distribution costs were scattered across a number of different departments and thus different budgets. It is only when a clearer view of marketing responsibilities is perceived, as suggested above, that such costs tend to be grouped together.

When the total distribution process is viewed as a system, less costly alternatives can often be identified. For example, many companies that originally rejected air freight as too expensive a method of transport have later discovered that its speed and security *vis-à-vis* sea freight can more than offset its greater price by saving on stock holdings, damage, loss and insurance.

Distribution cost analysis has also helped companies in decisions about which channels to use. Many companies have discovered that the cost of directly servicing small accounts is so high that they can never be profitable. This has led to such actions as surcharging small orders, utilising wholesaler networks or employing van selling, thus rationalising sales and distribution costs.

9:5:2   Controlling sales force expenditure

The sales force is usually a major element of marketing expenditure and, in industrial companies, usually the largest. The total cost is a function of how many salesmen are employed and how much each costs.

The only logical way to approach how many men are needed is to analyse the workload to be carried in terms of visiting customers and prospects. Figure 9:4 shows how this can be approached quantitatively.

How much each costs will obviously depend upon the labour market and the company policy. How the payment is made, however, can affect the financial risks and control of the company. The assessment of the

$$\frac{\text{Number of actual and potential customers} \times \text{call frequency}}{\text{Average daily call rate} \times \text{number of working days per year}}$$

Customer categories and call frequencies
Category *A* (over £50 000 a year)   500 × 12 visits p.a. =   6000
Category *B* (£25 000–£50 000 a year) 2000 ×   9 visits p.a. = 18 000
Category *C* (£10 000–£25 000 a year) 5000 ×   6 visits p.a. = 30 000
Category *D* (under £10 000 a year)   7000 × 32 visits p.a. = 14 000

                                                         Annual call total   68 000

Average daily call rate = 8
Number of working days
    Total days in year   365
    Weekends   104
    Holidays   15
    Sickness   5
    Training   10
    Conferences   5
    Meetings   11   150

Number of working days   215
Call total per salesman   215 × 8 = 1720
Number of salesmen required $= \dfrac{68\ 000}{1720} = 40$ salesmen

Figure 9:4   Calculating sales force size

balance between salary and commission will depend upon a number of factors such as the ability of the individual salesman to gain orders, the number of orders likely to be won in any period and the differences in potential between sales territories, etc. One important financial factor, however, is that whilst salaries are a fixed expense, commission is variable. Thus, the higher the percentage of total remuneration paid as commission, the less the risk to the company. When sales volume falls, sales costs therefore fall automatically. In smaller companies in particular, this fact can enable more rapid expansion of the sales force without consequently incurrring higher fixed costs.

9:5:3   Assessing promotional appropriations

Advertising and promotional costs are extremely difficult to assess because the results of the expenditure are so hard to measure. Although, as has been mentioned, all marketing activities are difficult to evaluate, it is usually possible to trace at least some direct result, for example, from employing a salesman even though there are other factors influencing his performance.

Because of the difficulties of assessing promotional spending, some companies decide the level quite arbitrarily by fixing an absolute amount or by taking a percentage of turnover. These approaches have the deficiency, already discussed, that they fail to recognise the causal relationships involved.

The most rational way of approaching the problem is what is known as the *task* method. This approach is concerned with assessing what goals are to be achieved and what level of promotional investment is likely to achieve them. It is first necessary to recognise the nature of promotion more clearly.

All forms of promotion, such as public relations, advertising, direct mail, exhibitions, etc., are methods of communication. Communication consists of transmitting a given message to certain people. It it can be specified what is to be transmitted to whom, a basis for goal-setting can be established. Furthermore, it can be seen that the different means of communication are suitable for different types of messages. Public relations messages, for example, are usually far less precise and detailed than direct mail can be. However PR will reach a far larger audience than direct mail for the same cost.

The different promotional techniques are suitable, therefore, for different types of communication. All are concerned with communicating with the market-place in order to move customers closer to the point of purchase. Such a concept of promotion has been formalised into what is known as the *spectrum of awareness* (see Figure 9:5) which at least demonstrates the inter-relationships within the promotional mix.

If the company can go further and quantify the number of people it wishes to have at each stage, for example, what percentage of the market should be aware of the product, it then becomes possible to calculate the cost of achieving that awareness.

Thus, the task method provides not only a more logical basis for assessing promotional expenditure but also a series of yardsticks by which results can be judged. Admittedly, there is no direct evaluation of the relationship between promotion costs and sales revenue but, as most companies have discovered, this is impossible to measure because

Spectrum of Awareness

	Current state of market	Desired state
Aware of product	50%	60%
of which Knowledgeable	25%	40%
of which Convinced	10%	20%
of which Bought	5%	10%

Notes
1 Market research is needed to quantify how much of total market is at each stage.
2 The target percentages will be derived from the marketing plans and it is on these that the promotional appropriation will be based.
3 Different promotional tools are needed for the different tasks, for example, PR, whilst capable of creating awareness cannot actually gain the order.
4 In order to quantify the goals, each stage must first be defined (for example, what constitutes "awareness"?). The percentages must be applied to the total market size and a media plan produced.
5 At the end of the period, further research should be conducted to assess whether or not the goals have been achieved, thus evaluating the effectiveness of the promotional expenditure.

Figure 9:5   Spectrum of awareness

of the integrated and complex nature of the marketing mixture. At least by this approach it is possible, through research, to establish if the right number and type of people got the right message and assess the value of that communication against its cost. That alone is surely a major advance over the arbitrary allocation of a fixed percentage of sales.

9:6   Conclusion

The problem of financial control in marketing is not basically one of lack of techniques. The monitoring of marketing activity can be improved by methods such as:

1 Discounted cash flow
2 Standard and marginal costing
3 Break-even analysis
4 Budgetary control
5 Management ratio analysis

The real difficulties are the relative unpredictability of the market-place, particularly in its reaction to promotional stimuli, the fuzziness of definition of marketing responsibilities and the lack of financial inform-ation and training amongst marketing people. If the nature of the environment can be understood and the available techniques applied with an awareness of their limitations, the financial control of marketing can be improved in most companies.

Chapter 10

Control of Production

P R Attwood, Professor of Industrial Engineering,
University of Benin, Nigeria

10:1 Production control objectives

In principle, controlling production means comparing production
results with the production plans and taking remedial action as necessary; however, this objective covers a wider range of activities in practice. Since every business organisation is a separate entity, the principle
of production control has to be adapted to suit its own activities,
personalities and resources. Consequently, it follows that the financial
control of production is most effective when the activities, personalities
and finances are analysed in the light of the objectives; their potential
can then be estimated and methods can be developed for achieving the
desired production levels. Control will be exercised successfully if the
income can be compared with the resource expenditure and assessed
in terms of value contributions. In this way, each item will be seen as
having a value to the enterprise and its relative importance can be
determined. Obviously, controlling production finances should commence with an appraisal of the most important costs first and continue
until all costs have been checked.

Large-scale production demands a kind of financial thinking that
helps managers to understand and interpret the over-all financial

progress. For this purpose, a form of production balance sheet is needed which reveals the value of all the production assets at a particular instance of time. Then, after the objectives for production have been defined, balance sheets for alternative strategies can be compared in order to prepare an operating plan with the greatest chance of keeping production costs and outputs in line with the objectives. This should be the prime purpose of production control.

10:2   Budgeting for effective production control

A budget is the basic financial plan for a production activity over a fixed period and it forms a framework for appraising the results and keeping them within the expected limits. Operating to a predetermined budget assures managers that the results are in accord with the over-all plan. Production control has a sound foundation when reliable production budgets are prepared, but no worthwhile budget can be prepared hurriedly.

At the outset, it should be realised that the more facts incorporated in a budget, the more effective it will be. Production budgets are most reliable when they are based upon factual operating costs—as is commonly known, stable conditions have the most predictable future. It follows that a stable production organisation has the greatest chance of success because costs will be relatively constant, varying only with normal economic trends.

Many companies prepare budget manuals to aid their production personnel in formulating operating budgets that are consistent throughout the organisation. A manual should include all the necessary instructions for preparing the budgets, plus other information, such as estimated sales for the period, anticipated profit margins and expected resource requirements.

The resources for production are known as the four Ms—*materials, machinery, manpower* and *money*. It is money that provides the finance for procuring the materials, machines and manpower that are directly responsible for the production outputs and income. Budgetary control can show a production manager how his costs relate to the anticipated break-even point, but he must apply his own operational control in order to rectify any discrepancies. Money is common to all the resources; therefore, it is an appropriate yardstick for comparing their value contributions. Controlling production means comparing production costs with the budget and taking steps to keep them in line where necessary.

10:3   How to control production costs

It is emphasised that the use of facts ensures effective control and costs are the financial facts for controlling production. Costs arise from using resources to make products for sale. They will become more meaningful when they are related to specific operations and circumstances; consequently, standard costing is valuable for controlling production. When preparing standards, they should be regarded as being pertinent to the most stable operating conditions that exist and this must be the aim of work standardisation.

Raising productivity is the over-all objective of industrial engineering and work standardisation was developed as a technique for appraising production inputs and outputs in order to determine production efficiency. Direct production costs are less variable when the work is standardised to ensure more effective control. Consequently, production control should be concerned with direct costs of production. These costs are materials, labour and direct overheads of machinery and supervision, and they can be controlled effectively when the resources required are standardised. Where materials are concerned, standard designs are effective for a range of conditions and the materials or finish can be specified accurately.

Work produces changes in materials so that they conform more closely to market requirements. It is performed by men or machines and the most controllable results are obtained from standard work performances. Standardising the machinery resource includes specifying types of plant and equipment, defining the limits of accuracy and maintaining machine speeds and settings. Standardising the manpower resource involves training the operators, specifying the skills needed and measuring the work content of jobs.

Industrial engineering has an important part to play in production control, especially collecting the information for standardising production, analysing its values, developing improved methods and strategies, measuring work contents, standardising workmanship and training personnel.

10:3:1   The importance of facts

Two types of fact are needed for controlling production; those concerned with making plans and those with measuring the results, because controlling means comparing results with plans. The first prerequisite of an effective production control system is accurate information from the shop floor describing production progress in relation to the plans. In this way, timely warnings will be given regarding the effectiveness of men and machines, particularly technical ability, training needs, labour troubles, machine breakdowns, materials failure, rejects, or the availability of materials, tools and components.

Since fewer facts are needed for controlling stable production, it is obvious that variable conditions give a production controller the most headaches. Paradoxically, the greater the number of facts that have been collected from a situation, the easier it is to standardise and the less variable it becomes. Fortunately, the same facts can be used for making plans as for measuring results and it is wiser to collect too many facts rather than too few.

When production standards have been prepared, the facts with the greatest bearing on production control are those that differ from standard, particularly inferior ones. Each fact is specific to a given situation and no two production control systems are identical. However, it is advisable to consider a specific situation for illustrating the fundamental principals of production control so that it can be explained practically. Once understood, they can be adapted to other situations and circumstances.

10:4   Example of assembly plant production control

In order to demonstrate a production control system in practice, the example of a heavy vehicle assembly plant is described below; it has been found to be eminently suitable for controlling both mass and batch production.

Control of production at the heavy vehicle assembly plant (HVAP) depended upon progressing the flow of information from the shop floor to the works manager's office. Production commenced after orders had been received from vehicle distributors and used to prepare the master production programme. Production programmes were the responsibility of the production controller in the industrial engineering department; they were prepared monthly and each was feasible for the resources available in the current month. After a programme was approved by the works manager, job cards were opened to put the production plan into practice.

In practice, the production of heavy vehicles was controlled schematically on a control board which was designed to display information collected from the workshops. The state of every job of work in the plant could be followed on the control board with coloured pegs that were updated daily.

10:4:1   Daily work sheets

The production shop managers were encouraged to control their departments along similar lines. All the information that was required could be collected from the production shops on daily work sheets; one of which is shown in Figure 10:1.

Each work sheet was an accurate record of the actual work done during a day in a work section of one of the shops. It recorded the number of hours worked by individual operators of the jobs allocated to the section. For control purposes the actual hours were compared with the standard hours for the jobs and the labour efficiency could be calculated for a section, a shop or the plant as a whole. Maintaining an acceptable labour efficiency was the responsibility of the man in charge of each one of these work areas.

10:4:2   Control information

The flow of information between the personnel in the system is illustrated by the flow chart in Figure 10:2. There are two primary circles of communication, one between the works manager and the distributors and one between the works manager and the shop floors. The types of information are shown on the flow lines.

1 *Production work.* The work information came from the chargehands in the shops, each was responsible for a gang of workers comprising a work section. They provided the following informations about jobs:

Shop:		Section:														
		Date:														
		Chargehand:														
		Job numbers and hours worked on each job													Total hours	
No. of men	Names of men	B/T	O/T	B/T	O/T	B/T	O/T	B/T	O/T	B/T	O/T	B/T	O/T	B/T	O/T
1																
2																
3																
4																
5																
6																
7																
Total hours B/T																
Total hours O/T														OK		
No. of production units																

Notes
1 Please write details of lost time against each man where applicable.
2 One production unit is the amount of work done by the section for one vehicle unit.
B/T = Basic time   O/T = Overtime

Figure 10:1   Daily work sheet

1   The work description
2   The number of units produced
3   The man-hours expended
4   The materials consumed

Work description. The name of the section related to the type of work done and the job numbers related to the work instructions that were issued. Basically, all work concerned the assembly of vehicle chassis or bodies.

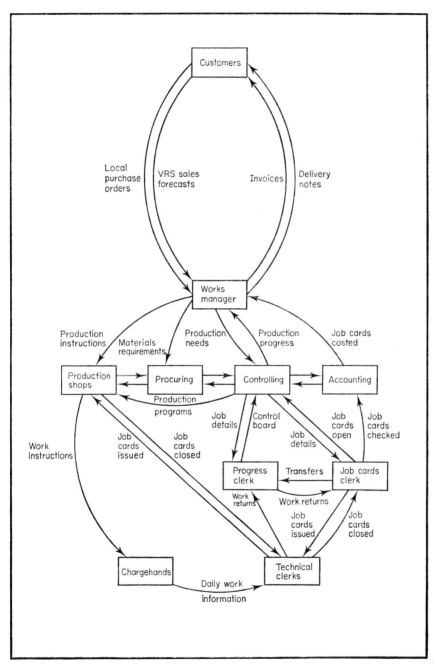

Figure 10:2   Production control information flow-lines

Production units. One production unit was considered to be a chassis or a body and the unit contribution of a work section was the amount of work that had to be performed on a chassis or body before it progressed to the next section. Each chassis was assembled from a kit, or pack, of components, but a body was assembled from parts that were manufactured in the plant.

Man-hours. A normal man-hour was the fair amount of work that could be done continuously by one man in one hour of time. A standard man-hour contained less work than a normal man-hour, because it included rest allowances. Accurate standard work times were obtained after measuring the work done, using time study.

Materials. In order to assemble a chassis or a body, its materials were issued by the stores and delivered to the work places by materials handlers. When materials were required, *stores issue vouchers* (SIVs) were made out and they provided the materials information for costing jobs of work.

Both the man-hours and the materials consumed by a job of work had to be entered on the job card which was a record of the work done for costing purposes.

2 *Production organisation.* A schematic organisation chart for the vehicle assembly plant is shown in Figure 10:3; only the functions directly associated with production are shown in detail. The flow of information commenced with daily work sheets which were completed by charge hands for the work sections; a summary of this information is as follows:

Job number. Each job was specific and defined by a job card number. The job card carried the work instructions and had provision for entering details of the work done with spaces for costing it.

Work section. The name of the work section described the nature of the work done.

Production units. Here the number of units produced during the day in question was entered, but a "W" was written if work was done but not completed.

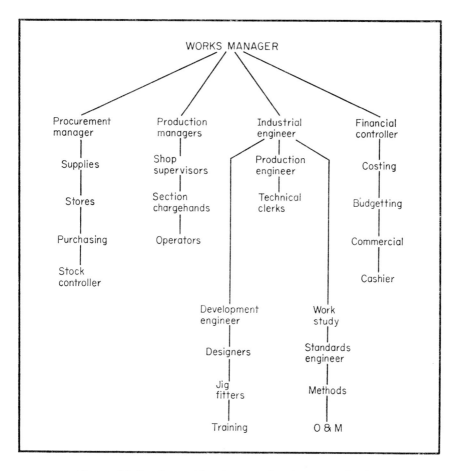

Figure 10:3   Assembly plant production organisation

Men. These were the named men in the work section who worked on the job numbers inserted.

Work duration. The hours worked on each job were entered so that the total work hours by jobs and by men could be checked.

Lost time. This was the unproductive time during the day and it had to be subtracted from the duration in order to obtain the true working hours by jobs.

10:4:3   Collecting production information

1 *Work returns.* The daily work sheets that were compiled by charge hands were collected by technical clerks and taken to the central office for analysing and presenting on the production control board. A technical clerk was assigned to each shop and his duties included recording the work done and the materials issued to each job. He collected the basic information from the chargehands in his shop before analysing it on a daily work returns sheet (see Figure 10:4).

SHOP:			DATE:			
			RECORDED BY:			
					MATERIALS	
SECTION	JOB NO.	MODEL	UNITS	TOTAL HOURS	MASTER SIV	SIV NO.
MEN PRESENT	DAILY HOURS		TOTAL WORK HOURS		SHOP EFFICIENCY	
ACTUAL HOURS AVAILABLE				STANDARD HOURS		

Figure 10:4   Daily work returns

The work areas in a production shop were called sections and each comprised a gang of workers supervised by a chargehand who was responsible for the original work times and materials information.

The labour times spent on each job were recorded on daily work sheets and the technical clerk prepared an SIV (stores issue voucher) whenever materials were required by a chargehand. Both the labour times and the materials issued had to be entered on the job cards (reverse side) so that the job could be costed after it was completed.

The information recorded on the daily work returns by the technical clerks was as follows:

1   *Date, shop and recorder's name:* each sheet was the work record for a particular day in a particular shop and it could be checked with the man who recorded it
2   *Section:* this column showed the names of the work sections that performed work on the jobs during the day
3   *Job number:* each job of work was specific and it was given a reference number which was the same as that on its job card
4   *Model:* this described the vehicle type on which work was done
5   *Units:* one production unit was recorded whenever the work contribution by one section to a particular vehicle chassis or body was completed
6   *Total hours:* this was the sum of all the work-hours spent on a job number in the section described
7   *Materials:* the materials issued to a job were authorised by a master SIV for standard jobs and attached to the job card, or a separate SIV was made out for consumable materials. Details of both were shown on the work returns sheet so that the information entered on job cards could be checked before they were closed by the works manager; the format of a SIV is given in Figure 10:5
8   *Shop efficiency:* the ratio of standard hours to total hours for all the jobs of work performed in a shop was its labour efficiency for the day and it was presented as a percentage on a graph in the central office. All shop efficiencies were shown on the same graph in different colours for comparative purposes

2 *Production progressing.* The daily work returns from the shops were used to keep the control board up-to-date by a progress clerk so that it could be consulted regularly in order to follow the progress of jobs through the plant. The objective of production progressing was to show at a glance how work on jobs was advancing, how shops were loaded with work and how to keep delivery dates.

8—FMH * *

Number...........

STORES ISSUE VOUCHER

Dept. ....   To ....   Date............

Job No. ....   Job .... Stores

Please supply the following items:

Qty Required	Description	Part No.	Folio No.	Qty Issued	Unit Price	Value
Remarks:					Total	

Cost Code............

Issued by..................   Date..............   Authorised by ....

Received by ....   Date..............   Stock Records posted by

....

Figure 10:5   Stores issue voucher format

Control of production

| Customer: | | Date opened: | | Job Card Number: |

Instructions:

Production Depts.	CHASSIS	PRESS	BODY	FOUNDRY	PAINT	MACHINE	TOTALS
Standard hours							
Actual hours							
Std. material costs							

Closed by...................................... Date..................

ACCOUNTS OFFICE DATE:

Depts.	Actual hours	Labour Costs	Indirect Expenses	Totals
CHASSIS				
PRESS				
BODY				
FOUNDRY				
PAINT				
MACHINE				
JOB INVOICE:		Actual materials cost		
Debit note:		Manufacturing transfer cost		
		Total cost		
Date:		Issue price		
Signed:		Margin (.......... % of Sales Price)		

Figure 10:6a   Job card (front)

203

JOB NUMBER..............

DESCRIPTION:

	MATERIALS					LABOUR TIMES		
Date	SIV No.	Qty	Description	Cost	Date	Section	Man-hours	Cost

Figure 10:6b   Job card (reverse)

Two kinds of information were needed for controlling the progress of work: the current position on each job and the precise costs involved.

1   *Job details:* The production control board showed the progress of jobs through the different work sections, commencing with the date of opening a job card. On job cards were detailed the work instructions, the production shops concerned and any special requirements of customers. The layout of the two sides of a job card is shown in Figure 10:6.

2   *Production costs:* The materials costs entered on any job card by the cost accountant were based upon the unit prices that were calculated

by the stock controller; labour-hours were costed according to the rates of pay for the workers involved and standard overhead expenses were calculated for each shop per hour, based upon annual expenditures and the available work-hours.

3 *Control board.* The progress of jobs of work was shown by coloured pegs on a wall-mounted peg-board. When a job was opened, its number and job description were allotted to a row of the board and a peg was inserted in the column representing a section as soon as work commenced there. The design of the control board is pictured in Figure 10:7 and it is in three parts to cover parts manufacture, chassis assembly and body assembly. For quick reference, the different shops were allotted different coloured pegs, but a fixed colour was used to show when a job was ready for transferring to another shop.

4 *Information flow.* Production control at the vehicle assembly plant depended upon the flow of accurate information from the shop floors to the central office through the production engineering and accounting departments. Initially, production instructions were given to the shop managers through the monthly production programme or schedule and they were followed by specific job cards. The production control procedure started and ended with the works manager who had authority over the whole plant. The information flow-lines are illustrated in Figure 10:8.

10:4:4   Presenting the production information

The industrial engineering department at the assembly plant provided a service to the production management with the over-all objective of improving the productivity of the plant through better utilisation of resources. Production control was a co-ordinated function that was performed jointly with production personnel. These included the shop managers, supervisors and chargehands assisted by the technical clerks, the cost accountant and the storemen.

The duties of the chargehands and technical clerks in the collection of information have been described; presenting the information was another function of production engineering that involved a progress clerk and the job cards clerk. The former man kept the production control board up-to-date and the latter supervised the opening, compilation and closing of job cards.

JOB DESCRIPTION			DIV.	MATERIALS SUPPLY		DIVISIONAL WORK AREAS						JOB COMPLETED
Job No.	Model	Starting Date										
			CHASSIS ASSEMBLY	Com-ponents	Acces-sories	Unpack	Cab Build	Frame Build	Paint	Final Assembly	Rectification	Transfer
			PARTS MANUFACTURE	Raw Materials		Shearing	Presswork	Fabrication	Machine Shop	Foundry	Paint	Storage
			BODY ASSEMBLY	Parts		Chassis Preparation	Body Assembly	Body Mounting	Paint	Trimwork	Rectification	Transfer

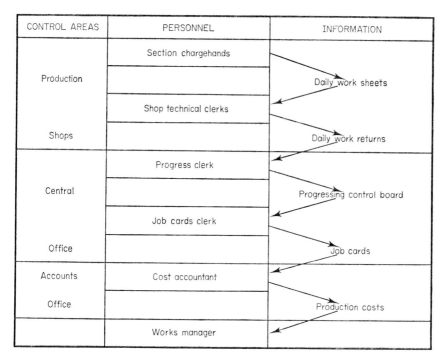

CONTROL AREAS	PERSONNEL	INFORMATION
	Section chargehands	
Production		Daily work sheets
	Shop technical clerks	
Shops		Daily work returns
	Progress clerk	
Central		Progressing control board
	Job cards clerk	
Office		Job cards
Accounts	Cost accountant	
Office		Production costs
	Works manager	

Figure 10:8   Production control personnel

1 *Progress clerk's duties.* The daily work returns from the shops were prepared by the technical clerks who brought them to the progress clerk each morning. Then they were presented on the control board with the aid of coloured pegs. The number and description of each job was written at the start of a row and a peg was inserted for each section where work was done; consequently, as a job progressed, more pegs were shown along the row. Completed jobs were removed from the board at the end of a month after checking that they had been taken off the work in progress list.

After displaying the information from a daily returns sheet on the control board, it was passed to the job cards clerk who used it to check the entries on closed job cards. Details of the vehicles that were completed and transferred to distributors were obtained from a daily transfers summary which was prepared by the job cards clerk; it is illustrated in Figure 10:9.

2 *Job cards clerk's duties.* Job cards were opened on the works manager's

Customer	Vehicle model	Chassis No.	Body type	Paint colour	Chassis job No.	Body job No.	In-spector	Delivery note No.	Unit price
						Total jobs transferred today			
						Number brought forward			
						Running total for the year			

Recorded by ....

Checked by ....   Date...............

Figure 10:9   Daily transfers job summary

instructions to the production engineer, under the following circumstances:

1 When a job was programmed for the current month
2 When a local purchase order was received from a distributor or other customers
3 At the beginning of each month for consumable materials in the shops and maintenance department

Details of each job card had to be recorded in the job card register, a page of which is shown on Figure 10:10, so that it formed an accurate record of all production work in the plant; it included the prices and costs of jobs for inspection by the auditor annually.

1	Job number																		
2	Authority																		
3	Customer																		
4	Description of job, code and related jobs																		
5	Vehicle model																		
6	Chassis number																		
7	Date job card opened																		
8	Date job card closed																		
9	Issue price																		
10	Labour costs and indirect expenses																		
11	Tax and materials cost																		
12	Delivery note number																		

Note: Each page is arranged horizontally in the Job Register and has many rows for the Job Numbers.

Figure 10:10　Page from the job register

Job cards were issued to shops by the technical clerks who returned them from shops when completed so that the job cards clerk could check the entries before sending them to other shops or the cost accountant, as appropriate. He also checked the transfer of vehicles from the plant in conjunction with the delivery clerk, who made out a delivery note for each vehicle leaving the plant. A copy of the delivery note later became the invoice.

At the end of each month a list of the work in progress was made and checked with the job register and the control board. The job cards clerk retained the job cards that were opened until they were ready for issue to the shops and he was the senior clerk in the production engineering office.

10:4:5   Using the information to control production

1 *Production costs.* The direct costs of production comprised the materials and the labour hours expended on each job plus the direct overheads. The materials and labour were recorded on job cards by the technical clerks and the overheads were apportioned to the working hours in each shop where work was done on a job.

The indirect costs were charged afterwards when the jobs were invoiced to distributors. Depreciation was charged as a straight-line expense over the length of life for plant or equipment.

2 *Cost control.* The job cards carried all the work details that were needed for direct costing; when work was done on a job in more than one shop, the costs were transferred from job card to job card if necessary. The cost of materials charged to jobs was the same as the unit price that was used for stock control purposes. A unit price was the mean price per unit of the items currently in stock.

3 *Budgeting.* The accounts office produced the annual budgets in conjunction with the commercial and production managers and the estimated operating costs were related proportionally to the expected production outputs. Items of capital expenditure that were needed for maintaining the production outputs had to be agreed at a management meeting before a proposal could be put to the board of directors.

Each production manager was expected to control his operating costs within the limits of the budget for his shop and it was essential to let him have monthly statements of his expenditure. It was considered vital for each manager to review his production costs regularly and to keep the accountant informed of special points at the monthly production meeting.

4 *Invoicing.* The second copy of the vehicle delivery note formed the invoice for the distributor or customer when the price had been inserted on it. Finally, the delivery note number was entered on the job card and in the job register for future reference.

5 *Production programming.* The control of vehicle assembly work was a process of comparing actual production outputs with the planned outputs presented in the monthly production programme which was based upon the orders that had been received. Each month, an estimate of the vehicles required by the distributors was prepared and the combined requirements were given to the works manager on a *vehicle requirements schedule* (VRS). These requirements were based upon the sales forecasts and it was the responsibility of the procurement manager to see that the assembly materials were obtained from suppliers.

When the production engineer received his copy of the vehicle requirements schedule, he obtained a summary of the stock available from the stock controller and then he accumulated this information on a production programme data sheet for each of the models that were assembled at the plant. A copy of a data sheet is shown in Figure 10:1. With the aid of a production programme data sheet it was possible to follow the procurement progress of a pack of chassis components from the time of ordering them to the month that they were put into production.

Assembling bodies on the chassis meant that the body parts had to be manufactured internally, for which short-term plans were needed; these were called schedules in order to prevent confusion over names. Schedules were developed from the over-all production programme, of course, but they specified the work in more detail for the foundry, press and machine shops. It was necessary to manufacture the parts for bodies in advance of assembling them so that they were transported to the assembly shops in good time; the production control system was designed to allow for this.

Information that was provided by the distributors formed the basis of production programmes and it was converted into production instructions when job cards were opened. Job cards were not issued until the jobs were ready to go into production and they were retained in the central office. Accessories that were not included in packs of chassis components, for example, tyres, batteries and lubricants, had to be procured additionally and this, too, was initiated by the production programme. Ordering chassis accessories depended upon the vehicle models programmed, the number of units required and the sequence for unpacking.

6 *Production programme.* The production engineer prepared a production programme for presentation at the production meeting that was held at the end of each month. The number of vehicles that were programmed for assembly was based upon the resources available,

standard work times and the distributors' requirements. Any surplus vehicles from the previous month, as with work in progress, were transferred to the subsequent programme.

7 *Bodywork schedules.* Bodywork jobs were scheduled on a weekly basis and work was assigned to machines or production lines in such a way as to ensure good productivity.

8 *Transferring vehicles.* When finished, the vehicles had to be given a pre-delivery check before transferring them to the distributors. A transfer section at the plant was responsible for handing over the completed vehicles as chassis with or without bodies. The last function of production control was to prepare an accurate record of all vehicles leaving the plant, which was done as a daily job transfers summary— see Figure 10:11.

9 *Production control requisites.* The control of production demands a continuous flow of pertinent information about the jobs in production; therefore, the first requisite is good communications. Verbal communications are fine for creating a happy working atmosphere, but written communications make the best work records. Unfortunately, workers have an aversion towards writing and production records must be kept to a minimum. Paradoxically, the greatest number of production facts are to be found at shop floor level, but they become diluted or modified as they rise up to the management level where they are vital for production control. Consequently, it is essential that the most important points are not lost during transmission. Omission or falsification can be prevented with simple paperwork.

At the heavy vehicle assembly plant, the system was straightforward and everyone was able to understand it, because it involved the personnel in a way that promoted teamwork. Trust and respect are the passwords for successful teamwork, but they can be learnt only from practical expereince of participating in the system.

The fundamental information for production control came from the workers on the shop floors through their chargehands and the technical clerks who analysed it for use by the production managers; then it was presented on the production control board in the central office. Factual information was transmitted with a minimum of paperwork and good cooperation was generated between the different personnel involved.

10 *Control paperwork.* Basically, two work sheets, a sales forecast, a job card and a transfers summary were the only paperwork needed for controlling production at the vehicle assembly plant. The information

PRODUCTION PROGRAMME DATA SHEET				SHEET NO.				
				SOURCES OF DATA: Supplies Department				
Chassis code	Vehicle model	Units per pack	PROGRESS DATES					
			In transit	Un- cleared	Broken delivery	Cleared	Month pro- grammed

= completed progress   Data recorded by:

Figure 10:11   Production programme data sheet

from these sheets was used to compare results with the plans presented in the production programme.

1 *Daily work sheet:* this was completed by the charge hands and summarised by the technical clerks for all the shops. Each sheet showed the jobs in progress in the different work sections and included the labour-hours and materials issued

2 *Daily work returns sheet:* the information given to the technical clerks by the chargehands was checked and analysed to obtain the current production position for each shop. It was taken to the progress clerk for updating the control board after the shop manager had been informed of the labour efficiency for his shop

3 *Vehicle requirement schedule:* the sales forecast for each month was prepared by models and the number of units required

4 *Job card:* this gave details of the job including work instructions, production shops scheduled, dates and costs

5 *Daily job transfers summary:* the final information needed for production control was full details of all vehicles transferred from the plant

10:4:6   Controlling production costs successfully

The planning of investments requires development of capital budgets, whilst the use of financial ratios and percentages helps to measure the effectiveness of spending the planned capital. However, the utilisation of liquid resources invested in raw materials, finished products, work in progress and debtors can be evaluated and production can be planned successfully by preparing operational budgets that are really cash forecasts for the near future.

The control of production costs is achieved by delegating the responsibility for specific budgets to the workplaces where the costs arise. Monthly statements of actual expenditures will show the people responsible for the work how their costs vary from their budgets. Then the production controller should prepare and issue statements which reconcile the actual achievements with the production plans as a whole. Over-all financial control of production is provided by studying abbreviated balance sheets in which budget percentages and ratios are compared with actual results.

Valuable information for preparing production budgets is given by work standards; with them, potential labour performance, machine operation, or materials usage can be measured realistically so that the relative values of different design specifications, product qualities and levels of resource expenditures can be controlled effectively.

Cost improvements result from reviewing the production resources continually: especially layouts, methods, tools, materials, designs and technical skills. Savings are maintained by revision of the production cost standards upon which control is based. Cost control is difficult to implement without practical measures for production performance that permit flexibility for minimising over-all costs. Instead of being rigid and restricting cost standards should motivate savings by giving supervisors room to reduce the total cost of operations within their control.

Cost performance has to be measured meaningfully if cost control is to be successful for two reasons: firstly, when supervisors know that their accountability is being judged they accept more personal responsibility for incurring costs and, secondly, measuring past performances can provide criteria for improving future performances.

Work simplification programs that are designed to get people thinking creatively about the work that they do will produce suggestions for improving it. Successful programmes motivate improvements and develop enthusiasm; they come from implementing suggestions of the people who will control them. Everybody is able to recognize cost improvements; therefore, producing savings is the best measure for judging a successful production control system.

Chapter 11

Control of Research and Development

A W Pearson, Director, R and D Research Unit,
Manchester Business School

Research and development is one of the major functional areas of a business. It is a consumer of resources, money, manpower and, in particular, highly skilled manpower. If these resources are utilised wisely and the resulting output is effectively translated into new products and processes it can be a major contributor to growth and profitability. But it is not sufficient to assume that increasing expenditure on R and D will necessarily lead an organisation or a country in this direction. Experience in the postwar period has amply demonstrated this. Japan, with a relatively small proportion of its gross national product allocated to R and D, has had an astounding growth rate, whereas the UK with a much higher proportion, cannot come anywhere near their perform-ance. Similarly, at the company level organisations like Marks and Spencers Limited and Tesco Limited would not be placed in the technologically-orientated category if judged on the number of qualified scientists and engineers (QSEs) that they employ, but their growth and profitability is the envy of many.

The reasons for this are many and varied, but a good deal of the anomaly can be explained by looking more closely at what is meant by R and D and the way in which it is used by different countries and organisations. For example, it may not be necessary to undertake R and D oneself if it is possible to purchase its results at an "economic" price from other organisations which are more skilled and more efficient in this activity. The choice between undertaking R and D at home and buying it in, whether by licence or otherwise, will be determined by the relative price of the alternatives, taking into account the costs of putting the R and D to use, that is, translating it into products and processes which will produce the economic returns.

One of the major tasks of those responsible for financial management of R and D is to ensure that the best choice is made in this situation. In order to do this it is necessary to have information about the needs of, and technological capabilities available to, the organisation. The first problem is to ensure that these are matched as far as possible and that systems and procedures are established which cover the different aspects of the management problem, such as evaluation, planning, selection and monitoring. Such systems must be designed in such a way as to provide an up-to-date picture of the financial situation regarding projected costs and benefits, while allowing the individual researcher and the team to which he may belong the maximum freedom to utilise the technological skills for which they are employed.

This chapter discusses some of the methods and procedures which are in use and are currently being developed by a number of organisations to handle these problems. Particular attention is paid to recent developments in the UK. The descriptions of particular methods are inevitably very short, and reference is provided to the source of the material so that more detailed information can be obtained about the characteristics of the methods and the way in which they are used. The importance of the latter cannot be too strongly emphasised. The value of formal methods is very much determined by the way in which they fit into and form part of the structure of the organisation.

11:1 Identifying capabilities and defining requirements

It has been argued by many people that the effectiveness of R and D is determined to a large extent by the way in which it matches the cor-

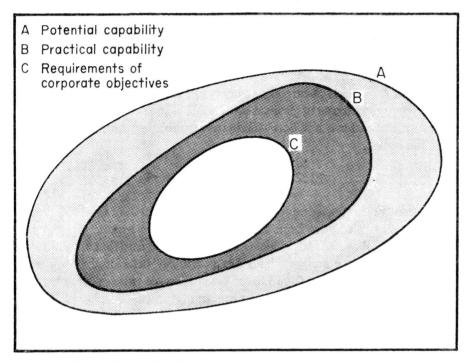

A Potential capability
B Practical capability
C Requirements of
   corporate objectives

Figure 11:1   Possible relationship between practical and
potential capabilities and requirements of corporate
objectives for a R and D laboratory
(Reprinted from *Chemistry in Britain*, September 1971)

porate objectives of the organisation. This has been neatly portrayed
as shown in Figure 11:1.[1]

In this case the curve C, portraying the requirements of corporate
objectives, lies wholly inside the other two. The situation in which C does
not overlap the other curves to any great extent can be easily visualised
and many organisations have suffered from such a situation in the past.
The current economic situation is changing this with organisations
paying more attention to the return which they are getting from each
of their activities. As a consequence, projects are being stopped, direc-
tions are being changed and other projects are being accelerated in order
to utilise more fully potential which exists within the organisations.
In order to realise this potential it is necessary to choose a set of projects
which provides a balance between the short and long term, between the
low and the high risk, between new products and process development,
and the support of well-established areas. In doing this it is vital to

choose a portfolio capable of providing a springboard from which the organisation can leap forward and take advantage of fresh opportunities which may come along, besides creating these opportunities for itself. Financial management starts with this aspect. It is no good attempting to evaluate projects accurately, to carry out detailed cost-benefit studies and to monitor costs of projects with a fine degree of detail if the areas and priorities have not been adequately established on a global basis at the outset.

11:2 Relevance analysis

In recent years considerable effort has been expended on this aspect and many companies have been very pleased with the results. One of the most promising methods which has come into use is that based on a form of relevance analysis. This has previously been used in military programmes, where it is found to have considerable value. More recently it has been applied to R and D programmes in other spheres. There

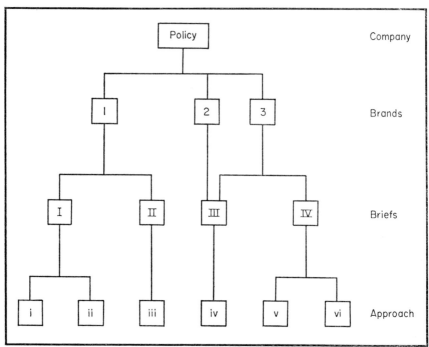

Figure 11:2   Relevance-tree for the company
(Reprinted from *R & D Management,* February 1970)

are many versions of this method, but one which has been developed and put into use tackles the problem of matching R and D to the company objectives from both ends, that is, from the company and from the R and D department.

11:2:1   Company viewpoint

From the company end this situation can be portrayed as shown in Figure 11:2.[2]

The tree is composed of a number of levels and the links between levels indicate clearly where direct inter-relationships exist. The logical follow-on to this is to attempt to quantify the strength of the links and hence to obtain a measure of the relative contribution of, say, different activities to the products they are supposed to support. However, it must be emphasised that great value is obtained from the use of relevance analysis even when it is not possible to assign accurate numbers to each of the links. The method is important because it highlights the linkages between activities and goods and shows up where differences occur.

11:2:2   R and D viewpoint

The situation can be looked at from the R and D end, as is shown in Figure 11:3.

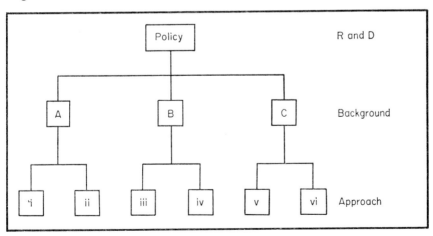

Figure 11:3   Relevance-tree for R and D
(Reprinted from *R & D Management,* February 1970)

Here the relative weighting given to the particular R and D area or background theme might be determined in the first instance by the amount of effort, measured in financial terms, which is allocated to the particular area. Indeed, at the present time many organisations are putting in a considerable amount of effort to identify and isolate a small number of background themes, to which they would like to see R and D orientated. As much as eighty per cent of future projects may be specifically related to these areas, and hence their identification is a major issue for both R and D personnel and top management in all functional areas.

11:2:3   Joint relevance-tree

It seems reasonable to conclude from the above that it would be useful to consider the two trees together and to identify the degree of overlap or otherwise, between the needs of the organisation, as defined by its objectives, and the direction in which R and D is moving, as defined by its emphasis on particular projects or programmes. This has, in fact, been done, as shown in Figure 11:4, and has produced very interesting results.

This exercise provides useful information about the degree of match, or otherwise, between the emphasis being given to particular areas by the R and D department and the needs of the organisation as seen in profitability terms. There will inevitably be some differences, and in a dynamic organisation there should be. The time-scales associated with R and D are different to other functional areas, and it is not necessarily a bad thing that R and D is looking further ahead than managers who must be concerned with profitability and cash flows in the more immediate future.

However, there have been many situations in which it is clear that changes of emphasis should be made in the research programs as a result of an exercise of this kind. This method of analysis is particularly useful for assessing the relative merits of alternative projects and programs of research in the more basic areas. In such cases it is very unusual to have any hard or quantitative data about the costs and benefits, and the choice must be made after consideration has been given to the potential contribution which such work, if it is successful, will make to the organisation's longer-term goals. Finally, it must be emphasised that the method of presentation itself, and the discussions which are

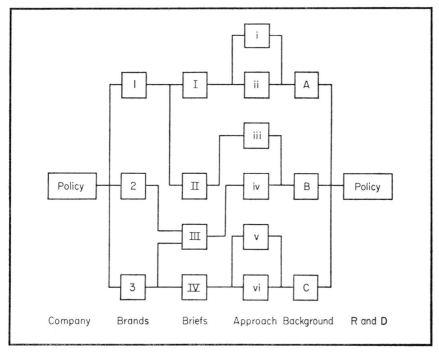

Figure 11:4   Joint relevance-tree
(Reprinted from *R & D Management,* February 1970)

encouraged in order to establish the basic framework of the tree, provide a useful means of improving communication in an organisation.

The use of methods of analysis and presentation such as relevance analysis enables large amounts of data to be neatly summarised and to be presented easily to senior people in different functional areas so that they can get an indication of the situation as it stands now and as it is likely to develop in the future. In situations where they have been used they have enabled the length of meetings in which top people are involved to be significantly reduced, by highlighting the important areas for discussion.

11:3   Project selection

At the departmental level it is necessary to discuss in more detail the allocation of resources to, and the progressing of, individual projects. To do this it is necessary to consider such factors as their costs and benefits, the likely technical problems, and the way in which they will fit into an overall portfolio designed to move the company in the direction in which it has chosen to go. A variety of methods have been suggested for this. Many of them have been specifically developed for particular organisations and it is quite clear that it is difficult to generalise about the value or otherwise of any one method or technique in this area. One thing, however, which must be stressed is that all formalised techniques and procedures, particularly those which provide numerical indices, are only useful in as much as they form a basis for discussion and provide background information for decision-making purposes. It is very unlikely and probably undesirable that such methods will ever replace the complicated network of informal and formal procedures which are now in use. It is to be hoped that they will assist management in what is inevitably a difficult situation by providing more useful information at various stages in the process. It must always be remembered that formulas and models are only as good as the information which is put into them, and there is a considerable amount of evidence to suggest that the level of accuracy of some of the information, in particular that relating to benefits estimates, is of a very inadequate quality for use in detailed mathematical models. However, the latter do have their place in structuring situations, in identifying important pieces of information which should be made available before major decisions are taken and in indicating to management the possible long-term consequences of decisions which they are making.

The majority of such methods require information not only about the R and D but about the utilisation and potential benefits. Hence they require information from a variety of people in different functional areas. This problem has been tackled in different ways by different organisations. Some have formed committees in which, at the very outset, proposals for R and D are debated by a group representative of finance and marketing as well as R and D. A number of organisations have set up specific groups which are responsible for providing a central facility in which evaluation can take place, and which perform an integrating and communicating function at the same time. They can call upon the people in the organisation who have the necessary skill to provide the information inputs and often make use of a set of procedures which allow a standardised approach to be taken to the problem of evaluation and selection.

Following discussion, each proposal is scored against a number of criteria. The rating (0—very poor to 4—very good) can be modified by a weight factor according to importance of the criteria. Both the weighting and the criteria used can be varied by the evaluation group. These are shown bracketed in the actual example below. This project is now reaching final development (as TIOS) and two overseas sales have been achieved so far.

Title: R.D.P.39. Submarine Torpedo Control System. Stage 1.
Aims: To establish requirements and outline system requirements for an improved system for overseas sales. To define programme and costs of further work.
Target Position: Ability to design and develop prototype.
Category of Study: Market oriented/Product improvement.

Evaluation Status: PRELIMINARY
Date: 12.11.68

SECTION 1. Relation to company policy, resources and technical considerations

Criteria	0	1	2	3	4	Weight Factor	Score	Remarks
A. Strategy and General								
A1 Relation to Company Aims		/				3	6	Support to s/m foreign sales
A2 Extent of Policy Directive		/				2	4	
A3 Gain in Know-How	/					1	1	Nothing outstanding at this stage
A4 Potential Publicity Value		/				1	2	
A5 Previous Experience			/			1	3	Experienced in T.C.S.
(A6 Relation to other Projects, R & D, etc.)				/		1	4	Building block for new p.v. sub work
				TOTAL SCORE			23	MAX. POSSIBLE 36
B. Resources, etc.								
B1 Rate of Spend				/		1	4	About £500/quarter
B2 Length of Study				/		1	4	3 months
B3 Labour Requirements				/		1	4	1 man
B4 Other Requirements				/		1	4	None
B5 Availability of Resources		/				1	2	Current lull; could soon build up though
B6 Sub-Contract Need				/		1	4	None
B7 Availability of Info.		/				1	2	Difficulty of quick answers on availabilities of equipment?
				TOTAL SCORE			24	MAX. POSSIBLE 28

Any General Notes on this Section

SECTION 2. Assessment of benefit, probability of success, and commerical factors.
Note For feasibility/information-gathering types of study, only part C need be considered. Part C is not for use where financial data, etc. is, *or should be*, known.
C. *Descriptive appraisal of likely benefit, value of study, etc.*

SCORE (out of 20)
(Reprinted from *R & D Management*, October 1971)

Figure 11:5　Formal evaluation using a check-list

11:3:1 Check-lists

Many organisations have found great difficulty in using complicated procedures, in particular mathematical formulations and manipulations; a simple check-list often forms the core of the system.[3] An example of one such check-list which is in current use is shown in Figure 11:5. It is clear that any such check-list must be specific to an organisation and that knowledge of its merits or otherwise will appear with use. It should therefore be modified and developed in use. A number of organisations have very successfully adopted this approach and it is certainly an introduction to selection which can be recommended.

11:3:2 Project scores

Check-lists can take on many forms and the introduction of weighting for the separate criteria is sometimes taken further by amalgamating the criteria into a project score. One such method[4] chooses the following five criteria as important:

1 Promise of success (P)
2 Time to completion (T)
3 Cost of the project (C)
4 Strategic need (N)
5 Market gain (M)

and suggests that each project should be given a numerical rating of one, two or three against each of these criteria. A score for a project is then calculated by multiplying the five numbers together:

$$project\ score = P \times T \times C \times N \times M$$

This project score then can be plotted against the cost of a project, A typical plot of a set of projects for an organisation is shown in Figure 11:6. It is interesting to note that the projects tend to fall within a cone-shaped area of fairly narrow angle.

This type of diagram provides useful information about the relative merits of individual projects and assists the decision-maker in selecting a set of projects which will provide a balanced portfolio. This approach

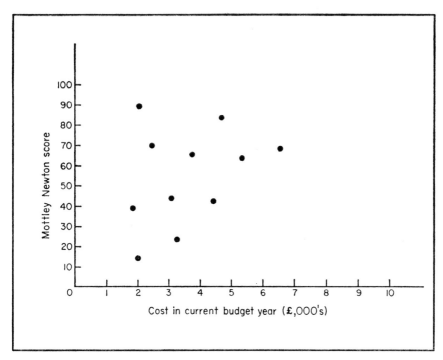

Figure 11:6   Example of a plot of a set of projects

is interesting, relatively simple and can be of use in a number of areas. It is, however, relatively vague, as are all rank indices methods.

11:3:3   Linear programming

Where the data is more hard and discrete and readily available it has been suggested that mathematical models of a more specific nature can be useful. One such model is that based on linear programming, and this has, in fact, been used in practice to some effect.

The basic linear programming format allows resources to be broken down into a series of categories; for example, capital and revenue can be treated as different accounts and manpower can be added in as a separately identifiable resource, if so desired. This degree of subdivision can be helpful in many situations as constraints can be placed on the availability of any particular resource in future time-periods and the choice of projects can be assessed against likely demand on this resource, taking into account the demands of all competing projects.[5]   A very

227

Project number	1	2	3	4
Wages cost	24	30	10	4
Capital cost	4	10	2	12
Benefit	35	60	30	28
Benefit/Total cost	1.25	1.5	2.5	1.75

Wages budget = 54

Capital budget = 14

Total budget = 68

Project number	1	2	3	4
Variable	x_1	x_2	x_3	x_4

Project constraints

$$x_1 \leqslant 1$$
$$x_2 \leqslant 1$$
$$x_3 \leqslant 1$$
$$x_4 \leqslant 1$$

Wage constraint $\quad 24x_1 + 30x_2 + 10x_3 + 4x_4 \leqslant 54$

Capital constraint $\quad 4x_1 + 10x_2 + 2x_3 + 12x_4 \leqslant 14$

Benefit $\quad 35x_1 + 60x_2 + 30x_3 + 28x_4$

Figure 11:7   Example of linear programming
(Reprinted from *R & D Management,* February 1970)

simple indication of the way in which a programme is set out can be seen by reference to an example in which capital and revenue accounts have been treated separately and budget constraints placed on each. A simple case in which four projects are under consideration and in which the capital and wages budgets are limited to fourteen and fifty-four respectively is shown in Figure 11:7, as is the mathematical formulation as it would appear in linear programming format.

This approach has not been used on any extensive scale and, in fact, considerable work is being carried out at the moment in a variety of situations in order to test its applicability. Some of the major problems likely to be associated with using this approach are those of data collection, but the model itself can be very useful in assisting and providing information about the type of data which is most relevant. It can also indicate the likely implications of choosing any particular portfolio on the resource requirements in future time-periods. This sort of information is of vital importance for longer-term planning in both the financial and the manpower areas.

11:4   Management information systems and multi-project monitoring

In every activity which involves more than one person there are likely to be communication problems, and these will increase with the size of the activity and the number of functional areas which are involved. A management information system should be designed to provide information for the people who "need to know". It should not become an indiscriminate dissemination of paper which does not lead to useful decisions being made. In this sense, it should be tailored to the organisation, taking into account its particular characteristics, the nature of the technology with which it is concerned, and the range of products and/or companies it serves. It should provide background information for a total management communication system and must be complementary to and not displace the project meetings and informal methods which are so much a part of the successful operation of any organisation. This has been widely recognised and has led to the development of a number of different types of system.

Basic differences tend to arise in the requirements for information, the output generated, the people to whom this is sent and, perhaps more important, the type of action taken as a result of the information. Some examples of the differences can be seen by reference to a number of systems which have been reported in the literature and which have been successfully introduced and used over a number of years. Consideration of these also indicates that there is some similarity of approach and that some generalisations can be made.

11:4:1   Defining objectives

One of the most important points to be made at the outset is that the majority of the systems in use require that a project should have a reasonably closely-defined objective, and it is interesting to note that more and more companies are reducing their open-ended commitment to research, and working much more on projects which have closely-defined end-products, both in a technical and a marketing sense. This has tended to mean that larger projects have been broken down into a series of sub-projects with intermediate milestones being clearly defined for planning and progressing purposes. The systems can be either manually operated or, in some cases, computerised. The basic requirement is usually an evaluation form on which the objectives of the project, the likely costs and time-scales and the likely difficulties are set out.

The information which is required for this exercise is collected from a variety of people and at this stage it is wise to involve marketing and finance, particularly where there is likely to be a heavy commitment to resources from these areas if the project is successful. Depending upon the size of the project it may also be necessary to obtain the active support of these people, in particular the marketing executive, to get financial approval.

11:4:2   Authorising expenditure

Generally speaking, R and D managers are able to go ahead with small projects to test feasibility, to develop methods and to look at new areas with their own authority, but there is a greater emphasis these days on the need to get authority for expenditure which is likely to lead to new products and processes as early as possible. In many companies this can only come from the marketing manager or co-ordinating body that is responsible to him, which will eventually be involved with the exploitation of the successful research. It is also important at this stage to obtain information about how the project is likely to progress and where the difficulties are likely to arise. The information is of value not only for evaluation purposes but also for future progressing of the project, and it cannot be emphasised too much that this second aspect is a very important one, as the identification of unsuccessful projects before a high level of expenditure has been committed is a vital issue to most organisations.

11:4:3   Bar or Gantt charts

In many situations simple planning mechanisms have been found useful to indicate the activities which must be undertaken and time-scales involved before a project is completed.

These often take the form of bar or Gantt charts, as shown in Figure 11:8. The length of the bars indicates the total duration of the activities and their position on the chart indicates the time-period over which they are scheduled to take place.

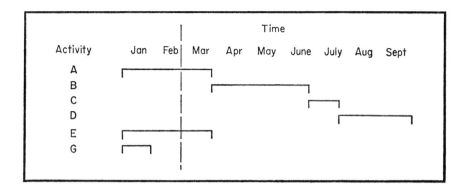

Figure 11:8   Bar or Gantt chart

11:4:4   Network analysis

In some situations, particularly for large and complex projects, it has been found valuable to make use of network analysis, although the use of this method in R and D has not been as extensive as the literature might suggest. One organisation has used the variation of network analysis based on a precedence diagram to good effect[6] and for projects of a more uncertain nature this appears to have some advantage over the more commonly encountered activity diagram, or arrow, method. The form of presentation used is shown in Figure 11:9.

The above methods of planning are of considerable assistance to management as they indicate the resources which are likely to be required during the course of a project. Hence they provide valuable inputs to the budgetary process as well as to forward planning with respect to other resources such as manpower and test facilities.

There will inevitably be uncertainty in any plans which are drawn up at the early stages in the life of a project, the extent of this depending to a considerable extent upon the type of project, the nature of the technology and the market environment in which the organisation operates. However, even simple plans can assist management in assessing the progress of a project and provide information about the most useful times at which reviews should be carried out.

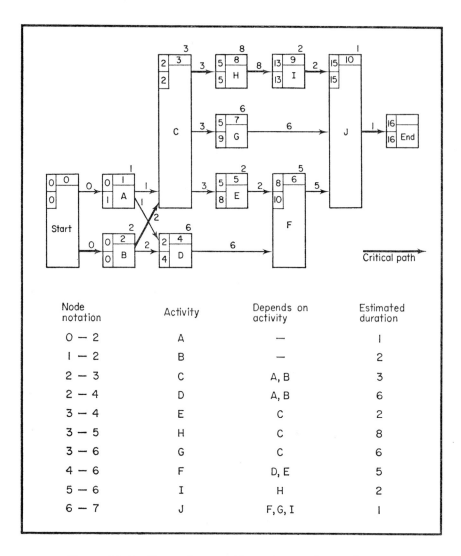

Node notation	Activity	Depends on activity	Estimated duration
0 — 2	A	—	1
1 — 2	B	—	2
2 — 3	C	A, B	3
2 — 4	D	A, B	6
3 — 4	E	C	2
3 — 5	H	C	8
3 — 6	G	C	6
4 — 6	F	D, E	5
5 — 6	I	H	2
6 — 7	J	F, G, I	1

Figure 11:9   Dependency table and precedence diagram
for an R & D project
(Reprinted from *R & D Management,* June 1971)

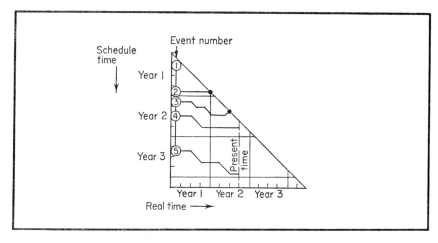

Figure 11:10   A slip chart, recording schedule changes

11:4:5   Slip charts

In order to facilitate the progressing operation a number of systems have been suggested. A very simple one, making use of a "slip chart" has been described in the literature,[7, 8] and variations of it are in use in a number of organisations. An example of such a chart is shown in Figure 11:10.

An essential feature of such a chart is that time appears on both axes, real time being on the horizontal and schedule time on the vertical. If the scales chosen for the time axis are the same, a line at forty-five degrees will meet both axes at the same date. The chart is simple to use and is fairly self-explanatory. When updated, it provides historical information about the progress of a project. Horizontal lines between review dates indicate that progress is on schedule. Movements away from schedule are clearly indicated by a change in direction of this line. If this change of direction becomes forty-five degrees and no corrective action is taken the project will never be finished. Movements between the horizontal and the forty-five degree line indicate the degree of slippage. The key to the use of a slip chart is an adequate definition of intermediate events. The time at which they should be reached, and hence the location of the events on the schedule axis, can be derived from bar charts or networks and the two methods of presentation, that is, plans and progress, can be portrayed side by side if so desired.

233

An alternative approach, which provides an extremely useful graphical output, has been developed and introduced by a major user of R and D facilities.[9] In this case projects, by their very nature, are considered to move through a number of stages. At the outset, the time at which a project is expected to reach each stage is estimated and this information is updated on a regular basis. The original estimates and updated information about the times which are required to reach each of these stages or "milestones" are then recorded on the same sheet and sent out to people who can take appropriate action as necessary. The format of the method of presentation is shown in Figure 11:11. The output can be sorted in a number of ways so that, for example, an individual section leader can have information about all his own projects. Information can also be fed to outside groups about the projects which are of concern to them, and this provides a very useful and relatively simple information system for both internal and external purposes and hence forms a useful integrating device between R and D and the market environment.

It is interesting and important to note that the majority of the systems in use for progressing projects request information about the reasons for any delays which occur. This indicates to management where the bottlenecks are occurring in the organisation, which, incidentally, are frequently due to lack of test facilities and lack of manpower. Indeed, the latter has tended to convince many organisations that they would be better progressing fewer projects and ensuring their viability than spreading their effort over a large number. It is also interesting that considerable emphasis is currently being placed on monitoring time, rather than costs, as the prime indicator of the progress of a project. The reason for this is that time can be a more meaningful variable for R and D, particularly if it is remembered that the costs of R and D are usually very much smaller than the costs of subsequent stages. This essentially means that lost time or overrun on projects can have tremendous implications for the organisation in terms of future cash flows and, in particular, that R and D which is too late may very well lose markets. In many situations the benefits which will be lost if the latter occurs will be considerably higher than any increased costs which would have been incurred if the project had been brought back on to an appropriate time-scale.

The methods which have been described above are relatively simple but effective. They allow a great deal of flexibility in use. They show

PROGRAMME HISTORY THE NUCLEAR POWER GROUP LIMITED

Programme key

1 Specification agreed	6 Rig commissioned
2 Equipment designed	7 Main test finished
3 Equipment ordered	8 Analysis complete
4 Equipment received	9 Report issued
5 Special development	* Stage completed

Site	Customer	S/leader	Project	File
B-2	COT	EAJ	P21/2/006	2345

Title: Pressure gradient effects on insulation for HTR Rig 1

Review date	1968 J A S O N D	1969 Jan F M A M J J A S O N D	1970 Jan F M A M J	Reasons for change
18 Dec 69	1 *	2 * 3 * 4 * 6 6	7	Laboratory manufacturing difficulties
14 Nov 69	1 *	2 * 3 * 4 * 6 6	7	Manufacturing difficulties
17 Oct 69	1 *	2 * 3 * 4 * 6 7 8	8	Foil welding problem
15 Sep 69	1 *	2 * 3 * 4 * 6 6		
14 July 69	1 *	2 3 4 6		Main order delayed in system
07 Jun 69	1 *	2 * 3 * 4 * 6		Drillings out for quotation
06 May 69	1 *	2 3 4 6		1st of two rigs, see also 2345A
10 Apr 69	1 *	2 * 2 3 4 6		More realistic delivery estimates
11 Mar 69	1 *	2 3 4		Reassessment of requirements
11 Feb 69	1 *			Requirements drawn up low priority week
13 Jan 69	1 *	2 3 4 6		Lack of effort

Figure 11:11   Computer printout
(Reprinted from *R & D Management*, February, 1970)

cumulative progress and they provide forward information for planning rather than only hindsight information. They can be used in a variety of ways and, in fact, the input to these systems can draw on other planning and control methods which have been suggested for particular projects; for example, it may be possible for the milestones in the second method to be derived from more detailed networks. However, whether the organisation uses this latter method or not will depend upon the ability it has to define, within a reasonable degree of closeness, the objectives of the individual project and to identify important stages through which it must progress if it is to be successfully brought to completion.

The most interesting point to be considered and perhaps the most important, relates to the person to whom the information should be sent, and what action should be taken, after it is received. On this question there is some disagreement, or apparent disagreement, which can be inferred from the way the methods are used.

Some organisations have tended to concentrate on exception reporting, with people being expected to take corrective action when costs or time fall outside given limits. Others have simply reported the information back to the individuals concerned and taken account of the fact that a great deal of interaction occurs at technical meetings, and by informal communication which will enable appropriate corrective measures to be taken without any need for formal control. The debate is not yet finished on this point, but in view of the uncertainty of R and D it would appear that the protagonists of the second system have good grounds for adopting their approach.

11:5 Handling uncertainty

Uncertainty is present in all R and D work but its magnitude differs considerably between organisations and also between different types of work within a single organisation. If it is accepted that R and D must be concerned about other functional areas, it follows that the nature and the extent of the uncertainty over the whole research exploitation process must be considered.

A number of organisations attempt to do this by requesting information at the evaluation stage about such factors as the probability of research success and commercial success. It is not easy to define exactly what is meant by these factors and how the information should be obtained in particular situations. Clearly, they must often be based on the subjective judgement of experienced people, assisted in some cases by mathematical models, for example, of market situations and competitive activity.

11:5:1   Ranking formulas and scoring methods

Having obtained such information there is no shortage of ranking formulas, scoring methods, etc., which have been suggested, and indeed used, for assisting the decision-maker in making a choice between alternative investments. Typical examples of such methods are the following:

1   *Carl Pacifico's method*

$$Project\ number = \frac{Pt \times Pc \times (p-c) \times VxL}{Total\ costs}$$

where Pt and Pc are the probability of technical and commercial success respectively, $(p-c)$ is the price minus cost, that is, the contribution per unit, V and L are the sales volume per year and the life of the product respectively.

2   *Solomon Disman's method*[10]

$$Project\ number = \frac{Pt \times Pc \times \dfrac{I_1}{(1+i)} + \dfrac{I_2}{(1+i)^2} + \ldots + \dfrac{I_n}{(1+i)^n}}{Total\ Discounted\ R\ and\ D\ Costs}$$

where I_n refers to the net income in the nth year of the project's life.

In assessing whether formulas of this type are likely to assist managers in making decisions under conditions of uncertainty it is necessary to consider the characteristics of the different situations in which they might be used.

If this is done it can be concluded that the formulae have some merit when the probability of technical success is relatively high, that is, the uncertainty lies in the market, and also where the uncertainty in the market is constant over time. The second point is fairly obvious. For example, if the uncertainty is very low in early years and high in later years it is not appropriate to discount all the cash flows and then multiply the resulting present value figure by an "averaged" probability factor. Clearly, uncertainty should be incorporated into the cash flows at the point where it occurs and most simple risk analysis models in the financial field take account of this. However, their use in R and D has been very limited to date.

The point about the use of such formulas only when the probability of technical success is fairly high is not so obvious. The reason is basically because subsequent probabilities are conditional ones, that is, the probability of marketing success is conditional or dependent upon the technical outcome. The two are not therefore independent, and, as such, cannot be multiplied directly together. In this case an alternative approach can be used, and the method of presentation and analysis is so useful and simple that it is seriously worth considering. The approach is one based on a decision-tree diagram and it clearly brings out the multi-stage nature of the process, as shown in Figure 11:12.

If it is necessary to produce a single ranking index for a project it is easy to calculate it from the decision-tree using the concept of expected value and the roll back procedure which has been well described in the literature.[11] Numerous computer programs exist for doing this and most of them allow the incorporation of cash flows on a time-base and allow these to be discounted by the appropriate factor to take into account the time-value of money. However, even if this calculation is carried out it is important not to ignore the information which is neatly presented in the decision-tree framework and which can be so helpful for forward planning purposes.

The diagram not only shows where the uncertainty lies and hence indicates where the problems are likely to arise; it also indicates the likelihood that resources will be needed in future time-periods. For example, if there is only a low probability of technical success then there is equally only a low probability that the heavy expenditure which might be required on production facilities and marketing facilities will be needed. If the uncertainty lies more in the market, then, in fact, the probability that funds will be required to launch the product is very high, and these are important points to bring out as early as possible, particularly from the financial planning point of view. The decision-tree approach, which is of great value from a diagrammatic point of view,

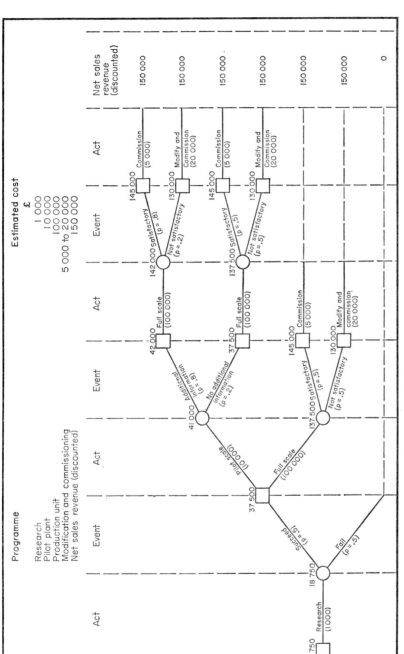

Figure 11:12   Decision-tree programme

can be very helpful in this respect, as well as being a useful means of communication between the various parties who will be concerned with the various stages from research through to ultimate exploitation.

11:6 Ensuring the effective utilisation of research results

The theme throughout this chapter has been that integration of R and D into the organisation is very important and that this will be best achieved if the research is chosen in such a way as to be within the objectives of the organisation, and if it is planned in such a way as to make available the resources for converting successful outcomes into new products and processes at the appropriate time. There is therefore a great deal of need for co-ordination throughout the organisation and for the involvement from the very outset of people who are not only concerned with the technical aspects but also with financial and marketing operations. This has been accepted in many organisations, but the form which the integration takes can vary. In some, integrating groups have been specifically set up, the people within these being specifically charged with the responsibility of considering the technical capability of the organisation and the potential needs of the market and trying to ensure that these overlap.

Another important feature of the changing scene in R and D management has been the movement towards the closer definition of objectives of projects with the reduction in the number which are open-ended. There has been a movement to appoint a project manager at the outset of all the work, whose responsibility is to ensure that it is progressed satisfactorily in the technical sense and that liaison is maintained with the people who will provide funds and with the market-place so that changes in the needs can be reflected in the direction of the project at the earliest possible time. It is quite clear that it is useless to continue research, however good it may be in itself, if the market for the product and processes has ceased to exist or if the financial resources will not be available for subsequent exploitation. The whole problem is one of continual interaction and feedback between the different functional areas.

11:6:1   Project-by-project funding

In some organisations there has been a movement over to the funding
of research on a project-by-project basis. This is in contrast to earlier
years in which a considerable amount of research was carried out with
block funds allocated by the organisation as a whole. This development
is interesting and can be very useful if not taken to excess, because it
ensures that the person who will use the results of the work is involved
at the earliest possible stage. His involvement includes paying for the
research and this is almost certain to encourage a greater degree of
interest and tends to reduce the time taken to diffuse the results of
successful research throughout the organisation and into use. However,
if this method of costing is adopted there are some necessary precautions
which need to be taken. For example, provision needs to be made to
allow some "slack" in the system. This might be achieved by allowing
the "contract" price to be higher than the actual cost of the research,
thus allowing some flexibility for the research director and his staff,
who are well qualified in their own areas, to develop pieces of work
which have longer-term potential to the organisation, the benefits of
which may not be immediately apparent to those who are responsible
for funding out of this year's budget. An alternative approach adopted
by some organisations allows for a certain percentage (often as high as
eighty per cent) of the research organisation's budget to be derived
from projects which are directly funded and which come within specified
theme areas. The remaining, say, twenty per cent is provided through
an overhead charge on operating companies and/or the group as a
whole and is allocated by the group through the R and D director.

There is some considerable need for thought here, because it is
impossible to generalise about the amount which should be allocated
for research of a more free-ranging nature. It will depend a good deal
upon the way in which R and D is seen in the organisation, the particular
role it is expected to play, how close to existing markets it is meant to
be, and how far it is going to be a determinant of future changes in
direction and strategy.

One thing that is clear is that the method which is chosen must be a
flexible one. It must operate through a series of checks and balances and
it must, in fact, bring benefits to researchers as well as to the market-
place. The aim should be to ensure that projects are not started and
stopped without good reason, that the markets which are being aimed

at are large enough to support the level of research which is being undertaken, that the finance will be available in the future to allow the research to be used usefully, and that researchers should be well enough aware of the market situation not to be delving into channels in which the company is very unlikely to be interested.

Perhaps one of the most important developments in the last few years has been that researchers have themselves been taking a more active interest in the market-place. They have become more interested and more involved in considering costs and benefits, if only in a global sense. The one danger is that they may, in fact, get too bogged down with an exercise in estimating and quantification and that people from all functional areas may become obsessed about information which is of dubious origin and spurious accuracy. On the cost side there is some evidence which suggests that the uncertainty is within manageable limits. On the benefit side there is still a great deal of information required before it can usefully be concluded that the evaluation models that are being brought in are likely to be of great use. What can certainly be said, however, is that there are many areas in which it is beneficial to establish objectives for any proposed research and to agree these with the various interested parties, for example, finance and marketing, at the earliest possible point in time. It is also possible to say that monitoring and progressing systems can be developed which will ensure that these objectives are more closely met, allowing movement towards the targets of given cost and time-scales better than in the past.

However, all of the current developments in the management of R and D cost money, and as such must provide an adequate return. Perhaps one of the biggest problems that has to be faced for the next few years is that of deciding on priorities in expenditure in these areas. This means that it is necessary to look more closely at how much should be allocated to such things as establishing the objectives of the organisation, establishing the long-term trends for R and D, modelling and identifying opportunities within these areas, carrying out detailed cost and benefit appraisals of projects and programmes, and introducing planning, progressing and information systems into the organisation. As the cost of research increases it will be of benefit to apply effort to each of these areas. The question of how much is as yet unanswered.

The methods which have been discussed in this chapter are those which are currently being developed and used by a number of organisations with a good deal of success. There are many more which might have been discussed, but they do not differ in general characteristics. Important differences arise mainly from the characteristics of the organisations in which they are used and the way in which they are operated. What cannot be emphasised too strongly is that new methods and procedures should be introduced in a sensible and progressive way. The aims of the system should be clearly defined, the progress towards these aims should be monitored and feedback should be taken into account. If this is not done there is a great danger that the end result will be a mass of paperwork circulating round the organisation, which provides little useful information and which does, in fact, confuse rather than contribute to improving the efficiency of the R and D activity, and, through this, of the organisation as a whole.

11:7   References

1 A G Baker—"Cost benefit analysis in R & D", *Chemistry in Britain*, September 1971.
2 J M Hubert—"R & D and the company's requirements", *R & D Management*, Vol. 1, No. 1, October 1970.
3 C G Milner—"Innovation in shipbuilding", *R & D Management*, Vol. 2, No. 1, October 1971.
4 C M Mottley and R D Newton—"The selection of projects for industrial research", *Operations Research*, November/December 1959.
5 D C Bell and A W Read—"The application of a research project selection method", *R & D Management*, Vol. 1, No. 1, October 1970.
6 R C Parker & A J P Sabberwal—"Controlling R & D Projects by Networks" *R & D Management*, Vol. 1, No. 3, June 1971.
7 A H Cooper—"How the Slip Chart Shows the Progress of Work", *New Scientist*, 15 March 1962.
8 R Benjamin—"Putting the Manager in the Picture", *New Scientist*, 28 September 1967.
9 R P Hardingham—"A simple model approach to multi-project monitoring', *R & D Management*, Vol. 1, No. 1, October 1970.
10 S Disman—"Selecting R & D projects for profit", *Chemical Engineering*, December 1962.
11 J F Magee—"Decision-trees for decision-making", *Harvard Business Review*, July/August 1964.

Chapter 12

Control of Overheads

Guenter B Steinitz, Management Consultant

The aim in the control of overheads appears to be simple. It requires the calculation in advance of what the costs ought to be and the monitoring of the actual costs so as to ensure that that is what they are.

In reality the problem is more complex and requires careful attention to matters such as deciding in the first place just what an overhead is, acceptance of individual managerial responsibility for its costs, the establishment of quantitative criteria before its incurrence and the establishment of standards to monitor the efficiency of the overhead activity.

12:1 Classification of overheads

A correct understanding of the meaning of overheads is most important, both for product costing and for the purposes of controlling expenditure. To answer the question "what is an overhead?" it is relevant to reconsider the customary practice of classifying costs into categories of *fixed costs*, *semi-variable costs*, *variable costs*, *direct costs* and *indirect costs*. It is a concept about which there is a great deal of confused thinking and which needs to be explained here in relation to the classification of costs as overheads.

Let us consider cost as follows:

1 *Direct Costs:* those which can easily be attributed to particular products or processes and
2 *Indirect Costs:* all other costs

Each can further be broken down into categories of:

1 *Variable costs:* those which tend to vary with volumes of output
2 *Semi-variable costs:* those which have some tendency to vary with volume of output but over a longer period and not in direct proportion
3 *Fixed costs:* those costs which are unaffected by variations in the volume of output

Figure 12:1 gives some typical examples of expenses in each category. Provided reliable standards have been set, it is relatively easy to control the variable costs, category (a), because they should rise and fall with output. Categories (b) and (c) are much more difficult to control. Therefore, the more costs that one can properly classify as variable, the easier they will be to control.

	Variable (a)	Semi-variable and fixed (b)
DIRECT	Direct materials Direct labour Sales royalties	Indirect materials Factory supervision Plant depreciation Plant maintenance
INDIRECT	—	(c) Post room Accounts department Management services Computer department

Figure 12:1   Classification of costs

12:1:1   Typical examples of expenses in each category

Likewise, direct costs, category (b), are usually easier to control than indirect costs, category (c), mainly because it is easier to relate cause and effect. For example, the question of whether or not to set up a factory supervision function is more easily related to its effect on profits than the setting up of a cost department can be. The former will have a calculable effect on productivity which can be evaluated more easily than the effect on company performance of the latter function. Therefore, it is desirable to classify as category (b) all fixed and semi-variable costs that can be properly related to a production process or selling activity.

It is those costs which fall into category (c) that are generally known as overheads. These include those expenses incurred in support of the main activities of the company which cannot easily be related directly to specific products, manufacturing processes or sales activities. For practical purposes one can view them in the context of:

1 Manufacturing, for example, production control, work study and inspection
2 Selling and distribution, for example, sales promotion, public relations, sales office and vehicle maintenance
3 General, for example, administration, personnel, computer and management services

In some cases it will be possible and desirable to attribute some of the types of cost listed above to production processes or products and opportunities for doing so should be sought. Failure to do so may lead to misleading information and poor decisions.

12:1:2   Example

A case in point was seen in a company manufacturing precision instruments. This company used a conventional system of standard costing. Costs were analysed by production department, and standard-hour cost rates were calculated by dividing the total budgeted departmental cost by the total budgeted productive hours of its direct workers. These standard-hour rates were then used to calculate product costs.

Examination showed that this method was extremely inaccurate. Batches were very small and the manufacturing time for most batches was exceeded by the setting time in widely differing proportions. Inspection was also a high proportion of cost and also varied considerably. The function of production control was such that many of the activities could have been attributed to identifiable batches of goods.

Instead, setting, inspection and production control were all treated as part of the factory overhead. By merging all these costs into departmental hourly rates the calculated product costs bore little relation to fact. Indeed, the whole departmental cost was based on a very small element, the actual process time. This was a classic case of the tail wagging the dog.

A new system was devised with setting, inspection and some production control treated as variable costs, giving much more accurate product costs and greatly improved control.

It is most important, therefore, when devising a system of control of overheads to include only those costs which cannot better be treated as direct or variable costs.

An overhead is, therefore, a cost which cannot readily be attributed to a product or production process and will tend not to vary with the volume of output.

12:2   Accountable responsibility

It is important to remember that the responsibility for control of expenditure lies not with the accountant but with management, and effective control depends in the first place on a very clear definition of each individual manager's responsibilities.

The responsibility for achieving the corporate profit objectives lies with management, which is, therefore, charged with preparing and executing the plans necessary for success. In the context of control of overheads management should bear full responsibility for the preparation of its own plans and budgets and their subsequent control.

Each manager responsible for incurring expenditure should be involved in the preparation of his budget and should be wholly committed to it before the beginning of each budget year. He should know what is expected of him and what resources he requires to achieve his objectives. The information should be quantified and set out for him in a way that he can understand so that he can become accountable for it.

12:2:1   The accountant's role

The accountant's role should be to provide the necessary financial advice, to assist management to quantify its plans and to provide quantitative data for purposes of control. His role will also include the provision of the machinery for preparing and co-ordinating the budget, but not for the figures therein except in an arithmetical sense and for those parts of the company for which he may have line responsibility. In some companies the co-ordinating role is performed by a budget committee with a budget officer, usually the accountant.

It is entirely wrong to leave the accountant to prepare the budgets with little or no commitment on the part of the manager responsible for incurring the expenditure.

It is also wrong, but not uncommon, for accountants to analyse expenditure by what seems to be a logical break-down of expense rather than by area of control. (Area of control means the activities for which an individual manager has full responsibility and can be held accountable.) For example, rather than have one heading for administration, with separate sub-headings for wages, stationery, telephone, etc., it is better to show separate headings such as:

1   Accounts department
2   Post room
3   Typing pool, or
4   Print room

which follow the responsibilities set out on the organisation chart. Each of these can be considered an area of control or a cost centre with a person specifically responsible for the "output" of the department and for all its expenditure. Control of these departments can therefore be achieved by monitoring both their "output" and their cost.

The nature of some categories of expenditure is such that they are not easy to control in the way outlined above. These could include items such as stationery, telephone, heating or lighting and it is easy to fall into the trap of devoting too much time and effort to their control. Clearly, the effort required to control the cost should not exceed the benefits thus derived. It is important to relate the cost of control to the value of the *benefits* and not to the total cost.

Where the expenditure is small, the best course is to give the responsibility to one person in the capacity of "watch-dog" whose job it is to ensure that the facility is not abused. Where expenditure is high then it may be worthwhile establishing a form of control either on a routine basis or by periodical investigations.

12:2:2   Cross-charging

A useful means of control of the use of an internal service is to charge for it. The cost of keeping records need not be high and the system can be very effective. This could be an appropriate means of controlling the effective use of a service such as management services department. Here the head of the management services department would still be accountable for his own department as a whole and its efficiency and total cost. His "clients" would be accountable for the effective use of his services and this could be controlled by means of a departmental "cross-charge." In some companies where this is done managers are still free to call on the services of external sources of management services but have to provide financial justification for their choice. This method is most appropriate where the cost of calculation is low, where the cross-charge is based on fact and where it is possible to establish genuine criteria for the users of the service to apply in their cost/benefit calculations.

Sometimes control routines are established to test the value of a certain activity or to test whether savings can be achieved as an *ad hoc* exercise. In these cases it is important to take out the control procedures when they have served their purpose. Most companies have obsolete control procedures operating in some part of their organisation.

Excessive costs can be incurred in collecting money from staff for personal services. In one company it was the practice to charge office workers for their tea. Each morning they would form long queues while the tea-lady calculated the change and poured the tea. Had she simply placed a free cup of tea on each desk, the value of time saved by the office workers would have considerably exceeded the cost of the tea. The person responsible for controlling canteen costs had not been in a position to take a sufficiently broad view.

For the effective control of overhead costs, management should, therefore, be made accountable for the "output" and expenditure of clearly defined activities. They should be responsible for the preparation of their budgets and should be entirely committed to them. In respect of services used by several departments, they should either be "cross-charged" if the level of expenditure is high in relation to the cost of the additional clerical work or, alternatively, the expense should become the responsibility of a "watch-dog" who is charged with keeping the cost within reasonable bounds.

12:3 Establishing quantitative criteria before incurring expenditure

In order to achieve effective control it is essential that quantitative criteria are established before the cost is incurred. This is particularly important where the cost has long-term implications. Take, for example, the purchase of a computer. If the decision is a poor one it is, of course, too late to do anything about it after it has been bought; the equipment is purchased or hired under contract, the software costs have been incurred, the department established. The marginal cost of retaining the computer and its related costs is usually lower than the cost of disposing of it or changing it. The same logic applies to other overheads, albeit usually to a lesser extent.

If a quantifiable case cannot be made this does not necessarily mean that the expenditure should not be incurred. Clearly, it must be recognised that some cases cannot be quantified and a value judgement must be made. An extreme example would be the replacement of a boiler which has burst. Quite clearly the company could not function properly without heating.

12:3:1 Monitoring

It is equally important that when the expenditure has been incurred and the activity is engaged the results are carefully monitored against the criteria on which the decision was originally based. In many cases the calculations must be based on assumptions and the quantities may be other than money. If, however, a case is made, it will then be possible in the years to come to monitor the costs of the activity against the benefit.

Take, for example, a decision to establish a public relations department. It may be engaged to deal with relations between:

1 The company and its customers and potential customers
2 The management and the workers
3 The company and the local general community

The benefits could be:

1   Increased sales volume
2   Improved labour relations
3   Lower recruiting costs (because the local community holds the company in high esteem)

Each of the above can be justified. Of course, it will be impossible to say with accuracy how much would be attributable to the public relations department and how must to other causes, and for purposes of the calculation some assumptions must be made. Provided the assumptions are recognised as such and provided that a suitable system of control is established, then it should be possible to make better decisions each year regarding the future of the PR function than would have been possible without the calculations.

12:3:2   Status

Too much attention to status, can result in excessive cost. In many companies a disproportionate amount of effort and discussion is centred around expenditure on chairs, desks, typewriters, carpets, etc. Mostly, the amount of money spent here is based on status rather than need. The size of desk is often a status symbol and typically a bought-ledger clerk is forced to do a balancing act at his inadequate table trying to cope with the many files, books and papers that he needs simultaneously. Simple method-study would demonstrate that this is a false economy if one calculates the cost of a desk over its life of twenty years compared with the reduction in efficiency of the ledger clerk. The same argument could apply in some cases to office equipment such as electric typewriters or calculators, which require less effort than manual machines and could well provide economies in wage cost far in excess of the additional capital cost spread over the life of the machine.

12:3:3   On-going overhead expenditure

What about the on-going situation? Most overheads really fit into this category. Conventionally budgets will be prepared each year and the only yardstick will be what was spent the year before. There is a great temptation to take last year's costs and add ten per cent but it is just as important to establish criteria for on-going overhead activities as for new ones. Failure to do so is the major reason why so many companies are incurring unnecessary overhead costs year after year. Not only are all activities accepted as being necessary to the company just because they were there the year before, but their costs are actually increased each year. In order to avoid the perpetuation of errors of judgement, questions such as these should be asked each year for each activity:

1 What is the "output" of this activity?
2 What would happen if we did not have this activity?
3 Is this what we really want?
4 Would we have a better chance of achieving our objectives if things were done in a different way?
5 Could they be done more economically? (that is, not necessarily more cheaply, but with greater cost effectiveness)
6 Is there any way by which we can improve the operation of this activity?

Most companies fail to do this. When business is bad there is a purge on overheads. A few years ago a major international company decided to reduce overheads by ten per cent and an edict went out to all departments that a ten per cent staff reduction was to be achieved within three months. The result was that those departments with "fat" were still able to function effectively despite the ten per cent cut, while the very ones which had been operating with the right number of staff had to reduce the service that they were able to give, with consequent long-term damage to the company.

Whenever possible the work content should be measured and compared with actual output on a regular basis. Clerical work measurement is now well established for office work and there are a number of techniques available for monitoring performance on a routine basis. Techniques are also well developed for controlling the efficiency of other activities, such as drawing office and maintenance work, and these are worth doing so long as the cost of control is kept low.

The dangers of not controlling efficiency are fairly obvious. In the first place the previous year's level of expenditure is not a reliable guide as to what it ought to have been and cannot therefore be a valid yardstick for the following year. Inefficiencies are perpetuated and can increase because they are not detected.

On-going overheads should, therefore, be reviewed each year not only in relation to the previous year's cost but also in relation to whether the activity is still desirable in its present form or whether it is required at all. Wherever possible, the work-content should be measured and the performance controlled by comparing the effort with reliable standards and with the output produced.

12:4 Controlling the overall level of overheads

It is essential to control the overall level of overheads in relation to the sales volume and gross margin. Even if each individual category of overhead appears to be at the right level it is still possible that the sales volume is insufficient to support the combined level of all overheads.

One major company in the electronics industry was very careful at the time of budgeting to ensure that overheads fitted into the total plan. When the sales budget was achieved there was no problem. Then, for several successive years actual sales fell short of the budget. Each year, as the months went by and the company consistently recorded below-budget sales it failed to adjust its overhead budget. Consequently, by the end of each year, even though overheads were within their own budgets, the company recorded very low profits. Had it been known at the time of budgeting that the sales volume would be as low as it ultimately turned out to be, the overhead budgets would have been set lower. The mistake was not that the company failed to meet its sales budget—this was beyond its control—but rather that it failed to react early enough to the change in the trend of sales.

To some extent this would be covered by a company which uses a system of flexible budgeting where the budgets for semi-variable overheads are geared to the budgeted level of output. The system provides for overhead budget levels to rise and fall with the volume of output, though not necessarily in the same proportion and usually in discreet amounts rather than on a sliding scale.

12:5 Utilisation of resources

There is a further aspect which is easy to overlook. That is the one of maximising the utilisation of resources. Take, for example, rent. For many companies this is considered to be a fixed cost over which nobody can exercise control in the intermediate term. Rent is written into the budget with the feeling that nothing can be done about it anyway. This may be true, but what can be controlled is the utilisation of space. This question should be examined regularly as it could apply equally to other fixed costs.

12:6 Summary of procedures

The control of overheads cannot be separated from control of other activities of the company, and should be an integral part of the company's system of budgetary control. As with other activities it is necessary to establish clearly who is accountable for what, and to obtain commitment from each manager for those areas of control for which he has accepted responsibility. A means of measuring and monitoring his output should be agreed. The way in which his expenditure will be analysed should be completely understood and agreed by each manager. The budgets will, of course, ultimately have to be accepted by the board. Figure 12:2 shows the procedural stages involved in controlling overheads.

In some companies there may be a budget committee whose responsibility it is to organise the budget procedures before submission to the board and subsequently to monitor progress during the course of the budget year, and which will probably wish to appoint a budget officer, usually the accountant or one of his staff, who will be responsible for the work of co-ordinating the budget and for doing many of the calculations.

The first task of the budget committee will be to review each of the overhead activities and reach agreement on the following main points:

1 The existence of each main overhead activity (for example, do we need our own print-room?)
2 The use and nature of each main overhead activity
3 The means by which its efficiency will be measured
4 The means of measuring its "output"

This preliminary stage sets the scene for the actual preparation of the budgets. Managers must be fully involved in their own budgets but the

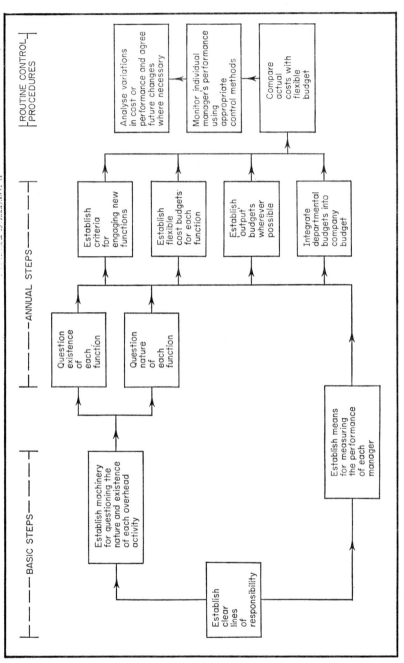

Figure 12:2   Diagram of procedural stages

budget officer will usually help to develop the preliminary budgets for each manager. This budgeting stage includes the submission of cost/benefit analyses for new activities which are proposed for the budget year. It also includes consideration of the utilisation of resources such as space.

These individual overhead budgets will then be integrated into the overall company budget, at which stage there would be a review of the total level of overheads compared with the budgeted gross margin. In the light of this review the budgets may be accepted, but it is probable that some revisions may be necessary for the company to achieve its profit objective. The expense budgets are then revised and agreed with the managers and it is possible that their outputs may have to be revised too.

There may be several cycles before the budget is finally completed with each manager committed to his own budget. Where flexible budgeting is in force he will receive a staggered budget for different levels of output.

During the course of the budget year actual costs, and where appropriate actual outputs, will be summarised by area of control and compared with the budget. In addition, wherever it is considered appropriate, there should be a control function within each overhead activity to monitor its efficiency. The accountant's role is to analyse the variances from budget in such a way that each manager can take the necessary corrective action as early as possible.

During the course of the year the accountant can play an invaluable role by presenting the figures to management at the earliest possible time, and by advising on the effect on profits of deviations from budget and of the financial effect of proposed new measures.

Chapter 13

The Internal Audit

*P C Elliott, formerly Manager, Internal Audit UK,
Shell International Petroleum Company Limited*

13:1   Concept

In a small business composed of an owner/manager and six employees it is apparent that the owner will be able to keep in close touch with all activities. If the business expands to a point at which each of the six is supervising another six it is still possible for the owner to keep in close touch by observation and through periodic meetings held at two levels. By the time another multiple of six level is reached communication is not quite so good, and when yet a further level is added (a total strength of some 1500) the owner and higher levels of management will be depending much more on what they are told than on direct knowledge of what each of the employees is doing, whether they are all working in the same direction, and whether the controls envisaged are operating in the way that was intended.

It is at about this point in size that management needs a full-time independent appraiser to review the activities of the organisation to ensure that effective controls are in operation and that the activities all form part of the objectives of the organisation. Statutory auditors will assist management in ascertaining that financial records, accounts and other statements are correctly kept and drawn up to reflect the progress of the business, but management needs to have something more than confirmation of the state of the business and the knowledge that money has been legally spent. It needs to know that controls are operating in all activities, helping to ensure that both people and assets are safe-guarded and used to the best advantage of the business and, for long-term growth and goodwill, to the best advantage of the community as a whole.

This function of independently appraising controls on behalf of management is the province of the internal auditor. Controls reviewed will relate to efficiency as well as to data, and to review these on behalf of management the auditor must think like management. Unfortunately the term "internal auditor" has a historical ring about it conjuring up an image of an employee filling a checking role with activities restricted to the financial function. The modern internal auditor appraises controls rather than acting as the control and is not confined to data records. The efforts of the Institute of Internal Auditors have done much to ensure that the responsibilities of an internal auditor are more fully understood and practised.

13:2   Organisation

If the internal auditor reports directly to top management, he will be in the best position of independence and will carry, without question, the appropriate status to review controls over all activities.

Partly for historical reasons, however, the internal auditor may often be found in organisations reporting to the senior financial executive and this is the reason for including a chapter on internal audit in this handbook.

The financial function is, of course, already giving a service to other functions and there is no reason why an internal auditor reporting within finance should be hampered in reviewing activities of other functions provided that he is given the full support of top management. There is, however, a danger that he may not be free, then, to express himself fully on financial activities. A necessary safeguard against such an impediment is for it to be agreed, and included in his terms of reference, that the internal auditor has the right of direct access to top management should he feel that this is warranted.

13:3   Terms of reference

Recommended responsibilities of the internal auditor were set out in a statement approved by the Institute of Internal Auditors' Board of Directors in 1947 and revised in 1957 and 1971. The revised statement is included as an appendix to this chapter. It is, of course, necessary for every management to decide on the particular terms of reference which it proposes to give its internal audit department.

Terms of reference, after agreement, should be produced in writing giving a firm base for planning, staffing and carrying out internal audit work without objection and resentment from those responsible for activities to be audited. The work of internal audit is not easy. It is, after all, an inspection and people normally resent being inspected. A very careful path has to be trodden ensuring that controls are reviewed and that the organisation's policies are being carried out without giving the impression that the internal audit department is either criticising policy or that it will be making adverse criticisms on decisions taken which could only have been proved wrong after the event. The work of a good audit team with full management support will be appreciated as something leading to improved profitability, and, therefore, of value.

13:4   Staffing

It will be clear from the preceding sections that internal auditing is a responsible job, involving contact with senior staff and requiring skill and tact in personal relationships. Having decided on the establishment of such a department, it would be folly to staff it with people incapable of the performance required.

Opinions differ as to whether internal auditing is a profession in itself or whether it is a useful step in the career development of those with future management potential. Whether the more senior positions of the internal audit department are filled with those having a career in internal auditing or not, it is generally agreed that this department affords an excellent training ground for those with potential early in their careers and, with the department's interest in all activities, shorter-term recruitment should be made for the lower levels, not only from those having a financial background. It is usual to have a majority of

261

staff with accounting qualifications as it is no accident that basic training in accounting disciplines instils the "control mindedness" needed for successful internal audits. The perfect internal auditor would, perhaps, possess both accounting and engineering qualifications, but such staff are not in plentiful supply. A balance can be achieved by a mixture of staff from different functions in appropriate proportions.

In addition to "control mindedness" and the usual virtues, the internal auditor needs perseverance, empathy and a logical approach with analytical ability. Given staff of this calibre, qualified by examination or by experience, internal auditing has the best opportunity to meet and maintain its objectives.

Those employed on internal auditing early in their career should not serve too long, say about two years. This time is sufficient for them to gain an insight into many aspects of the organisation, to learn and carry with them throughout their career the value and basic requirements of good control, and to contribute significantly to the work of the department. A longer term may lessen their enthusiasm. The movement of good staff into internal auditing together with promotion of many on leaving it, will be an excellent advertisement and will banish the earlier images of internal auditing as a department where finance staff finish their working years.

The number of staff required is determined after an initial planning stage with subsequent annual review; this is dealt with more fully in the next section. The correct order is to decide on the terms of reference, list the activities covered to satisfy the terms of reference in the form of a plan, then estimate the staff required to carry out the plan.

There is a temptation to draw on internal auditing staff in emergencies. Whilst in certain circumstances it is "all hands to the pump" it should be remembered that the internal audit department has a job to do as much as any other department; to use it as a reserve staff force will lower its performance and make it less attractive to the better recruits.

13:5   Planning

All business activities need a plan and a budget, and no exception should be made for internal auditing.

13:5:1 The audit plan

The activities to be covered in accordance with the terms of reference should be listed; the headings are preferably restricted to the main and first subordinate activities but should give sufficient detail to allow estimates of audit time to be made.

The review of all activities each year, regardless of the stability of organisation, adequacy of controls or chance of loss or profit improvement, is wasteful and a decision should be made regarding the time-cycle over which the activities are to be reviewed.

It may be considered appropriate to cover all activities over a two-to-three-year time-cycle. This does not preclude reviewing any of the activities more frequently as may be necessary. An example of a plan is shown in Figure 13:1.

Having established the time-cycle, columns are drawn to the right of the activities, one for each year of the time-cycle, with an additional column for noting the year or quarter when last covered. As a refinement the first year may be broken down into quarters.

13:5:2 Calculation of staff numbers

An assessment of the plan in terms of audit man-days, including travelling time, is now made in order to determine staff requirements. Initially, timing is rather difficult to assess but, as experience is gained on actual audit timing, estimates will improve. After adding the man-days audit effort for each year in the time-cycle some adjustments to allocation of audits within the years may be necessary to give a more even distribution of effort. Staff requirements can now be estimated, not forgetting that audit time as shown on the plan, although the major part, is not the whole part of staff activity. An allowance is needed for leave, sickness, training courses and *ad hoc* requirements. In a later section it is recommended that internal audit staff keep time-sheets; time-sheets summarised for previous years will help in estimating both audit time and the additional allowance.

Assuming that audit effort is eighty-five per cent of the whole, a simple calculation gives the staff required. A very rough yard-stick for numbers is that, for an average mixture of staff and labour in a concentrated area, one internal auditor per thousand employees is an expected ratio. In a scattered area, when head office control is effectively

Project	Last covered qtr/yr.	Current year	Current year + 1	Current year + 2
Manufacturing				
Raw material			x	
Labour			x	
Processing			x	
Packaging		x		
Plant			x	
Costing and statistics				x
Safety and security		x		x
Environment		x		
Marketing				
Representatives				x
Agencies				x
Avertising		x		
Costing and statistics			x	
Market research		x		
Transportation				
Fleet			x	
Maintenance			x	
Safety and security			x	
Costing and statistics		x		
Administration				
Personnel				x
Secretarial				x
Estates			x	
Canteens				x
Communications		x		
Computing Systems				
Computing centre			x	
New systems		x	x	x
Operational systems (selected)		x	x	x
Finance				
Accounting		x		
Costing		x		
Budgets			x	
Credit control		x		x
Banking				x
Payrolls			x	
Taxation				x

Figure 13:1   Example of an audit plan

weaker and much audit travelling is involved, the ratio may be expected to increase up to one internal auditor per five hundred employees. Numbers of internal audit staff in excess of these figures indicate, *prima facie*, use of internal auditing as a control (or a checking function) rather than as an appraiser of controls.

13:5:3   The budget

The budget for the coming year can now be prepared. This will include:

1   Salaries (plus on-cost for pensions schemes, etc.)
2   Travelling expenses
3   Training courses
4   Computer time
5   General share of overheads

Budgets, if required, can also be prepared for further years in the time-cycle, but owing to the many changes that take place in organisation and activities it is best that the plan be prepared afresh each year over the new audit time-cycle.

13:5:4   Management agreement

Approval from management for the budgeted cost of the department and the broad plan within the agreed terms of reference is next required. The budget may be the particular responsibility of one member of management, but the plan needs to be discussed with management as a whole if controls on all activities are subject to review.

Under the section on reporting it is recommended that the chief internal auditor sits down periodically with management to review audit effort and progress against the plan. Such a meeting prior to each year can be used to review the new plan. Copies should be circulated before the meeting, giving management the opportunity to review activities covered and the proposed timing, possibly leading to adjustments in timing, staffing and costs.

After agreement of the plan and the budget, the chief internal auditor is in a position to adjust staffing ready for the coming year. He is also

265

in a position to calculate the estimated average cost of an audit man-day, by dividing the budgeted cost of the department by the planned audit man-days. This is a very significant figure and can be used quickly to assess the limit of time that can be reasonably spent on audits having regard to the possibility of benefits that may arise, either from preventing loss or improving profit in other ways.

13:6 Audit programmes

Many people are familiar with the "old style" audit programmes that detail the various work to be done, leaving columns to the right for initialling at each audit. This is not the way to interest staff nor is it the way to get the best out of the internal audit effort.

Admittedly, there are basic steps of a protective nature in certain audits that need to be on file for reference, but a sound approach is for the chief, or a senior, auditor to sit down with the proposed audit team a short while in advance of the review to prepare an audit programme. The programme will set down the audit objectives first, followed by the detailed steps that are foreseen to achieve the objectives, leaving room for adjustment as the audit progresses.

13:6:1 Operational auditing

The term "operational auditing" was coined to distinguish the broader, or management, audit from the previous protective audits that are usually associated with stocks, cash, payroll and so on. Audits, however, do not fall neatly into one of the two categories, operational and protective. Rather, they involve a difference in approach and no internal auditor should proceed with any type of audit without an operational approach. Two routine examples clarify the position:

1 *Petty cash*. Many auditors have counted petty cash and have obtained satisfaction from the agreement of the cash-in-hand with the records but without regard to:
   (*a*) the average level of cash held compared with requirements
   (*b*) the availability of drawing facilities at the right times and in the right places
   (*c*) the inadequacy or over-adequacy of security arrangements

2 *Stock.* An internal audit of stock should include not only tests that the protective controls are operating but also that:
  (*a*) levels are maintained in accordance with optimised calculations to ensure that unnecessary working capital is not tied up and that business is not lost through failure to supply
  (*b*) stocks are stored adequately as a protection against deterioration as well as loss
  (*c*) stocks are available at the right time and kept in the right places
  (*d*) stocks are stored tidily and with sufficient room for ease of access
  (*e*) thought has been given to the equipment necessary for efficient storing and movement of the stocks

It is emphasised that the internal audit is an appraisal of controls and not the control. Hence, routine cash counting and stock checking should be carried out by staff other than from the internal audit department. The internal auditor will, however, appraise the controls by reviewing work of the checkers and carrying out spot tests.

13:6:2 The internal audit and other functions

Both management and the internal audit department, more familiar with appraisal of controls in the finance function only, may ask the question "what contribution can be made by the internal audit department in other functions?" The question is partly answered by picturing oneself managing the activity under consideration and thinking of the controls needed (the complete answer can only come from the investigation with this principle in mind). Two further examples given below, which are outside the historical field of internal auditing, may help to clarify this approach:

1 *Manufacturing*
  (*a*) Is the right product of the right quality manufactured in the right quantity at the right time?
      Control from statistics of marketing requirements and processing supported by marketing research and product testing
  (*b*) Are the factories in the right places?
      Control from knowledge of the source and availability of materials and labour and where the products are to be sold, supported by optimisation studies

(c) Is it cheaper to manufacture than to buy?

Control from costing compared with knowledge of the cost of purchase (there may, however, be strategic reasons demanding an own-manufacturing process)

(d) Is the manufacturing process as economical as it should be?

Control from work studies covering processing, plant utilisation and the availability of raw materials; comparison with other yard-sticks

Control from review of work satisfaction, job environment, safety and incentives for employees

(e) Are there controls over pollution during processing and safeguards for recipients of manufactured products?

Control from regular inspections and tests coupled with research

2 *Marketing*

(a) Is the right product of the right quality offered for sale in the right place at the right time?

Control from market research and customer acceptance and comparison of returns of profit margins

(b) Is the right packaging used and are safety precautions clearly stated in the local language?

Control from market research and experiments with different types and colours

(c) Is the market fully tapped and is the image as good as it should be?

Control through advertising in various media and assessment of results

Control through recruitment and training of representatives

Control through customer satisfaction in dealing adequately with complaints and minimising errors

(d) Is the marketing activity as economical as possible?

Control through work studies and costing, review of travelling and representation expenses, optimisation of stock carried.

The above lists can, of course, be extended but they may be sufficient to indicate the value to management of reports confirming the satisfactory nature of these controls compared with the old style report that merely stated that "x" tools or "y" products had been lost or misapplied. Good controls automatically highlight any significant losses of the latter nature.

13:7   The investigation

Very occasionally, when fraud is suspected, an investigation has to be carried out without warning. In all other cases the usual courtesies can be extended. The overall plan is agreed with management but the actual date of the audit will not be known until nearer the time. Notice of the date should be given to management and there should be sufficient tolerance in the plan to avoid descending on an activity at peak periods or at a time of emergency. The auditor, or the audit team, will start with the appropriate level of management supervising the activity, having cleared all higher levels before and having obtained the appropriate introductions.

The auditor will ask for a quick review of the department, thus becoming aware of organisational and other changes since the last audit and gaining some knowledge of proposed changes. It is useful if he discusses the audit objectives with the local management and gives a broad picture of the program, which may lead to useful adjustments in the approach. He should ask for introductions to those people he expects to contact during the investigation.

Controls cannot be appraised without knowledge of the activity. He will therefore gather the facts and ask appropriate questions to obtain a good picture of the activities. A complex operation is better understood if it is flow-charted. Flow-charts should be kept as simple as possible, using symbols with the minimum of narration, produced as useful working papers rather than works of art involving the cost of several man-days or -weeks.

The activity may involve the use of land, buildings, plant, equipment or people to move or change physical things or data. When the movements or changes are comprehended, the established controls can be reviewed, safeguarding the continuing useful existence of the assets and employees, their efficient usage in the operations involved, and on the movement or changes of that which is processed.

The established controls now need to be tested to see that they are working as intended. In clerical operations it was once the fashion to select a week's or month's transactions which were checked in detail. Recently the fashion has changed to the use of statistical sampling techniques, on the theory that a random sample of calculated size taken over a whole period gives a sample more truly representative of the whole and, therefore, gives a better test than one of a block period selected at random.

13:7:1 Audit in depth

Before discussing the comparative merits of these methods, mention should be made of another internal audit technique known as audit in depth. In this technique a record or voucher is selected, not merely to test the authorisation and accuracy of the supporting documentation, but to carry out an investigation of one item right through the organisation.

An earlier vouching technique compares with an audit in depth as follows; where there is an item of cash expenditure, consisting of the cost of photographing a piece of equipment, amounting to £75:

1 *Vouching technique.* Find the original invoice supporting this payment, checking that it is made out in the name of the organisation, properly authorised, currently dated, cancelled and that appropriate discounts have been taken
2 *Audit in depth technique.* Carry out vouching technique; check expense account to which it is carried; ascertain the budget unit (or cost centre) bearing the charge; visit the budget unit to discover the purpose of the expense (for example, advertising), whether it is within the approved budget (for example, was this within the province of the budget unit?), how the photographer was selected (possibly the charge includes unnecessary travel and accommodation), how the photograph was used; review the controls operating along the route

Such audit in depth may open up areas for future investigation of considerably more importance than the item of £75, for example, clarification of departmental responsibilities, the existence of an advertising policy, procedures and the general cost-consciousness of the departments concerned. These are the type of questions that the owner of the business would want answered if he had time, and a report on these aspects is of much more interest to management than trivial errors arising from the recording of the item of expense.

The internal auditor cannot carry out such an investigation sitting at his desk or within the accounting department. He should use the record properly as a record of something real that has happened and should go to the point of activity to further his investigations. Worthwhile investigations often start from trivial items of expenditure or income and it can be short-sighted to review only items exceeding a certain figure.

13:7:2   Random sampling

Audit in depth is a time-consuming technique and, with this in mind, the comparative merits of block period, statistical or other random sampling methods for testing established controls can be considered. All three methods have their uses.

Selecting a block period has the advantages of covering all items for a period, it is simple and vouchers are normally easier to find.

The statistical sample gives a random and representative review of the whole period but the method is not so simple and vouchers are harder to find.

Neither of these methods lends itself to audit in depth because transactions are too numerous. The best method for this technique is a truly random sample but restricted to a much smaller number than the statistical sample.

The small random sample is also of value in testing non-clerical controls, for example, an employee may be checking weights of filled packages; the random selection of a few items by the internal auditor for re-checking will give an indication of the value of this control.

The internal auditor should be aware of all these techniques and select the one, or combination, appropriate to the job in hand with regard to the extent of the audit operation after the selection has been made.

Proper working papers must be kept in good order, in detailed support of the review and recommendations to be made in the report.

13:8   Reporting

Some managements prefer verbal reports. It is recommended, however, that written reports are always produced following an internal audit review. These lead to better disciplines in the audit department, there is no opportunity for argument on what recommendations were made and there is a greater likelihood of success in follow-up. The report should set down the objectives, note the salient points of the review, make recommendations and, above all, be brief.

The internal auditor is reporting to management and the report must be of interest to management. A lengthy report, however good, will be passed down to a lower level for consideration. The report is no place to list trivialities; minor errors discovered should appear in the working papers and be discussed and corrected on the spot. The fact that a large percentage of errors was discovered would, if appropriate, be noted in the report as a salient feature.

All internal audit reports should be discussed in draft with the department audited. This is an added check that the facts have been gathered properly, that the emphasis is right and that recommendations are sensible. When the local management disagrees with an important recommendation, its viewpoint should be noted in the report with the recommendation.

The report should be finalised as rapidly as possible so that it is still fresh and relevant. It is usually accepted that it should be distributed to the department or section head audited and the next superior in line. If the internal auditor reports within the financial function it does not necessarily follow that reports on other managements should always go to his senior. To whomever he reports, he should be appraising controls on behalf of top management and his independence of all executive functions should be apparent. This can be aided by the internal auditor sitting in committee with the management as a whole two or three times a year. He can then offer a brief review of his investigations, prompt action where follow-up of the recommendations has been unnecessarily delayed, report on his performance compared with the plan and review future plans as necessary.

Where the organisation is large, having several major locations, this procedure can be followed with advantage at each of the major locations.

Follow-up of recommendations is vital. If the report has been agreed with managements, the recommendations become theirs and it is their responsibility to implement them. However, the internal auditor should review follow-up action and bring pressure to bear when this is inadequate.

13:9   Auditing of computing systems

(*a*) *Introduction*

Most textbooks on this subject are orientated to the external audit approach. Internal audit is responsible for all activities and reviews controls on both efficiency and data. The internal auditor, therefore, is interested in the controls on all systems. He will pay greater regard to data processing systems than to mathematical systems because, apart from the smaller chance of his making an effective contribution, mathematical systems are, generally speaking, conceived by employees already organisationally independent of the executive function.

Auditing of computing systems includes the auditing of the general controls operating in the computing department as well as in the systems themselves; the lack of elementary precautions to safeguard equipment and information can jeopardise the best of systems and, in any case, the computing department, as a budget unit, needs to be reviewed as much as any other activity.

Systems are created, *inter alia*, to control assets outside the computing department so that the points to be reviewed in these will be, firstly, the effectiveness of the controls created by the system to operate on those assets and, secondly, the controls built into the system, whether manual, mechanical or electronic, to ensure proper processing of data within the system.

Systems are expensive to create and expensive to alter. It is therefore good common sense for the internal auditor to involve himself in, and comment on, systems during development as well as in relation to systems that are working operationally.

In summary of these requirements, the internal audit review of computing systems may be considered to fall into three parts:

1 Review of the computing department as a budget unit and the general controls operating in relation to staff, equipment and information
2 Review of systems under development, looking at the effectiveness of the proposals and the controls envisaged within them
3 Review of operational systems for accuracy and effectiveness

External auditors are, significantly, coming much nearer to an efficiency audit in their reviews of the first part than they have thought it appropriate to apply to any other activity. Some, however, have so far restricted their investigations to the third part, and have then carried out these reviews only on financial projects. Internal auditors should complement rather than duplicate the work of external auditing and the greatest value from the internal audit department can come from the review of the controls in the computing department and in new systems. Good controls and disciplines in the computing department not only lead to efficient safeguards on, and usage of, staff, equipment and information, but also to effective systems development and subsequent operation.

13:9:1   Audit of the computing department

Controls to be reviewed will include those on:

1   Division of responsibilities
2   Purchase and hire of equipment
3   Fire precautions and general security
4   Stand-by equipment
5   Fall-back procedures
6   Usage of equipment and information
7   Acceptance of systems for development (for example, feasibility studies and justification statements)
8   Standards of documentation
9   Testing of new systems and subsequent amendments
10   Training
11   Normal administrative responsibilities

13:9:2   Audit of systems under development

After the new system has been thought out, but before detailed programming and testing begins, the project leader in charge of the systems development should prepare documentation in accordance with laid down standards and send copies to the user department, internal and external auditing functions. A meeting should be held soon after for a review of the system and controls proposed to be included.

The internal auditing department will examine the system, consider its effectiveness and, after breaking it down into its different sections of activity, review the controls helping to ensure that only accurate, properly authorised input is accepted for processing, that no information can be added or lost after acceptance, that master files and amendments are authorised, that the processing is correct and that the output, whether visible or invisible, is correctly distributed.

With knowledge of other facets of the organisation, the internal auditor may be able to suggest further integration to satisfy other requirements.

The internal auditor will also review the statement of justification for the development. A typical statement is shown below:

	£
Expected benefits (detailed)	10 000 p.a.
Estimated cost of operating new system	6 000 p.a.
Net estimated benefit	£4 000 p.a.
Cost of development	£8 000

Unless there is a recovery of development costs in a reasonably short period—two years in the above example—there is unlikely to be recovery at all as, owing to changes in equipment and requirements, major redevelopment occurs quite frequently with EDP systems.

13:9:3 Audit of operational systems

Internal auditors do not check programs in detail. Errors in programs are either accidental or made with intent to defraud. If accidental, the application of proper testing routines or the controls built in to the operational system will discover them. If made with intent (which will be more difficult if there is proper segregation of duties and good supervision) they will not be documented and will remain undetected if the normal controls are not sound. The job of the internal auditor, as for other activities, is to appraise controls and not act as the control. He will appraise controls by reviewing the organisation and the system, selecting items for following through the system, using, perhaps, test-decks to compare results with those expected, and using the computer itself for random selection of items from master files and so on.

As for manual systems he will choose the technique most suitable to the requirements. Various audit packages now exist to help select random items from master files, to sort and compare information and to prepare reports. Nearly all published accounts of so-called computer frauds indicate the absence of basic controls so that, had the system been manual, similar frauds could have been perpetrated even more easily.

13:10   Comparing benefits with costs

Internal auditors should keep time-sheets to the nearest day or half-day. The purpose of the time-sheets is to obtain audit job-times and to be aware of, and control, training, leave, sickness and other absences.

The audit job-time in man-days can be multiplied by the average cost per audit man-day to arrive at a job cost. This is the debit side of the profit-and-loss account and is fairly easy to determine. The credit side is rather more difficult as it consists of losses discovered and recovered that would not otherwise have been found, of reduction in costs or improvement in income as a direct result of recommendations made, of losses that would have occurred if it were known that there would not be an internal audit appraisal, and finally, of the value in training staff with a future career in the organisation. For his own satisfaction if not for his superior's, the internal auditor should endeavour to evaluate some, if not all, of these benefits. His job, in a nutshell, is to help improve the profitability of the business and the assessment of the worth of this activity is the sort of control that he looks for in others.

13:11   Appendix

The Statement of Responsibilities of the Internal Auditor issued by the Institute of Internal Auditors is as follows:

13:11:1   Nature

Internal auditing is an independent appraisal activity within an organisation for the review of operations as a service to management. It is a managerial control which functions by measuring and evaluating the effectiveness of other controls.

13:11:2   Objective and scope

The objective of internal auditing is to assist all members of management in the effective discharge of their responsibilities, by furnishing them with analyses, appraisals, recommendations and pertinent comments concerning the activities reviewed. The internal auditor is concerned with any phase of business activity where he can be of service to management. This involves going beyond the accounting and financial records to obtain a full understanding of the operations under review. The attainment of this overall objective involves such activities as:

1   Reviewing and appraising the soundness, adequacy and application of accounting, financial and other operating controls, and promoting effective control at reasonable cost
2   Ascertaining the extent of compliance with established policies, plans and procedures
3   Ascertaining the extent to which company assets are accounted for and safeguarded from losses of all kinds
4   Ascertaining the reliability of management data developed within the organisation
5   Appraising the quality of performance in carrying out assigned responsibilities
6   Recommending operating improvements

13:11:3   Responsibility and authority

The responsibilities of internal auditing in the organisation should be clearly established by management policy. The related authority should provide the internal auditor full access to all of the organisation's records, properties and personnel relevant to the subject under review. The internal auditor should be free to review and appraise policies, plans, procedures and records.

The internal auditor's responsibilities should be:

1   To inform and advise management, and to discharge this responsibility in a manner that is consistent with the Code of Ethics of The Institute of Internal Auditors
2   To coordinate his activities with others so as to best achieve his audit objectives and the objectives of the organisation

In performing his functions, an internal auditor has no direct responsibility for, nor authority over, any of the activities which he reviews. Therefore, the internal audit review and appraisal does not in any way relieve other persons in the organisation of the responsibilities assigned to them.

13:11:4   Independence

Independence is essential to the effectiveness of internal auditing. This independence is obtained primarily through organisational status and objectivity:

1   The organisational status of the internal auditing function and the support accorded to it by management are major determinants of its range and value. The head of the internal auditing function, therefore, should be responsible to an officer whose authority is sufficient to assure both a broad range of audit coverage and the adequate consideration of and effective action on the audit findings and recommendations

2   Objectivity is essential to the audit function. Therefore, an internal auditor should not develop and install procedures, prepare records or engage in any other activity which he would normally review and appraise and which could reasonably be construed to compromise his independence. His objectivity need not be adversely affected, however, by his determination and recommendation of the standards of control to be applied in the development of systems and procedures under his review

PART THREE

The Financial Environment

Chapter 14

Presentation of Accounts

George R Thomson, Financial Consultant

This chapter is concerned with accounts required by law to be published for the use of people outside the business. It is the duty of the auditors to ensure that the legal requirements, which vary according to defined classifications of businesses, are met.

The minimum requirements are a balance sheet which shows assets and liabilities at the end of a company's most recently completed accounting period (normally a year) and a profit-and-loss account which shows the profit or loss made in that period. These two documents should reflect the total financial results of the business to which they relate.

The law, currently the Second Schedule of the Companies Act 1967, lays down the content of both the balance sheet and the profit-and-loss account. A quoted company, the shares of which are dealt in by a recognised stock exchange in the UK must comply with further regulations issued by the Council of the Stock Exchange.

What is not laid down by the law is the way in which the contents of accounts should be presented or precisely how "the true and fair view" required by Section 149 of the Companies Act 1948 should be given. Some additional requirements asked for by the Stock Exchange Council attempt to be more specific but even these allow for a great degree of elasticity. The major accountancy bodies give their members detailed guidance about some aspects of presentation. Generally, however, the growing complexities of ill-defined attempts at legislation and the difficulties of valuing all kinds of considerations in an era of changing money values mean that, in some aspects of presentation of accounts, there are nearly as many responsible viewpoints as there are accountancy firms.

It follows that there is a wide field of manoeuvre, after all statutory and some non-statutory minimum standards have been fulfilled, available to management in the actual presentation of accounts.

14:1   Objectives

In deciding its presentation management has to consider appropriate objectives. The minimum objective is to show proprietors how their funds have been utilised and what profits have been made. This can be said to have been achieved by presenting a balance sheet and profit-and-loss account which shows "a true and fair view" of the state of the company's affairs. "The true and fair view" implies an appropriate classification and grouping of the various items involved and the consistent applications of generally accepted accountancy principles. The law also requires that annual accounts show figures for the preceding as well as the current year. Consistency is insisted upon by a further legal requirement that there must be disclosure of any material changes in the accounting treatment and a statement of how such changes have affected the current and the previous years' figures.

A manager who is also a controlling shareholder, with only a few unsophisticated relatives as minority holders, may be right in judging that presentation should end at this point. Before doing so he should take other considerations into account. Is the business likely to need outside cash, either through borrowing or through an extension of the shareholding? Is it likely to acquire another business or be acquired by one? Will death duties or other reasons make it desirable to sell existing shares, either privately or through a stock market flotation?

In any of these (and in numbers of other) cases the accounts are going to be scrutinised by sophisticated outsiders. They will want to know the answer to a number of points which are not covered by minimum statutory requirements. They will almost certainly wish to see accounts for some years previously. Indeed, it is a legal prospectus requirement that at least five years' figures must be produced by a company seeking to raise money in the market. Application for a stock market quotation normally has to be supported by ten years' figures.

Bearing these factors in mind, it is obvious that the objectives of a presentation of annual accounts should take note of many things beyond the immediate objective of producing a single year's figures economically and with the least fuss possible. Financial management should regard presentation as being an important element in promoting the general image of a company. Presentation is concerned with good public relations. Properly done it confers many benefits.

The main benefits can be listed as follows. Firstly, against any given economic background, to make it easier and cheaper to borrow money or to attract new capital either from existing or new investors. Secondly, to make it cheaper and easier to expand by acquisitions or to get better terms from a merger. Thirdly, to make it easier to resist an unwanted takeover bid. Many other, less tangible, benefits accrue even down to helping individual salesmen to sell a company's products.

Financial managers of the majority of big stock market quoted companies are aware of these factors and would regard it as failure on their part not to carry the point with any higher managerial executive.

Technically the accounts are only being presented to shareholders, as in the case of the individual controlling head of a family business mentioned above. The latter may only have to publish for circulation to one or two people. The big public company will have many thousands of shareholders all of whom have to be circulated. The essential objectives of presentation are the same.

In the nature of things the big publicly-quoted company will be more complex than the small family business. Statutory requirements insist on a greater degree of disclosure, and other organisations, such as a stock exchange, require further disclosures.

What is scarcely germane in modern circumstances is the number of shareholders. For weal or woe it is simply a fact that a greater proportion of thousands of shareholders in a quoted company is no more likely to be sufficiently interested, or knowledgeable, in the study of accounts than the one or two members of a family business. And, because it requires a vastly greater effort to communicate with and herd together a multitude than a taxi-cab load, the theoretical concept that a business is owned by a democracy of proprietors (shareholders) seldom has any relevance in practice.

Only short-sighted managers would take the view that, because this is so, shareholders should not be told more than is necessary. Institutional investors (the insurance companies, investment trusts, unit trusts, pension funds, etc.) are invariably large shareholders who can exercise considerable influence. The financial press is a powerful force in guiding investment thinking and is very much the champion of the private investor.

Both of these forces will be highly critical if they suspect that relevant information is being withheld unnecessarily and their criticisms will be echoed throughout the investment world.

14:1:1   The degree of disclosure

Obviously, a prime objective of presentation should be for accounts not to lay themselves open to suspicions and criticisms which can blight a company's financial standing for years after the original causes have been put to rights. It follows that careful attention should be given to the degree of disclosure.

The general principle should be that disclosure of significant information should not be avoided unless it can be shown that it would damage a company's interests. The most thorny aspect of this is non-disclosure on the grounds that the information would be of value to competitors.

In a few cases, usually concerning consolidation of overseas subsidiaries' accounts, Board of Trade absolution from full disclosure can be given. In others permission can be obtained from the Council of the Stock Exchange not to give such items as a full breakdown of turnover. Exemptions like these confer the highest guarantee that the case for disclosure is unarguable. Where such exemptions have been given the fact should be stated clearly.

In all other cases the best criteria to be followed is for a financial manager to ask himself: "Could I justify non-disclosure to an intelligent third party such as an investment manager of an institution or a city editor?"

The majority of companies recognise today that the tide of political, trade union and investment opinion in favour of the fullest reasonable disclosure continues to flood even more strongly. It is almost a quaint thought that, until the 1967 Companies Act insisted upon it, many companies refused to disclose their total sales on the plea that this would be damaging.

Obscurantism on this scale, or even the suspicion of it at a far lesser degree, wins no marks. Today it merely arouses suspicion, which is the mortal enemy of confidence.

Only one degree less dangerous to a company's image is when non-disclosure can lead to ridicule. For instance, it is no good telling a city editor (for the sake of convenience this character will serve as an archetype for any influential person whose opinions count in deciding a company's financial rating) that disclosures of a certain figure would be giving aid and succour to a main competition if the city editor can pick up a telephone and discover that the competition is well aware of the figure concerned.

Even if such tales, and there are many, do not get into print, they are enjoyed as jokes among the financial coterie.

In all this it should be remembered that the normal professional inquisitor of accounts is a reasonable chap who has a wide experience of the problems involved in their presentation. He will understand, for instance, a reluctance to split an overall figure on research and development down to a level at which the precise spending on development of a potential product, which cannot be marketable for several years, will give valuable information to the competition.

What he will want to know is how, overall, research and development has been treated in the accounts. If it is being written off profits as it is incurred, published profits will be conservative. If it is being capitalised (in other words, being put into the balance sheet as an asset), there will be a day of reckoning if the project fails to become commercial.

The majority of larger companies today have interests in different areas of a single industry and, in many cases, in totally different industries. In the case of quoted companies, the accounts are expected to give a clear indication of the division of profits and turnover between these different interests.

Even when such treatment is not mandatory it is often desirable. A financial analyst tends to use comparative statistics as measures of managerial efficiency. Where he is not fully in the picture his judgements may be quite unfair but, none the less, damaging.

14:1:2   Example

Two companies are both in the food supply industry. Company A shows a profit of £1m from sales of £25m. Company B shows the same profit from sales on only £14m. The analyst may jump to the hasty conclusion that Company B is more efficient.

Company B, however, gets all of its sales from retailing. Company A sells only £5m retail on which it earns £500 000. The remaining £20m of sales comes from wholesaling, which involves big turnover and small margins. A profit of £500 000, on two-and-a-half per cent, from this source is quite acceptable.

Given the additional information the analyst will realise that he is not comparing like with like and will revise his first judgement. Of course, it can be argued that he would have revised his first judgement anyway through other statistics such as the return on capital employed. But there is no virtue in letting him puzzle out the position for himself when a simple line of explanation makes everything clear.

14:1:3   Explanatory notes

Disclosure usually involves a short explanatory text to elaborate the bare figures. To attempt do this directly against every item which calls for elaboration in the profit-and-loss account on the balance sheet would give a muddled and unpleasing result.

The presentation of accounts like the presentation of goods, should aim at aesthetic appeal. The typographical lay-out deserves as much consideration as that bestowed by a newspaper editor on the appearance of his front page. Maximum simplicity and clarity are the keynotes.

For this reason it is normally desirable to confine the profit-and-loss account to a single page and the balance sheet to a single page or, at most, to two opposing pages.

Further disclosure should take the form of notes which should be numbered clearly against each relevant item. For ease of readership, those appertaining to profits should be on the page or pages immediately following the profit-and-loss account. Similarly those to do with assets and liabilities should follow immediately after the balance sheet.

Because of the complexity of legislation, accountancy procedures, stock market requirements, international complications and the differing nature of businesses it is impracticable in a chapter of this scope to give an example of every accountancy figure which may call for an explanatory note. The items which most frequently do so are listed under their appropriate headings in what follows.

GENERAL TRADING LIMITED

Trading, profit-and-loss and appropriation account for the year ending
31 March 1970

	£
Trading account	
Sales (See Note 1)	240 000
Less: Expenses (not specified in detail (See Note 2)	223 000
Trading profit for the year	£17 000
Profit-and-loss account	£
Trading profit for the year (as above)	17 000
Less: Debenture interest	1 000
Profit before tax (See Note 3)	16 000
Corporation tax	7 000
Net profit for the year after tax	£9 000
Appropriation account	£
Net profit for the year after tax (as above)	9 000
Less: Ordinary dividend	5 000
Retained out of the year's profit	4 000
Add: Unappropriated balance brought forward from last account	16 000
Unappropriated balance carried forward	£20 000

Figure 14:1   Profit-and-loss account

14:2   Profit-and-loss account

It is assumed that the reader is familiar with the way in which the profit-and-loss account classifies items.[1] An example is shown in Figure 14:1. Certain items which may call for additional disclosure in the form of notes are:

14:2:1   Sales

Note 1. These can be subdivided into different categories such as printing, engineering, leisure activities, etc., with or without disclosure of proportionate profits and capital employed in each subdivision.

Another subdivision may be into UK and export sales or overseas companies' sales with relevant profits.

14:2:2   Expenses

Note 2. These can be specified in greater or lesser detail in the actual accounts. Loan interest is often an important item and, where this is so, a figure should be given.

14:2:3   Tax

Note 3. Where a taxation figure varies substantially from the percentage norm, and particularly when it differs from the percentage of other years (after allowing for actual changes in overall company taxation), an explanation is desirable.

A high tax figure can result from a number of factors. A company may derive considerable income from trading overseas in areas of high taxation. Depreciation may have been applied in excess of that allowed by the Inland Revenue. The Revenue may have caught up on tax undercharged in previous years.

A low tax figure can result from the opposite of any of the factors in the last paragraph. Or it may result from losses made in previous years. In the latter case it is desirable to indicate the extent of the remaining relief to be expected from this source.

14:3   Balance sheet

There are two accepted methods of presenting a balance sheet.

14:3:1   Account format

The older *account* format consists of opposing columns. On the left is itemised the share capital followed by reserves (which together comprise shareholders funds). Then come long-term liabilities followed by current liabilities.

14:3:2   Net asset format

The other method, which has been gaining ground in recent years is the *net asset* format.

In this case the same figures are shown in a single column vertical tabular form. Shareholders' funds are followed by other long-term funds and then totalled to produce a figure of capital employed. After this come fixed assets and net current assets. The latter figure is derived from an inset table listing current assets and liabilities with the latter being deducted from the former to show working capital.

Although the same figures are used in both presentations the resulting balance sheet total in the account format is lower to the extent of the current liabilities figure.

In the net asset method it is becoming increasingly common to use a form of presentation which shows no detail in the face of the statement. All detail is supplied in the form of notes.

Examples of both methods are shown in Figure 14:2, with the net asset format with detail indicated in note form.[2]

In the example below, Note 1 would show the share capital, with additional information of the number of shares and their par denomination. It would also show the authorised capital since the difference between authorised and issued capital gives a clear indication of the board's intentions to issue new shares without specific approval from existing shareholders. It would also detail reserves. In a more complex company there would be a subdivision into general reserves and capital reserves.

Note 2 would detail loans giving their amounts, interest rates and repayments dates. Today it is normal to give a subdivision between long-term loans of more than five years' life and short-term loans due for repayment in less than five years.

Note 3 would subdivide fixed assets. The property figure would differentiate between freehold and leasehold and a further refinement could be to indicate the duration of various leaseholds. It is normal to indicate whether the property figure is at cost or valuation and to give dates of revaluations. Depreciation would be shown in greater or lesser detail. The remaining fixed assets are also frequently capable of subdivision with the relevant depreciation figures.

GENERAL TRADING LIMITED
Balance Sheet 31 March 1970
"ACCOUNT" FORMAT

	£			£
Share capital		*Fixed assets*		
100,000 ordinary shares	100 000	Freehold property		50 000
		Fixtures and equipment		
Reserves		at cost		
Profit and loss account	20 000	*less* depreciation		30 000
Shareholders' funds	120 000			80 000
Long-term liabilities		*Current assets*		
Loans	20 000	Stock	40 000	
		Debtors	35 000	
Current liabilities		Cash	15 000	
Corporation tax	7 000			90 000
Creditors	18 000			
Ordinary dividend	5 000			
	30 000			
	£170 000			£170 000

"Net asset" format
(with details removed and included in notes)

	Notes		£
Shareholders' funds	1		120 000
Loans	2		20 000
Capital employed			£140 000
Fixed assets	3		80 000
Current assets		£	
Stock	4	40 000	
Debtors		35 000	
Cash		15 000	
		90 000	
Less: Current liabilities	5	30 000	
Net current assets			60 000
Net assets			£140 000

Notes to accounts
Notes 1–5 to the accounts would include the appropriate detail relating to each item.

Figure 14:2   Balance sheet

Note 4 might contain a subdivision of stock and should certainly give the basis of its valuation.

Note 5 would detail current liabilities which, in more complex companies, would have several more headings than in the example. Typical items are hire-purchase contracts due within one year, loans and deposits repayable within one year and, of course, bank overdrafts.

14:3:3   Notes on accounts generally

Where the affairs of a company are complicated, which is invariably the case with large holding companies, there is a danger that the notes to accounts will be so numerous and so lengthy that sheer mass will defeat the object of illuminating the figures.

This problem can be minimised by devoting a page immediately preceding the accounts to a description of the accounting policy being pursued.

It is important to remember that notes on the accounts form part of the accounts themselves and, like the balance sheet and profit-and-loss account, are subject to the reports of independent auditors.

14:4   Directors' report

This does not, strictly speaking, form part of the accounts of a company, but is an important element in presentation. Indeed, the report and the accompanying chairman's statement, which most companies issue each year, are likely to be more widely read than the accounts themselves.

14:4:1   Contents

Because of this it is usual to give a brief summary, in the simplest form, of results for the year. Any major changes in the company's structure should be listed, such as acquisitions or disposals of assets, and it is desirable to give reasons for these.

Unless dealt with separately in the chairman's statement, the report is expected to give a review of operations during the year, an indication of trading to date in the current year and some comments about future prospects.

The report offers great scope for presentation. The growth of a company can be shown by simple charts and graphs of such items as sales and pre-tax profits over a number of years. Many reports show a ten-year record of important extracts from the accounts. Where these include earnings and dividends per share it is important that adjustments should be made for scrip issues and rights issues.

Well presented graphs, diagrams and statistical surveys are undoubtedly a desirable feature of a report. The sophisticated analyst is grateful to them for the toil which they save him. The unsophisticated small shareholder finds them meaningful in a way in which the actual accounts could never be; they help to make him feel more truly a real member of the company.

The bulk of a directors' report normally consists of volunteered information. In addition, certain information, not all of it of an accounting nature, must be shown if not shown elsewhere. For instance, the report must show the directors' individual shareholdings at the beginning and the end of the accounting year. It may be that a substantial reduction is shown in the holding of a director. He may have given shares to his children, or he may have sold them in order to make safer provision for death duties or for some compelling business reason.

In such a case it is obviously desirable that an explanation should be given. Equally, it is undesirable that the fact should appear to be tucked away in some obscure corner or in unduly small type. Such treatment would be sure to arouse suspicion.

14:5 Conclusions

The presentation of accounts should take into consideration the various categories of people who will be reading them, the various interests of these categories and their relative importance. The broad categories are shareholders, small and large, the financial press, employees, potential investors, creditors, customers and the Government.

The wider the potential readership, the more desirable it is to make disclosures well in excess of statutory or Stock Market requirements.

The result should be a successful financial public relations operation which enhances the company's image in commercial and investment circles.

14:6 References

[1] The subject is dealt with comprehensively in *The Meaning of Company Accounts* by Walter Reid and D R Myddelton, from which the example in Figure 14:1 is taken.

[2] Figure 14:2 is taken from *The Meaning of Company Accounts* by Walter Reid and D. Myddelton.

Chapter 15

Sources of Finance

P M E Springman, Consultant, Heidrick and Struggles

The methods of estimating the company's overall financial requirements for working capital and capital expenditure have been discussed
in earlier chapters. This chapter examines the methods of financing any
deficit when the cash flow generated by the company exceeds its overall
financial needs and describes the sources from which this finance is
available. All company policies and plans are interdependent, whether
they concern development, marketing or production, because each
decision must be assessed in the light of its effect on the company's
overall financial position and its capacity to borrow external funds.
Although the broad financial objectives of any company are easy to
formulate they need to be quantified in respect of the company and the
industry concerned to arrive at a company strategy. This is necessary
for the following reasons:

1 To ensure that the company has an adequate level of finance for
the company's present and future level of trading, including any
loan repayments, after considering all sources of capital, retained
earnings, and long- and short-term funds.
2 To decide on the overall level of borrowings which it is safe for the

company to assume, based on the stability of its past level of earnings.

3   To maintain a proper balance between long- and short-term capital, so that long-term requirements are financed by long-term capital and temporary, fluctuating requirements are met by short-term borrowings.

4   To match the requirements for finance with the sources best suited to the company's needs.

5   To use the assets of the company to the best advantage by improving the return on capital, by controlling the level of working capital (stocks, work in progress, debtors and creditors) and by ensuring that these levels are kept in balance with sales turnover.

6   To increase the present and future value of the shareholders equity by maximising present and future earnings per share, after considering the risks and rewards involved. This in turn requires decisions on, firstly, the dividend policy to be adopted, and, secondly the level of gearing to be adopted; that is, the level of overall borrowings in relation to the company's net worth.

7   To build up good banking relationships, which enable the company to use its borrowing base to the best advantage by adopting financial policies, which make the company a good lending risk, by prompt repayments of loans when they become due, and by keeping the banks informed on the company's financial position.

8   To revise the overall plan, when either conditions within the company or external market conditions could cause the company's present or future capital requirements to become out of line with its financial resources or borrowing capacity.

15:1   Identifying the type of finance required

The principle sources for loan finance are the London, Scottish and Northern Irish Clearing Banks, other banks such as merchant banks, overseas banks, discount houses, and finance houses. Other sources for finance are pension funds, insurance companies, factors, specialist financial institutions and export finance houses. The largest source of permanent finance is the Federation of Stock Exchanges of Great Britain and Ireland, through which both existing and new companies can make issues of shares to the public.

A company, seeking external finance, has to decide which type of money is best suited to its needs after considering the following factors:

1 The period
2 The reason
3 The cost
4 The risk

15:1:1   Period of the loan

Using the same definitions as are used in the gilt-edged market, the various loan periods are as follows:

1 Short-term loans: 1-5 years
2 Medium-term loans: 5-15 years
3 Long-term loans: over 15 years

The period of the loan required by the company can only be decided upon after considering the overall financial position of the company both now and in the future. However, the period for which the loan can be obtained will depend on the risk to the lender.

15:1:2   Reason for the loan

The borrower should be very clear in his mind why the finance is required. Is it needed to finance a genuine expansion in sales in an existing or new field of activity or is further finance required because inflation and a low profit margin have not allowed the company to finance its existing business? Most financial institutions consider that a company should be able to finance out of retained earnings: product improvement, replacement of plant and machinery, and the increase in working capital required through inflation. A recent article in *Management Today* states that firms which are unable to generate enough cash to meet their needs can only offer two explanations. Either their profitability is defective making them a suitable case for management treatment or their needs legitimately exceed the existing means of the business.[1] If finance is wanted to enable the management to correct past errors or because profits have not been sufficient to pay dividends,

297

then a lender will wish to make sure that the company is likely to overcome its existing problems.

15:1:3   Cost

Clearly, the cost of the finance is of paramount significance and has to fit into the company's overall strategic plan. The cost can vary considerably with different types of finance; this is considered later in the chapter.

15:1:4   Risk

One of the Research Reports commissioned by the Bolton Committee of Inquiry on Small Firms, considered the reasons for the refusal of finance to small firms.[2] It concluded that those requiring finance for aggressive reasons, such as expansion or diversification, were far more likely to obtain finance than those needing money for defensive reasons.

The lender will always consider the level of risk and whether the firm will be able to repay both the interest and the capital within the time-scale agreed. The period, the interest rate and the amount of the loan offered, and whether any loan is offered at all, will depend on the following factors:

1   The capital structure and liquidity. The lender will expect that the current ratio will be between 1:1.5 to 1:2.0 (that is, that current liabilities are covered by current assets by this ratio). The loan capital must also be in balance with the shareholders' equity (share capital and reserves). Long-term loans of between one-half to two-thirds of the shareholders' equity are usually permitted by the institutions, provided that the interest is covered by earnings between four and five times.

2   Management. The past record of the company must show an increasing record of earnings. In addition, the management must have the correct experience if it is venturing into a new field of activity.

3   Industry. The prospects for the industry should be favourable.

4   Security. The company must be able to offer the correct type of security. For this reason it is easier to raise money for financing

assets, such as factories or debtors, which can be more readily turned into cash, than it is to finance the purchase of specialised machinery and stocks which may only be able to be sold at very reduced prices.

15:2   Short-term funds

15:2:1   Relationship to long-term requirements

The company must decide the proportion of long-term to short-term funds it requires to finance its operations. To a certain extent the mixture will depend on the cost of finance and its availability to the borrower. However, the company will be liable to encounter liquidity problems unless its long-term assets (that is, fixed assets and permanent working capital for stocks, work in progress and debtors) are financed by long-term capital (that is, long-term loans, equity capital and retained earnings). The excess of long-term finance over long-term assets in 1968 was 1.6 for quoted companies and 1.8 for small firms.[3]

When considering the method of financing short-term requirements, attention should be paid to the effect of any such arrangements on any long-term financing which the company may wish to negotiate at a later date. This is especially true for debentures which normally require a limit to overall borrowings which may or may not include factoring, hire-purchase and acceptance credits. The debenture holder would also have to agree to postpone his charge if the company intends selling its book debts to a finance house.

Financing long-term assets by borrowing short-term money has been risky since the war because of frequent credit squeezes. Throughout this period ceilings have been imposed on bank lending and the banks' liquidity has been reduced by requiring the clearing banks to make special deposits with the Bank of England. During these periods of restriction, overdrafts have been reduced or maintained in a period of inflation. These restrictions have weighed very heavily on small firms which depend to a great extent on bank borrowing. Although priority was allowed for exporting firms, no priority was given to indirect exporters.[4]

Since the publication of the Crowther Report, the Banks have tended to raise their lending rates to higher levels for more risky loans, and also to discourage "hard core" overdrafts. It is therefore becoming even more important for firms to forecast their financial requirements accurately over a three- to five-year period, so that they can raise the most appropriate finance for their needs at the lowest cost.

In Chapter 4, the short-term financial facilities available from bank overdrafts, bill finance, acceptance credits, suppliers' finance and factoring accounts receivable were discussed, leaving only confidential invoice discounting, block discounting and export financing to be dealt with in this chapter.

15:2:2   Confidential invoicing discounting-factoring

Unlike the straightforward factoring of accounts receivable, the customers do not know of the arrangement, as the client deals direct with them. The factor is assigned the book debt and has recourse to the client as the factor does not assume the credit risk. An interest charge is made on the balance outstanding, but no charge is made on sales turnover. There is no requirement that all business in a given period must be factored and irregular use can be made of the arrangement. A minimum annual turnover of £100 000 is required with a minimum loan of £10 000. The current charge is 15% p.a.

The factor is usually prepared to advance up to eighty per cent of the invoice value and will give the client a bill of exchange for the balance, maturing on the invoice due date. As the factor has direct recourse to the client, he is interested in his financial position and a three-year record of profits is usually required. The quality of the management and the level of financial control are also considered important. Guarantees are usually required from the directors on the proper performance of the terms of the agreement.[5]

15:2:3   Block discounting

A retailer wishing to offer instalment credit to his customers as in the motor trade, can either act as an agent for a finance house and receive a commission or make an agreement direct with the customer. In the latter case, he can sell the agreements in blocks to a finance house at an agreed percentage, often seventy-five per cent of their collection value. This loan is repayable over the period of the agreement and as payments are collected from the customer by the retailer they are remitted to the finance house.[6] The rate quoted is always a flat rate, which can be roughly converted into the true rate on the reducing balance of the debt by multiplying the flat rate by 1.8. Thus, $6\frac{1}{2}$ to $8\frac{1}{2}$ per cent flat rate converts to 12 to 15 per cent true. Rental agreements covering domestic or industrial equipment can also be financed in this manner.

15:2:4 Export finance

The principle methods of financing exports are through the following organisations:

Export Credits Guarantee Department (*ECGD*). This government department now covers about a third of all United Kingdom export trade, by offering the following insurance cover on export risks:

1 Comprehensive cover. Up to ninety per cent of any political risk and up to one hundred per cent of all other risks on sales on deferred terms, provided that all the exporters business is first offered to ECGD for a period of at least a year.
2 Supplier credit. The department will also insure, in the same manner, an exporter who sells on deferred payment terms and who borrows from a British bank to bridge the period from shipment to payment.
3 Buyer credit. A British bank will also be guaranteed the repayment of any loan to an overseas buyer who uses the loan to make prompt payment to a British supplier. This arrangement is also being extended to provide lines of credit to foreign buyers who wish to place orders with unrelated United Kingdom suppliers.

Joint Stock banks. The banks have agreed with the Bank of England to finance one hundred per cent of all ECGD-covered transactions at Bank rate plus half a per cent for comprehensive buyer and supplier credit policies.

Commercial banks. These institutions will provide advances against overseas debts, documentary credits and bill discounting.

Discount houses and overseas banks will provide bill discounting facilities.

Merchant banks can provide a line of acceptance credits to overseas buyers on which a United Kingdom company can draw or the exporter can negotiate a line of acceptance credits for any goods exported.

Finance houses offer an export revolving facility for exporters to finance extended credit (90–180 days) to agents or distributors for financing stocks or debtors. Up to ninety per cent of the amount outstanding can be made available on a weekly basis. Extended credit is also available for capital goods manufacturers for periods of between one and three years, subject, usually, to the customer making a down payment. This avoids the necessity of the customer approaching a finance house on his own account. Another variant is the Amstel Club, where the finance house insures with ECGD and assumes the credit risk.[7]

British Export Houses Association. The members of this association provide the following services:

1 Confirming Houses, accepting full responsibility as principals for the payment of the United Kingdom seller and may also undertake shipment and arrange insurance
2 Buying Indent Houses, acting as agents for overseas customers
3 Merchants who buy and sell other people's goods on their own account
4 Manufacturers' Export Agents, acting as sole agents in certain territories for a manufacturer's products and selling on his behalf
5 Factors providing the same services abroad as they do at home[8]

15:3   Medium-term funds

15:3:1   Term loans

These loans are for a fixed period, between five and seven years, which can be extended up to ten years. Repayment is over the period of the loan at fixed dates and the loan is secured by a floating charge. The minimum size of the loans made varies, between £20 000 and £50 000. The rate of interest can be as high as Bank Rate plus 4 per cent. As the loan is not repayable in advance of its due dates, the bank has to satisfy itself as to the credit standing of the borrower. The investigation is more extensive than for bank overdrafts, as the commitment is for a longer period. Accounts for the last three years are required as well as forward cash flow projections for at least the same period, to ensure that the loan can be repaid on its due dates. The following factors are usually considered:

1 Managerial ability
2 Past success in forecasting sales, profits and cash flow

3 The level of financial control. Up-to-date comprehensive accounts
4 Past earnings record and future prospects
5 The financial structure, taking into consideration such factors as any evidence of overtrading and the level of proprietor's stake in the company
6 The security available
7 The viability of the project, a small range of untried products being sold to a few unreliable customers would not be considered to be a viable project

As the banks are tending to charge higher rates of interest on "hard core" borrowing, term loans are likely to be in greater demand. These loans require a higher level of financial control than has been usual for the semi-permanent bank overdraft, as the repayments have to be made on the due dates.

Term loans are obtainable from the joint stock banks, merchant banks, finance houses and from other banks.[9]

15:3:2 Instalment credit

Hire-purchase. Hire-purchase is used for hiring an asset for between eighteen months and three years or longer. As soon as the repayments and the interest due have been repaid, the asset is sold to the purchaser for a nominal amount. An initial down payment is usually required. The hirer usually has the option to complete before the end of the contract. The interest rate is fixed for the period of the agreement and is at the current true rate of twelve to fifteen per cent. The type of equipment suitable has a life longer than the loan, is easily identifiable and has a known resale value. It should have a high earning potential to generate sufficient cash flow to enable the loan to be repaid over the period fixed. The Inland Revenue considers the equipment to be the property of the hirer, who is entitled to the allowances due but only on the capital amount paid to date. The interest paid is deductible from profits but the purchase price is treated as a capital item.
Credit sale. A loan is made to the client to purchase an asset which becomes his immediate property. The tax position is preferable as the borrower is entitled to all the capital allowances in the year of purchase.
Leasing. Plant and equipment can be leased for a fixed rental for a fixed period—the primary period. At the end of this period the cost of the equipment and the interest due will have been repaid. Then the

equipment is leased for a nominal amount for a further period. The leasing company owns the equipment and is able to offset the capital allowances against profits. The rental is therefore lower and the amount paid by the lessee is fully deductible for tax. This is an advantage over hire-purchase, where only the interest amount is tax-deductible. If the lessee purchases the asset after the primary period some tax relief may have to be repaid. Leasing is not considered to be borrowing but leasing agreements must be noted in the accounts.

These three methods are different ways of financing the purchase of plant and equipment. In most cases the directors of small private companies will be required to give personal guarantees as security for hire-purchase agreements, and sometimes for leasing agreements. The credit standing of the company is important as the hirer has no wish to repossess the equipment and the hire-purchase company will usually wish to see accounts for the last three years. In the case of hire-purchase agreements for small companies, the amount of the loan, including any other liabilities, is usually restricted to one half of the owners share in the firm. Current assets are also expected to be between one-and-a-half and two times current liabilities. However, the profit record is more important than the assets and a firm with poor earnings will not be able to borrow up to this level.[10]

15:3:3   Euro-currency loans

These loans are usually only available to internationally-known companies of very high financial standing and are usually for a period of five to ten years. The firm must earn sufficient foreign currency to cover the interest payable over the period of the loan.

15:3:4   Sources and comparisons

An article in the *Investors Chronicle* examined the relative costs of purchasing an item of equipment by leasing, hire-purchase and by using a bank overdraft.[11] Over a three-year period, assuming current rates for hire-purchase and leasing and an overdraft rate of eight per cent, leasing is the cheapest method, but outright purchase is the most economic over a ten-year period. The article also recommends that prospective lessees should read the fine print of the agreement to see whether the proceeds of the final sale of the asset are fully reflected in the leasing charge. For information on medium-term finance of unquoted companies, see section 15:6.

15:4 Long-term funds

15:4:1 Sale and leaseback

The company sells the property to a pension fund or to an insurance company, which leases back the premises to the seller. The term of the lease is usually from twenty-one to forty-two years, with rent reviews at seven-year periods. However, with the present rate of inflation, rent reviews are being required in some cases after five years. The rents charged are between six and seven per cent per annum on the purchase price for shop premises and from ten-and-a-half to eleven-and-a-half per cent for industrial premises. The type of property considered would be shop property in first-class shopping areas and industrial property in trading estate situations. Specialised single use buildings, such as hotels and theatres, are not normally considered. Age is important, as well as the condition of the building and its appeal to an alternative user in case the lessee defaults on the agreement. The lease requires the lessee to insure the building and to keep it fully repaired. The lessee has to pay his own legal costs and is liable for capital gains tax on any capital profit on the sale.[12]

15:4:2 Mortgage debentures

Insurance companies and pension funds also provide loans secured by a first fixed charge on freehold property and on leasehold property with more than twenty years of the lease to run from the end of the mortgage. The minimum loan amount is between £25 000 and £50 000. The loan offered is between fifty and seventy per cent of the current value of the property, depending on its age, condition, location and the possible alternative use of the building. The type of building on which the institutions are prepared to lend is precisely the same as the type they are prepared to buy on a sale or leaseback agreement. The term of the loan is between twenty and twenty-five years with no option on early repayment. As well as the security of a first fixed charge, the lender often requires a capital redemption or endowment policy to be taken out by the

Company for the amount of the loan. Personal guarantees are sometimes required from the directors of small firms.

The interest rate is usually fixed for the term of the loan and is about half a per cent more than the rate for a first-class debenture with comparable maturity but this will depend on the viability of the company. The lender has no wish to have to repossess and relet the property and will therefore satisfy himself on the financial standing of the company and the purpose for which the loan is required. Interim accounts for the current period and audited accounts for the last three to five years and a forward cash flow statement will be examined by the lender so that he can satisfy himself that the loan can be repaid.

A small mortgage scheme is also in existence with a minimum loan amount of £15 000 to £20 000 for a term of between five and fifteen years at an interest rate of between one and two per cent above the normal mortgage rate. Repayment is made by means of equal annual instalments with a penalty if early repayment is required. The borrower pays the lender's and his own legal costs and survey fees, which usually amount to about three per cent of the loan amount. Merchant banks, estate agents, insurance brokers, solicitors, accountants and financial consultants act as agents for companies which wish to arrange mortgage finance or sale and leaseback agreements.[13]

15:4:3 Debentures

Companies can raise loan finance by means of a debenture, secured by way of a floating charge on the assets and undertaking of the company, with a collateral charge from its subsidiaries which have power to charge their assets as security for the loan. The company and its subsidiaries are referred to as the "charging group." The terms of the debenture are contained in a debenture trust deed and an insurance company, bank or pension fund are appointed as trustees if the debenture is quoted on the Stock Exchange.

The term of the loan is usually between twenty-five and thirty years, as insurance companies, which are the main subscribers for debenture issues, require a long maturity date. Repayment can be allowed during the last five years. The loan can be repayable in full on maturity or a sinking fund, cumulative or non-cumulative, can start after an initial holiday, of perhaps five years, to redeem a proportion of the loan before maturity.

Other secured borrowings, such as priority borrowings (first fixed charges), pari passu bank borrowings (with a floating charge ranking equal to the debenture) and all other debenture stock, including any further issues, cannot exceed sixty-six-and-two-thirds per cent of the share capital and reserves of the charging group. The share capital and reserves are adjusted to include any property revaluations, less any capital gains tax liability, and to exclude any intangibles. However, no increase in secured lending can take place unless, in addition, the total interest on the priority borrowings and the debenture stock is covered five times by the average consolidated net profits of the charging group for the last three years, pre-interest and tax.

Further priority borrowings ranking prior to the debenture are limited to fifteen to twenty per cent of the adjusted share capital and reserves of the charging group. The overall borrowings of the charging group, including secured and unsecured borrowings such as acceptance credits, are often restricted to one-and-a-half times the adjusted share capital and reserves of the charging group. There are also restrictions on selling or disposing of the whole, or a substantial part of, the assets of the company without the trustees' permission. Assets are not allowed to be transferred outside the charging group, if this causes secured borrowings to exceed sixty-six-and-two-thirds per cent of the net assets of the charging group.

The financial standing, earnings, and the security offered, determine the amount which can be raised. For reasons of marketability, £3 million is considered to be the minimum size for a publicly-quoted debenture. The interest payable should be covered at least four times by earnings and the principal amount at least two-and-a-half times by assets.

The striking price and coupon for a debenture, will be related to the gross redemption yield on a similar dated gilt-edged stock. Treasury Stock $8\frac{3}{4}$ per cent 1997 at present yields 9·41 per cent to redemption, and the differential in yield between gilt-edged and debenture stocks is between $\frac{1}{2}$-1 per cent, depending on the quality of the stock.[14]

15:4:4   Unsecured loan stocks

Large credit-worthy companies prefer to issue unsecured loan stocks as they have greater control over their assets within the restrictions imposed by the trust deed. The earnings and asset cover must be satisfactory because the lender ranks as an unsecured creditor on liquidation. However, a well-secured loan stock can offer better security than a poorly-covered debenture. For instance, an unsecured loan stock issued by a property company and covered adequately by first-class properties, let to well-established firms, is often preferable to debentures secured on specialised buildings, machinery and stocks. In the latter case, it is possible that book value will not be realised on liquidation. The gross redemption yield is between one quarter and one half of one per cent above the debenture rate for a similar stock. The term is normally between twenty and twenty-five years and there are similar restrictions, as in the case of debentures, on overall borrowings, on loans ranking in priority to the loan stock, and on the disposal of assets.

15:4:5   Convertible unsecured loan stock

A convertible, unsecured loan stock is a deferred rights issue and is often used to raise finance without diluting the earnings attributable to the ordinary shareholders. For this reason it has been used frequently in take-overs to allow the bidder time to rationalise the operations of the two companies and to raise the total earnings above the sum of the two parts.

The loan can be wholly or partly convertible into shares at either a fixed or a variable price at certain fixed dates within a period.

The conversion period will often start three years after the issue of the stock and end within seven to ten years. The starting conversion price will normally be about fifteen per cent above the current market price. The coupon rate at present for such issues is between eight and ten per cent, but the rate will depend on how favourable the conversion terms are. The interest rate can be increased after the conversion period has expired but the terms should be sufficiently attractive for conversion to take place. Otherwise shareholders may not be so interested in the next issue the company makes and, in addition, the company's market standing may suffer.

The Stock Exchange requires that all issues having an equity element should first be offered to the equity shareholders unless they have agreed in general meeting to some other proposal. There are also specific requirements laid down for convertible issues which must be observed, unless the Quotations Department consents to alternative arrangements.[15]

The issue of a convertible loan stock overcomes the reluctance of the investor to hold fixed interest stock in a period of inflation. Furthermore it allows the company to raise money when market conditions are unsuitable to an equity issue and at a price above which a rights issue of ordinary shares could be made.

15:4:6   Other loans with equity rights

Loan stocks can be issued with subscription rights attached to them, which entitle the holders to subscribe for ordinary shares at a fixed price in the future. The company therefore keeps its loan stock intact and, in addition, receives the proceeds of the new subscription. However, in certain issues all or part of the loan stock can be surrendered to pay for the new shares. Multiple convertibles can also be issued, which allow the holder either to convert into equity or into a short-dated stock.[16]

15:4:7   Governmental finance

The Department of Trade and Industry has powers under the Local Employment Acts to make grants and loans available to those firms which are prepared to provide continuing employment in areas of high unemployment in England, Scotland and Wales and which have been designated as development areas. These grants can be made to cover the initial costs of moving to a development area, towards the cost of new plant and machinery and for up to twenty-five per cent of the cost of building a new factory or factory extension. The Department will also build a factory or an extension for rental or deferred purchase in the development areas. Grants are also available to key workers who are transferred temporarily or permanently to these areas.

Information is obtainable from the Department or from its Regional Offices. There is a similar scheme for Northern Ireland and information can be obtained from the Ministry of Commerce.

15:5   Stock Exchange quotations

15:5:1   Advantages

A company which has obtained a public quotation for its shares has access to the capital market for raising additional loan or equity finance.

If the shares are quoted on the London and the Regional Stock Exchanges, as well as being dealt in on the London market, the shares will be traded on the following exchanges:

1 The Midlands and West Stock Exchange (Birmingham)
2 The Northern Stock Exchange (Manchester)
3 The Scottish Stock Exchange (Glasgow)
4 The Belfast Stock Exchange
5 The Irish Stock Exchange (Dublin)
6 The Provincial Brokers' Stock Exchange (York)

A private company can raise money for expansion or for funding a bank overdraft through a mortgage, a sale or leaseback, or through an institution which will finance private companies. This stage is normally reached when the existing shareholders have no more capital to invest and when retained earnings and bank loans are insufficient for the needs of the company. Provided the company is able to go public it may find that this method is preferable to raising loan capital, which is always expensive for private companies and as the lender will often, in addition, require conversion rights into equity. Furthermore, the company may not be at a stage when it can raise sufficient loan capital for its needs. It is often advisable to leave sufficient security unencumbered so that a loan can be raised if the company runs into unforeseen difficulties. On the other hand the bank may wish to reduce its loan if its security is reduced by another loan, whereas an issue of shares broadens the equity base of the company and its borrowing capacity.

A public quotation also gives the company greater publicity, because it has a wider market for its shares and as its progress is reported in the financial press.

In addition, the shareholders of a family company are given the means whereby they may raise money for paying estate duty. A quotation also avoids the possibility of an asset valuation under the Finance Act 1940, where the deceased, within five years of his death, had control over the company, owned more than fifty per cent of its share or loan capital or received more than fifty per cent of the dividends. Provided that more than thirty-five per cent of the shares are held by the public, the company is able to avoid a shortfall assessment as it is no longer a close company.

A public company can also acquire another company by issuing shares and/or loan stock to the shareholders of that company. However, on the other side, if the directors and the family lose control, the company can be taken over. The directors are also accountable to the public for their performance and must be prepared to bear the criticism if it is not up to the expectations of their shareholders.

15:5:2   Methods

There are a number of methods by which securities can obtain a quotation.

A prospectus issue. This is an offer of shares to the public at a fixed price, which raises new finance for the company. A full prospectus is required and is subject to the approval of the Quotations Committee of the Stock Exchange.

An offer for sale. A prospectus is issued. The sponsor for the issue, a merchant bank or a broker, buys shares from the existing shareholders and sells these shares to the public at a fixed price.

An offer by tender. A full prospectus is required. Either the company or a sponsor offers shares to the public. However, only a minimum price is fixed and the applicant states the number of shares and the price he is prepared to pay. Although, in theory, the sponsor will accept bids in descending order of price until the issue is fully subscribed, in practice a lower striking price is fixed which will give a good spread of shareholders. Where there is no comparable company, this method can be used to allow the market to make the appropriate valuation. Instead of a very large premium over the issue price in the case of a fixed price issue, the benefits of a very popular issue are enjoyed by the company rather than the "stags." However, the process of selection required to see that there are sufficient shareholders to make an orderly market makes it unpopular with the City institutions.

Placings. Where the proposed issue has a low capitalisation and is likely to be of little interest to the public, the sponsor will purchase or subscribe shares and then sell them to their clients. At least thirty-five per cent of the issued amount of equity capital should be placed and not less than twenty-five per cent of the amount placed should be offered to the market. The costs are lower because the requirements for advertising are less than for a full prospectus issue and no underwriting is required.

Introductions. Where a private company already has a reasonable number of shareholders or where there is already a quotation for a company's shares on another Stock Exchange, an introduction may be allowed. If large blocks of securities are being offered, then a full prospectus offer for sale may be required to ensure an orderly market. The public must hold thirty-five per cent of the issue and that these holdings should be spread amongst sufficient shareholders (about 200) to ensure a free market. The broker to the introduction will normally arrange for a supply of shares to be available from the existing holders, unless there is a free movement of shares from another Stock Exchange. This method is used principally to obtain a quotation for the shares of foreign public companies.

Rights issues. Where a quotation already exists for the shares of a company, further capital can be raised by making a rights issue to the existing shareholders. The shares are normally offered at a discount of between fifteen and thirty per cent below the existing market price to ensure acceptance. If the discount offered is within this range, about thirty per cent of the existing market capitalisation can be raised. The issue is normally underwritten so that the company is sure of obtaining the money if the market falls for any reason just prior to the issue.

Other issues. Securities are also quoted on the Stock Exchange for the following reasons:

1 When a company makes a capitalisation issue to existing shareholders by capitalising reserves (a free, scrip, or bonus issue).
2 When a company makes a takeover offer to the holders of another company's shares which are already quoted, or if a company issues shares in consideration for assets acquired, that is, if it acquires shares in a private company.
3 When shares are issued to satisfy conversion rights or in the exercise of options.

15:5:3 Types of share

The principle types of shares quoted on the Stock Exchange are as follows:

Preference shares. The Company's Articles of Association define any preferential rights which the preference shareholders have over the ordinary shareholders as to dividends, the distribution of assets in a liquidation and voting rights when the preference dividend is in arrears.

The dividend rate is usually fixed and is either non-cumulative or cumulative. A cumulative preference share is entitled to be paid any dividends in arrears from previous years before the ordinary shareholders receive any payment. Some preference shares are redeemable and others have rights of conversion into ordinary shares. Since the advent of corporation tax, companies have, wherever possible, exchanged preference shares for unsecured loan stock, as loan interest is a tax deductible expense, whereas dividends are paid out of taxed profits.

Ordinary shares. The ordinary shareholders are entitled to the earnings of a company and to the assets after all preferential rights have been satisfied.

Public dislike and the unwillingness of the institutions to underwrite and to subscribe for such issues, has resulted in the majority of new issues now being for fully-voting ordinary shares. Deferred shares which rank after the ordinary shares for dividend and capital rights are sometimes issued. Preferred shares rank prior to the ordinary share capital and are sometimes issued to institutions, providing a mixture of loan and equity finance for private companies.

15:5:4   Limitations

The various requirements of the Companies Acts and of the Stock Exchange are designed to ensure that investors are protected against fraud and that sufficient and accurate information is made available for the public to be able to make an informed decision on the merits of any security. In addition, the Stock Exchange is concerned to avoid a false market in any security through either an excess or a shortage of stock, during the period of initial trading in a new security. After an issue, the Stock Exchange regulations are designed to protect existing shareholders' rights.

For this reason, the overall valuation of a company's shares must be more than £250 000, and any one issue must have a value in excess of £100 000. Sponsors will normally be unwilling to handle the issue of the shares of any company with net profits (pre-tax) below £100 000. Some merchant banks have fixed this level as high as £200 000 to £250 000. The Stock Exchange usually requires that thirty-five per cent of the issued equity of the company is in the hands of the public to ensure a good market for the shares. In addition this level of public participation avoids a close company status for the company and the possibility of shortfall direction by the Inland Revenue. Preferential treatment in any issue is limited to shareholders and employees and then to only ten per cent of the amount offered.

15:5:5 Valuation

The valuation placed on a share being issued depends on the following factors:

1 The industry and its outlook
2 Its past record of earnings
3 The earnings forecast
4 The comparison of the prospects of the company with other similar shares and their outlook
5 The reputation of the company, its management, its products (This illustrates the importance of good image-building prior to a public issue)
6 The financial position of the company, including its asset backing, gearing, etc.

It is very likely that the shares will be offered at a lower price than the shares of similar companies which are already quoted because the company is unknown and as thirty-five per cent of the equity is being offered at one time. Using average prices over a period, a survey showed that market discount averaged 17.7 per cent on a sample of 24 offers for sale and 26.8 per cent on a sample of 19 placings. Market discount was higher for smaller issues, but the samples were not large enough for any strong inference.[17] The sponsor is responsible for setting a price at which the issue can be underwritten and which will result in a premium on the issue price when dealings begin. Too great an initial premium (over twenty per cent) for whatever reason, has reduced the company's proceeds from the issue. However, a discount on the issue price which is maintained for a period, damages the market image for the company and will prevent it from issuing any more equity, for a considerable period except at a substantial discount.[18]

15:5:6 Costs

The costs of an issue are made up of the following expenses: advertising, printing, accountants fees, legal fees, quotation fee, commissions to the sponsor, stockbrokers', underwriters and the receiving bankers' fees. The following figures on London quotations in 1969 can be taken as a guide:[14]

Group	Number of issues	Average amount paid by public	Costs as percentage of amount raised
Placings up to £200 000	3	£142 417	15.0%
Placings £200 000–£500 000	8	£319 161	6.7%
Offers £200 000–£500 000	13	£372 248	9.3%
Offers £500 000–£750 000	12	£623 275	7.0%
Offers £750 000–£1 250 000	10	£951 537	5.2%
Offers over £1 250 000	13	£3 374 854	3.1%

15:5:7 Time-table

The Bank of England exercises control over the timing of new issues of £3 000 000 or over to maintain an orderly new issue market. In this case the sponsoring broker has to apply to the Government Broker for Impact Day, which is the day on which the terms of the issue are made known to the market. There is, at present, a six-months queue for new issues. A time-table is contained in *Company Share Quotations*[20] which shows that the actual drafting of the prospectus and other documents should begin about forty working days before Impact Day. However, this assumes that all the preparatory work has shown that an issue is a feasible proposition. There may well be considerable work involved in restructuring the company's share capital, acquiring associate companies and minority holdings in subsidiaries, etc. In addition, it is useful if the sponsor, whether it be an issuing house or a broker, is given time to become familiar with the company, so that it can understand the company and see that the public is given a fair picture of the company and its prospects. The timing of the issue can also, to a certain extent, be planned to take place when the market is in a receptive mood.

The directors should realise that they are financially responsible to any shareholder for any loss resulting from a mis-statement in a prospectus. Sufficient time should be allowed to sort out any problems well in advance of the planned date of issue. In case of any delay temporary financing should be arranged well in advance to cover the company's financial requirement until the issue can take place.

15:6   Unquoted companies

15:6:1   Specialist financial institutions

Specialist financial institutions, such as merchant banks and special investment companies are interested in providing finance to private companies with growth potential which cannot justify a public issue, but yet still require finance. Some institutions wish to realise their investment within a period of five to seven years, but others wish to turn over their money within three years. Some are interested in high-technology companies, while others are interested in backing solid, well-managed family companies. A list will be found of specialised financial institutions at the end of this chapter.

15:6:2   Types of finance

The majority of institutions are interested in providing a mixture of loan and equity finance, so that they can enjoy a capital gain when the company is finally floated on the Stock Exchange.

The types of finance provided are as follows:

Nursery finance. Institutions and some stockbrokers are prepared to make finance available to private companies with pre-tax net profits of between £100 000 and £150 000, which intend going public within a three year period.

Development capital. Private companies with net profits (pre-tax) of around £50 000 are of interest to the specialised financial institutions if there is a strong possibility of a public issue or a disposal in five to seven years. Companies with lower profits are sometimes considered if they are likely to achieve a very fast growth. A potential growth in profits up to a level of £100 000 to £150 000 is required to justify an investment.

Venture capital. Start-up situations, in which the institution is required to finance a new company, are occasionally considered if the management has shown an excellent record in the same field in another company. The financing and development of inventions is not usually considered by institutions as they feel unable to evaluate the possible success of the project. The National Research Development Corporation and Technical Development Capital (a subsidiary of the Industrial and Commercial Finance Corporation Limited) sometimes finance these types of projects.[21]

15:6:3   Terms

The terms considered will depend on the size of the company, its management, the financial position and the risks involved. In nearly all cases, a mixture of loan and equity financing is used. The size of the equity holding required depends on the risk, but is usually between twenty-five and thirty per cent. Restrictions are imposed on the company to protect the minority shareholders' rights and a director is often appointed to the board. The period for investigation, negotiation and for the drafting of agreements is usually four to six months, but his will depend on the sophistication of the company's accounting, budgeting and forward planning systems. The rejection rate is extremely high, over ninety per cent.[22]

15:7   Conclusion

An efficient system of financial forecasting is essential so that a company can know what amount and type of finance it needs, for how long and for what purpose. Decisions can then be taken in the light of the company's overall requirements instead of making piecemeal decisions. As a broad generalisation, a new or a young private company with little or no earnings record should be financed by equity. Interim requirements should be financed through bank or other types of short-term lending. Convertible loan or debenture stocks should then be used to finance projects where earnings from the investment are not immediate; this avoids diluting the equity in the early stages. After a period of expansion, the assets generated can be used to retire the debt or else more equity can be raised through a public issue. A public company with a high price/earnings ratio can then use its equity to buy earnings and/or asset situations.

At all times, the financial balance of the company should be preserved so that it has a reserve of borrowing capacity to deal with unforeseen situations and so that it keeps within the accepted financial ratios appropriate for its type of business.

15:8   References

1 "What Debt does to Profits", *Management Today* (July 1970), p 100.
2 Committee of Inquiry on Small Firms, Research Report 5: *Problems of Small*

Firms in Raising External Finance; the results of a sample survey. A study by the Economists Advisory Group directed by John M Dunning (HMSO, 1971), pp 42, 61-62.

3 Committee of Inquiry on Small Firms, Research Report 16: *A Postal Questionnaire Survey on Small Firms; An Analysis of Financial Data by M Tamari* (HMSO, 1972), pp 6-9.

4 Report of the Committee of Inquiry on Small Firms: Chairman J E Bolton, CBE, DSC. Cmnd 4811 (HMSO 1971), paragraphs 12.14–12.18 and 12.21.

5 See Committee of Inquiry on Small Firms Research Report 4: *Financial Facilities for Small Firms—a study by the Economists Advisory Group directed by Dennis Lees* (HMSO, 1971), pp 195-18.

6 See *Financing Your Business* (Engineering Industries Association, 1968), pp 29-30.

7 See *Financing Your Business*, pp 37 and 52.

8 See *Financial Facilities for Small Firms*, pp 42-49.

9 See *Financial Facilities for Small Firms*, pp 84–95. Bolton report, paragraphs 12.31–12.39.

10 See *Financial Facilities for Small Firms*, pp 160–170, 178–184.

11 "Equipment Leasing: Weak Points in the Argument," *Investors' Chronicle*, (14 January 1972), p. 133.

12 See *Financial Facilities for Small Firms*, pp 109–116.

13 See *Financial Facilities for Small Firms*, pp 120–122 for details of the scheme.

14 See "The Debenture Market: Crying out for Business", *Investors' Chronicle* (2 December 1971), p 916.

15 *Admission of Securities to Quotation—Memorandum of Guidance and Requirements of the Federation of Stock Exchanges of Great Britain and Ireland*, The Council of the Stock Exchange, 1969, pp 7, 90-93.

16 *Company Share Quotations* (Fielding, Newsom-Smith and Company, 1972), p 46.

17 See *Financial Facilities for Small Firms*, p 155; and see *The Comparative Efficiency of Methods of Issue* by A J Merrett and G D Newbould, The Manchester School, January 1966, p 2.

18 *The New Equity Issue Statistics*, issued by Singer and Friedlander Limited, give details of the premium or discount on the issue price for each new issue in the previous two years. The statistics are published quarterly.

19 The figures are from *Company Share Quotations* (Fielding, Newsom-Smith and Company, 1972), p 19.

20 *Ibid*, pp 30-31.

21 See *Financial Facilities for Small Firms*, pp 50-55.

22 *Ibid*, pp 127-156.

15:9   Some sources of capital for private companies

Henry Ansbacher and Company Limited
Arbuthnot Lathams and Company Limited
William Brandt's and Company Limited
Bankers Trust International Limited
Charterhouse Development Limited

County Bank Limited (National Westminster Bank Limited)
European Enterprises Development Limited
Gresham Trust Limited
Guinness Mahon and Company Limited
Hambros Bank Limited
Hill Samuel Limited
Industrial and Commercial Finance Corporation Limited
Ionian Bank Limited
Keyser Ullman Limited
Kleinwort Benson Limited
Lazard Brothers and Company Limited
Midland Montagu Limited (A joint company formed by the Midland Bank Limited
    and Samuel Montagu and Company Limited)
Morgan Grenfell and Company Limited
Old Broad Street Securities Limited
N M Rothschild and Sons Limited
J Henry Schroder Wagg Company Limited
Singer and Friedlander Limited
Small Business Capital Fund Limited
Sterling Industrial Securities Limited
S G Warburg and Company Limited

Chapter 16

The Stock Market Rating

I: Enhancing the Corporate Financial Image

Stanley Gale, Managing Director, Shareholder Relations Limited

Few areas of financial application that are common to all public companies offers such large potential reward for such comparatively small outlay and effort as the implementation of effective corporate financial communication. The purpose of this chapter is to detail the advantages, to describe how financial communication is effected, to indicate the causes of non-effect and to outline the mainstreams whereby corporate financial status may be enhanced.

16:1   Main advantages of communication

There are half-a-dozen easily identifiable main advantages that result from a properly conducted financial public relations programme, as follows:

1   A higher price for the the company's shares than would otherwise be the case

2 Access to cheaper finance and greater availability of funds
3 A more orderly market in the company's shares and other securities thereby avoiding unjustified fluctuations in stock market prices
4 Enhanced shareholder loyalty, both institutional and private
5 A far better foundation from which to repel undesirable takeovers
6 Improved sources of reference in the form of newspaper cuttings and magazine articles in a variety of libraries, including those of the credit rating agencies, bank intelligence departments, etc., which may be referred to other organisations for commercial, as well as financial purposes

16:1:1 The investor

The main advantages to the investor in a company which is well understood and well thought of are obvious. His investment will be worth more and there will be a better merket for it, making disposal easier for him. But the major gain to the shareholder is also the major advantage to the management—the much improved efficiency that the company may enjoy, leading to greater opportunity and increased profits.

16:1:2 Management

It is not difficult to imagine the consequences for a company that is underrated in the stock markets by as little as fifteen per cent. It will be open to take-overs by competitiors on a share exchange basis and it cannot sensibly arrange acquisitions by share exchange on its own behalf. If it pays only half of one per cent extra for finance, on a capitalised basis it will amount to tens of thousands or hundreds of thousands of pounds.

Compared with its competitors it has had imposed upon it an enormous disadvantage despite the fact that the company may, intrinsically, be better managed in all respects than those with which it is unfavourably compared.

Many private companies that go public do so with one of their main objectives being to obtain easier access to large-scale finance and to increased opportunity for expansion by acquisition. To fail to follow through with effective financial public relations is to negate to an extent the potential benefits to be obtained from the exercise.

322

The company which has the correct financial rating may acquire others by acquisition with advantage to earnings per share, can obtain its finance at cheapest possible rates, is much less likely to be bid for by marauders, and, if it is bid for, will merge on its own terms or be able to mount an adequate and effective defence.

The wastage involved in inadequate financial recognition may truly be a millstone, for, whilst the example given above was that of a company fifteen per cent underrated, it is common to find public companies underrated by twenty, thirty, forty and even fifty per cent.

16:2   Channels of communication

Possibly the greatest single cause of ineffective communication is misunderstanding of the target at which it should be aimed and a lack of detailed knowledge about the channels of investment information and motivation.

In financial communication it is essential always to remember that over ninety per cent of total stock market investment is undertaken on somebody's advice. The primary target is, therefore, investment advisers. They are stockbrokers, investment analysts, investment managers, the press, bankers, solicitors and accountants. If they think well of the company and if you are able to inform them in a manner that enables them to make an accurate evaluation of the company and its potential, then the corporate status will be established at its correct level.

The press performs a dual function. Apart from direct advice to readers, on which a reasonable proportion of investment decisions are made, it also influences and informs investment advisers and provides library and research material which may help to form opinion long after publication date.

The statistical services, which provide investment information, both historical and current, to investment advisers and the press are a very important link in the communication channel. The diagram in Figure 16:1 displays the channels of financial communication.

Just as it is important to appreciate that the main target is investment advisers it is also imperative to realise that investment analysts and city editors receive more than two hundredweight of investment reading matter per week. The message needs to be presented with above average

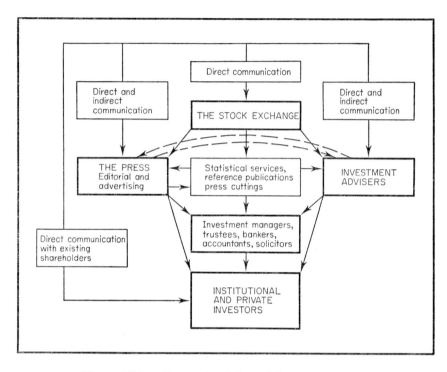

Figure 16:1   Channels of financial communication

ability if it is to receive above average attention or to avoid being overlooked in the mass.

Obviously, the most important financial communications are those that are sent by companies directly to their shareholders, the Stock Exchange and the press. This is an area where great differences arise between those companies that capitalise on the corporate financial status to the full and those that fail to make noticeable impact.

16:3   Communication deficiencies

In most companies the responsibility for financial communication falls upon the chairman, the managing director, the financial director or the company secretary, usually acting in consultation with each other. In many cases however they do not adequately understand investment, in the sense that investment knowledge is required, or communication in this specialist field.

The problem is that in all other fields of company activity the board may call upon trained staff to execute boardroom policy in a highly effective manner. However, in the field of investment analysis, mass communication and financial press relations, most boards do not have trained specialists at hand to advise and implement.

This difficulty is compounded by the fact that most directors are denied the chance to learn by experience, since the occasions on which they are concerned with financial communications are so infrequent that relevant experience, in a field that is always changing anyway, is difficult to accumulate.

Many boards of directors seek the opinion of accountants or their auditors. This is generally a mistake because they do not understand the science of investment analysis or communication either, and by training and practice they are inclined to advise minimum legal disclosure, which is the opposite of what is required.

Impact in financial statements is frequently lost by esoteric presentation. It is a common mistake to assume knowledge on the part of the reader of past events and circumstances.

In financial announcements it is much better to assume that every shareholder is a new shareholder, especially since financial status is established by investors other than existing investors whose contribution is limited to a decision not to sell.

There is a widespread tendency on the part of company directors reporting on events that are as familiar to them as the proverbial lines on the hand to assume similar familiarity on the part of others. They may be surprised to discover how frequently very little is known about them in detail.

16:3:1   Inadequate disclosure

The biggest barrier of all to effective communication is that of inadequate disclosure. This is where effective status-building falls down time and time again. It is a hurdle that is erected in the boardroom and which can be dismantled only in the boardroom. It is useless to perfect the distribution of financial information, to present it with clarity and impact, to reach the right people at the right time, if meaningful fact is withheld in the first place.

Investment decisions are predominantly based on what is to come rather than what has past. The company that is underrated through inadequate disclosure will remain underrated until such time as adequate information is forthcoming.

Much of the apprehension on the part of directors in the field of disclosure is unwarranted and has been demonstrated so to be by past events. The big improvement in financial reporting by companies commenced with the 1948 Companies Act, was carried on by the 1967 Act and accelerated by the hard work and guiding encouragement on the part of the Society of Investment Analysts, the press and the Institute of Chartered Accountants. There is no evidence that the great increase in the volume of information disclosed has noticeably harmed companies.

Company directors will usually know, better than most others, when their company is underrated. They will have a thorough knowledge of the industry or industries in which they operate, be well-informed about competitive companies within those fields and, probably, be in possession of inter-firm comparisons in greater or lesser detail.

A general assessment may be made from the comparative historical records of earnings and dividends per share, dividend yields and earnings yields, degree of profit fluctuation and, most important of all, the future prospects of earnings per share.

Read in conjunction with stock market prices and compared impartially with other companies, or with stock market averages, there is rarely much doubt in a boardroom as to the company's status.

The price/earnings ratio will provide a good rough indication of status but is not always fully understood by many company directors and is increasingly being questioned by financial analysts. It should not be taken in isolation and used as an undisputed measure of the company's financial status.

16:4 Effective implementation

Effective financial communication is a matter of reaching the right people with the right message at the right time. In order to achieve this it is necessary to fully understand investment advisers and what motivates them. It is also necessary to understand the press and to ensure that announcements reach newspapers swiftly, comprehensively and in easily assimilated form.

It is essential to bear in mind the target—the investment advisers—and important to realise that, to achieve effect, the messages must make an impact on people who are *not* existing shareholders.

16:4:1   Background knowledge

Effective implementation requires a quite detailed knowledge and understanding of investment, newspapers and communication, which means that it requires time expenditure and constant application—more time than is practicable or reasonable to expect a board of directors to devote to it *en bloc*. In any event split knowledge and split experience is ineffective.

The extent of the knowledge required, and the extent of the time required in order to keep abreast of changes and development justifies one of the following or a combination of item 3 with item 1 or 2:

1 Nomination of one of the directors to be responsible for financial communication
2 Appointment of an individual with suitable qualifications
3 Retention of the services of a specialist financial communications consultant to advise the board in detail

It is difficult to be specific on the amount of time required since the variation is large. In very big organisations, giant multi-national corporations, etc., the full-time services of one person would be justified. This would include full routine liaison with the press and financial analysts. In most other companies the time requirement would probably amount to something like five to seven man-hours per week, say one working day.

The person responsible for the detail and the work involved in remaining fully informed, whether it be an internal representative or outside consultant, should concentrate on the following:

1 Establishing and maintaining an effective chain of communication for the distribution of financial announcements
2 The procedure and practice involved in liaison with the financial press
3 The procedure and practice involved in liaison with financial analysts

Effective communication with investment advisers and the financial press is easily understood, although a lot of application and study is necessary if it is to work with effect. It consists of discovering, in depth and detail, what is required by financial analysts and financial reporters and then providing it.

The person responsible for financial communication must himself become part-analyst and part-reporter. He must read the financial columns of newspapers, the specialist financial magazines, stockbrokers' circulars and financial reports. He must do this widely and continuously. By intense reading of the financial press he will become aware when investment reports are issued or recommendations made on investment matters, the suggestions of which he will adopt or adapt and provide through his own company. He may, in addition, obtain great assistance from the various guiding publications issued by the Society of Investment Analysts and the Institute of Chartered Accountants. He will obtain extremely valuable assistance from person-to-person discussions with analysts and financial reporters by assimilating their points of view.

If a director, it is essential that he looks at everything to be issued by his company from the analysts' and reporters' points of view rather than his own as a director. He should ensure that statistical cards and investment reference books carry accurate information and that the information is the most meaningful and the most informative from the point of view of an investment consultant who will study those sources as part of the process of deciding for or against investment in the company.

The specialist financial public relations consultants are predominantly former financial journalists. Their methods of operation vary slightly but the largest and best known among them have established systems of press and analyst liaison and their advice may be sought with confidence.

16:4:2   Presenting the information

When presenting financial information it needs to be carried out with above average ability if it is to be materially noticed in competition with news from some 5000 other publicly-quoted companies. This does not mean it needs to be more sensationally produced in printed multi-colour pamphlets—entirely the reverse.

There is no better substitute for Stock Exchange and financial press announcements than the straightforward duplicated statement which is produced with maximum speed and maximum security, thus conforming to Stock Exchange requirements on speed of disclosure.

Such statements may be given impact by a combination of the following:

1 Reveal more content than is required. Reveal all that can reasonably be disclosed at the time for the purpose of more accurate evaluation by city editors and analysts
2 Wherever possible, time the statements in advance to appear when there is minimum competition for newspaper space. This involves not only the choice of day on which to hold the board meeting, but the choice of the hour also
3 Consideration of additional distribution, through press advertising and direct mail
4 A clear, easily assimilated statement with all relevant comparisons so that financial reporters are enabled to report more fully and more conclusively in the extremely short time available
5 The use of forecasting the forward look, so much sought by analysts, should be kept in mind. It is extremely important

Company financial statements issued in this manner will be more interesting because they contain more information. They will be more interesting to journalists who, as a consequence, will give them greater coverage. Announcements will arrive in time to be handled conveniently without undue haste, when there is a comparative shortage of publishing material. They will contain a message more meaningful to analysts and will appear in the press at a time when there is relatively less competitive material to diffuse their interest.

16:4:3   Use of advertising

They may be accompanied by advertised material, giving the board announcement in full as distinct from the editorial versions that will appear in the editorial columns.

The publicity that such statements receive is not to be compared with those which contain minimum disclosure and are made on the wrong day of the week at the wrong hour of the day.

When financial communication is carried out properly it develops an accelerating effect as more investment advisers start looking at the com-

329

pany and the company receives requests from investment analysts and journalists for information or facilities for visiting the company.

16:4:4 Press relations

It is essential however, to maintain the shareholder relations effort on a constant basis. It is not sufficient to put concentration into occasional outbursts when things are going well.

In most instances the amount of time devoted to press relations is a comparatively small amount of the total time expended on financial public relations; but it is extremely important and corporate status will be enhanced far more rapidly with good press relations.

As with analysts, good press relations will be brought about first by finding out what newspapermen want, and then providing it. Financial reporters work at terrific speed. Time considerations and clarity are the main factors and availability is also very important. Reporters quickly lose patience with companies that issue releases when the directors that issued them are not available to comment, amplify or clarify. Nothing kills press relations faster than the words "no comment" or "not available".

The person responsible for the detail and mechanics of financial public relations should so arrange press relations that financial journalists are known personally by the senior directors of the company. When press people and company directors are known to each other the press will more willingly approach the company for information. This leads to more accurate reporting and greater coverage. It minimises the costly risks involved in communication, since the person-to-person contact will result in clarification of anything that is ambiguous or capable of misunderstanding or misinterpretation.

A situation must not be allowed to develop which involves uncertainty. Good effect comes from constant guidance. If things are going much better than previously indicated, this fact should be made plain in an announcement, as should the reverse.

16:4:5 Preliminary profit statement

The Annual Report is the most important of all routine financial communications but the greatest effect is normally brought about in the preliminary profit statement, usually issued several weeks in advance of the Annual Report.

Preliminary statements are reported on in the press far more widely than Annual Reports. Information of immediate investment value should be included in the preliminary statement as well as the Report. If otherwise, a false market would have existed in the share during the time between publication.

Preliminary statements have press appeal. Annual Reports have analyst appeal. An adequately reported preliminary statement will result in greater readership of the report by analysts.

The effective Annual Report is that which is produced with maximum disclosure in mind, following the recommendations of the Society of Investment Analysts and Institute of Chartered Accountants.

The cost involved in implementing effective communication is minimal, it may be achieved for a few thousand pounds per year, a tiny fraction of the increase in capital value of a company's equity that may come about as a result of it.

II: Evaluating Company Share Prices

Stanley Gale, with case studies in price-earnings ratios contributed by Peter Baker, Assistant Director, N M Rothschild and Sons Limited

Part I of this chapter emphasised the advantage to corporate management of ensuring that the quoted equity of a company is correctly valued in the stockmarket.

This section indicates how analysts evaluate equities, with particular emphasis on that aspect which is most relevant to company directors in forming an opinion on the stock market value of the equity of their own company.

Many boards of directors are frequently of the opinion that the equity of their company is currently too cheap and it is by no means uncommon to find the contrary opinion that their company's stock is over-priced. The information in this section is intended to enable them more accurately to form an opinion, to avoid the more common pitfalls and to compare more effectively the value of a share in one company to those in others.

16:5   Sources of information

The information that most analysts take into consideration is readily available in respect of a large number of companies through the special analytical cards issued by Extel Statistical Services Limited 37-45 Paul Street, London EC2A 4PB; Moodies Services Limited, Moodies House, 6-8 Bonhill Street, London EC2A 4BX, and other similar services.

With kind permission of the Exchange Telegraph Company Limited, a description of the information and ratios included on their analytical cards is reproduced as follows:

Ten-year tabulations showing, for industrial companies:

1   Share capital and total capital employed and the percentage of each class to the total
2   Employment of capital
3   Quick assets and liabilities

4   Debtors and creditors and the ratio between the two
5   Stock and its ratio to turnover
6   Capital changes tabulated in chronological order and amount raised by the issues
7   Turnover and its ratio to the capital employed
8   Net profit before tax as a percentage of turnover
9   Tax charged and its percentage of the net profit before tax
10 Net asset value per share both actual and adjusted
11 Percentage earned on equity capital both actual and adjusted
12 Dividends paid on equity capital both actual and adjusted
    (The adjustments in the above refer to both scrip and rights issues)
13 Earnings are further adjusted to eliminate the effect of investment allowances and again to allow for all scrip and rights issues
14 Record of all dividends—times covered by profits (earnings)
15 Earnings and dividend yields, calculated on the price of the shares on the day following the publication of the report and accounts: these are compared with the group yields on the same day (so far as it is possible) given by *The Financial Times—Actuaries Index*
16 Highest and lowest prices adjusted for both scrip and rights issues
17 Adjusted earnings, dividends and prices shown in graph form with indicator bars showing the annual range of prices reached
18 Special ratios and figures are produced for other groups of companies, for example, banks, hire purchase finance, insurance, investment trusts and property companies

Exchange Telegraph has been providing information of this kind for decades and its card information system has been developed to meet a widespread demand.

16:6   Methods of analysis

Various analysts have, of course, developed other methods of assisting in evaluation which may have real, or imaginary, advantage, but it is impracticable for the average director or, indeed, finance director to concern himself with providing other than the universally used information and ratios.

From the practical point of view any director who wishes to understand more fully the use to which the information can be applied can do no better than begin by obtaining analytical cards from one or more of the various card services. These analytical cards are not produced for every public company but the choice is wide and some suitable selection will be available. The usefulness of the information and the ratios are obvious and the application is a matter of common sense.

The methods employed by investment analysts to assess the prospects of one sector of industry against another and the factors they take into account to determine investment timing or switching are not relevant to the average company director who is mainly interested in following the stockmarket assessment of the shares in his own company on a continuing basis. From the practical point of view there is very little that boards of directors can do in these statistical exercises other than to provide the information.

It will be observed that the universally used information is obtained from published balance sheets, stockmarket prices and other sources of fact and is thus unalterable. Two analytical yardsticks deriving from these are earnings per share and the price earnings ratio.

16:6:1 Earnings per share

Earnings per share is the most important of all investment considerations. Unlike the price earnings ratio it is easy to understand and simple to explain. It enables analysts and investment advisers quickly and accurately to assess how efficiently the directors utilise the company's equity capital and to measure precisely the company's progress, or otherwise, from year to year.

Earnings per share indicates those companies that are growing bigger just for the sake of getting bigger—a 100 per cent increase in earnings is of doubtful value to investors if the equity base has also been doubled by new capital, resulting in nil increase in earnings per share.

Earnings per share (abbreviated as EPS) are easier to explain than achieve. Equity earnings can be expanded by borrowing money on fixed interest terms and then putting the cash to work for a higher return than is paid on the borrowed money. That may be sound or it may be unsound and standard investment analysis enables an assessment to be made of which it is likely to be.

Earnings per share is, therefore, not the be all and end all but it is mightily important and investment analysts are constantly seeking situations in which equity earnings are soundly based, with the issued amount of equity restricted to the minimum, resulting in satisfactory increases in earnings per share, with the prospect that this situation is likely to continue.

Any director who has served a company in which he has a large equity interest will be thoroughly familiar with the relevance of earnings per share. Bluntly stated it means no more than getting the maximum amount of money out for the minimum amount put in.

The way in which directorial policy can effect earnings per share is obvious—money should never be raised by expanding the issued equity unless a sound alternative is not available and, even then, it should be avoided except where the issue of additional equity will have the effect of increasing the earnings per share on the enlarged equity capital.

16:6:2   Price/earnings ratio

The price/earnings ratio is a very different matter; it is well known throughout industry that the p/e ratio measures the "status" put on a company by the stock markets.

Whilst this view is correct lack of appreciation of the combination of numerous factors that contribute to the p/e ratio leads to incorrect interpretation. The outcome is that many directors imagine their company's status to be lower than it really is and others, who are flattered by apparently above-average ratings, will eventually find them no more than ordinary.

The p/e ratio is derived by dividing the stock market price by the earnings per share. If it could stay as simple as that, interpretation of the p/e ratio would be by straightforward comparison. The company on a price earnings multiple of twenty would, obviously, be more highly regarded than others on fifteen or ten.

The problem in interpreting the p/e ratio begins with the realisation that whilst earnings per share remain static (until re-established by the next profit announcement) the share price is moving freely, reflecting optimism and pessimism, not only on the company's prospects but also on the stock market as a whole.

Stockmarket prices are attempting to anticipate and there comes a time during the year when the share price is regulated by the anticipated new earnings rather than those announced months previously.

If increased earnings per share are expected the share price moves ahead in anticipation and when the higher price is divided by the last announced earnings, now months or perhaps nearly a year old, it results in an increased price/earnings ratio. This is where many company directors go wrong. They look at one sector of the stock market, the field in which they happen to be interested, and compare the ratios of a number of companies operating within that sector without making sufficient allowance for such factors affecting the ratios they are studying. Or directors of a company that was on a p/e ratio of, say, fifteen, feel quite happy to see an improvement to, say, eighteen only to see it drop back to fifteen again when increased profits are announced and the higher earnings per share is divided into the share price in place of the smaller, former figure.

Analysts attempt to overcome this aspect by making an estimate of forward earnings per share and use this figure as a divisor of the market price, thus working from a projected p/e rather than the historic p/e.

Dividend policy affects the p/e ratio. It will frequently be found in comparing equity investments that a company with high profit retention has a lower p/e ratio than another which is distributing a higher proportion of profit as dividend.

This is because dividend yield considerations are effecting the market prices and income consideration is leading to higher demand for the shares in the company paying the higher dividend. From management's point of view this is a question of judgment. The company distributing a higher proportion of profit may eventually find itself forced to raise new capital, or new equity capital, with adverse effect on earnings per share. The company with higher retentions may be able to avoid this situation, in which case the company which formerly had the higher p/e will end up with the lower. All these facets should be taken into consideration when comparing the status of one company with others.

Just as the right p/e is important from the viewpoint of corporate management, so, too, is the judgment of the "correct" p/e an essential part of the professional investment managers' task in valuing equities.

Similarly, just as it is inadequate for company directors to attempt to assess the status of different companies by a simple comparison of p/e ratios, it is altogether too superficial for the analyst to advocate the purchase of low p/e stocks because they look "cheap", or to avoid high p/e stocks because they look "dear". It is a question of deciding, from the viewpoint of the investor, what is the "right" p/e for the stock in question.

16:7   Examples of price/earnings ratio and earnings per share variations

The remainder of this chapter deals largely with case study examples of how the p/e ratio varies on different stocks and examines the reasons for these variances. This indicates something of the methods used by analysts with the objective of obtaining a truer comparison. It should also enable the company director himself to achieve more accurate interpretation and show how factors quite remote from the control of management sometimes substantially affect p/e ratios.

The method used here has the effect of excluding the complications caused by overall stock market movements or overall sector movements by taking the average p/e of the market or the average of a particular sector as the base of 100, shown on the graphs in Figures 16:2 and 16:7 as a thick black horizontal line.

This thick black horizontal line straight across the graphs therefore represents the average for the stock market or sector and by charting the p/e of a particular company against it a clear picture emerges of the company's status *relative to the market (or sector) as a whole*. This relative p/e analysis is of considerable greater value than to assess the p/e in absolute terms.

A similar exercise is carred out on earnings per share. The average of the stock market is taken and this average is represented by the same thick black horizontal line as represents the average p/e. Again, the earnings per share of a particular company may be taken and plotted against the stock market average.

Each graph thus shows the average p/e and the average earnings per share of the stockmarket as a whole and the p/e and earnings per share of a particular company *relative to the average*. From the graphs one can immediately see whether a company's p/e and earnings per share are better or worse than average.

Additionally, it is also immediately apparent when divergences occur; thus the graphs show quite clearly when relative earnings per share are

337

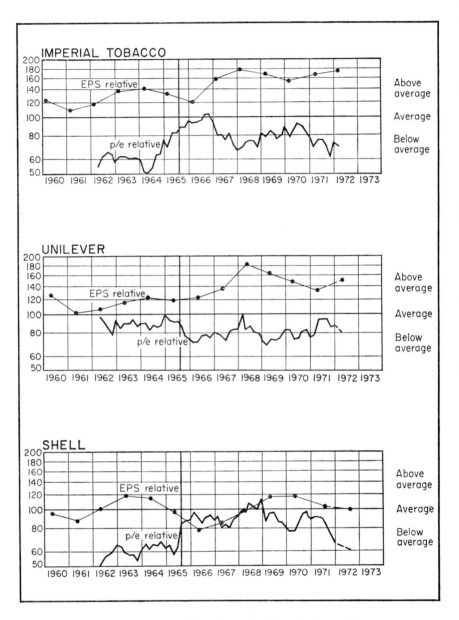

Figure 16:2   Examples of stocks historically trading on
price/earnings ratios lower than average

Vertical black line represents introduction of corporation tax
Comment is restricted to period after introduction of corporation tax

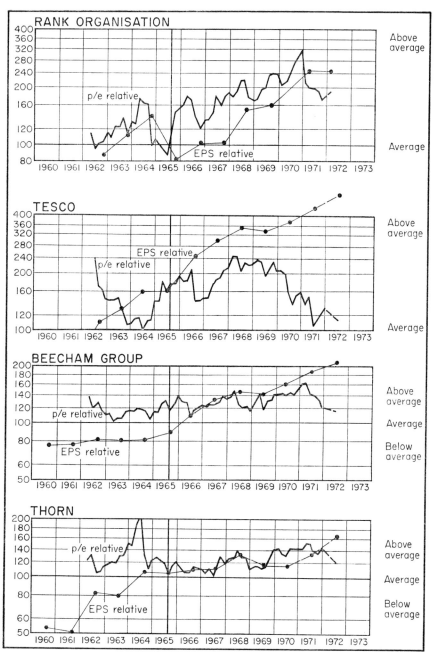

Figure 16:3   Examples of stocks commanding
consistently high price/earnings ratios

Vertical black line represents introduction of corporation tax
Comment is restricted to period after introduction of corporation tax

increasing whilst the relative p/e is falling and vice versa. Since, in ordinary circumstances, the relative p/e and the relative earnings per share should move approximately in line, divergence implies that special factors are exercising effect and it remains for the analyst or company director only to establish what they are.

The case study examples that follow are all based on leading stockbrokers, Wood Mackenzie and Company's excellent studies in "relative analysis". As shown in Figure 16:2 Imperial Tobacco, Unilever and Shell have consistently been valued below the market average p/e, despite quite good growth records in earnings per share. The reasons for this are various but important among them are (as regards Imperial Tobacco) the "unfashionable" nature of tobacco as an investment with the attendant "knocks" on health grounds, causing concern as to the long-term dependability of tobacco profits.

The rating of Unilever has been, and is, held down by the even lower p/e rating of the "twin" company, Unilever NV, which has resulted in continuous pressure as United Kingdom institutions switched out of the cheap Unilever stock into the cheaper Dutch sister company.

Similar pressure is also an influence on Shell's low p/e, where Royal Dutch, the sister company in Holland, has traded on an even lower p/e basis. The p/e's applicable to the US international oil companies, which have tended to be below average, have been an additional influence on Shell's p/e.

It may thus be seen that there are often external influences beyond the

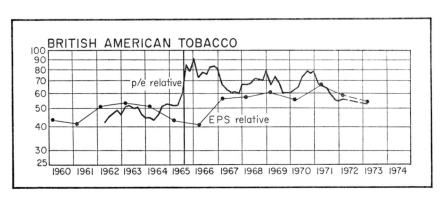

Figure 16:4   Example of stock substantially re-rated downwards

Vertical black line represents introduction of corporation tax
Comment is restricted to period after introduction of corporation tax

control of corporate management which affect a stock's p/e. It is notable that, in the case of the Rank Organisation, how a strong earnings growth relative was accompanied (logically enough) by a major re-rating of the p/e relative from 100 in 1965 to over 300 at the end of 1970. This combination (representing the investor's dream involving a re-rating "status play" on top of increasing EPS) led to a rise in the share price of nearly 500 per cent between 1965 and 1970. On the other hand, 1971 saw a sharp downward re-rating of Rank's p/e relative which, exceptionally for the stock, led to its share price under-performing the United Kingdom market generally throughout 1971. The downward re-rating was basically attributable to the anticipation of, and subsequent effect of, rather disappointing interim results in 1971, from what the market considered an outstanding growth company. When the market values a stock on a high p/e, it is a tough fact of stock market life that the market (perhaps unreasonably) demands consistently outstanding results if the rating is to be maintained.

There are several points of interest in the graph on Tesco. Note the major p/e re-rating in 1967, in the first leg of the 1967/69 bull market, from a p/e relative of 150 to a relative rating of over 240 (which, compounded by EPS growth, resulted in a rise in the Tesco share price from under 30p to over 90p in the course of one year). It will be noted that the Tesco p/e relative remained above 200 during 1968/69 but has fallen sharply in status since the top of the 1969 bull market. During 1970 and for the first half of 1971 the share price accordingly under-performed the market, despite a continued excellent growth of earnings per share. In the second half of 1971, the price of the stock began again to out-perform the market.

Beecham is another example of a growth stock where the market, rightly or wrongly, has re-rated the multiple downwards, despite continued earnings growth, which clearly was not up to the best expectations of the weight of professional investor opinion.

The quality of Thorn's profits growth (*quality* of earnings means the reliability of the *source* of the profits: for example, a "dealing" profit is a low "quality", whereas rental income, be it property rental or television rental is of high "quality") has led to its above-average rating, helped by the anticipated growth of colour television in the United Kingdom. Note how the p/e rating of British American Tobacco has fallen from a p/e relative of just under 80, at the end of 1970, to a p/e relative of around 54 in March 1972. The share price at end 1970 and March 1972 was about the same (300p) despite the sharp rise in the market overall during this period. This static price at a time of generally rising equity prices (the *Financial Times All Share Index* was up just under 60 per cent over this period) is reflected in a falling relative p/e ratio. In addition to the low p/e rating historically accorded to tobacco shares "BATS" has suffered from devaluation of the dollar in 1971, which had the opposite effect on BATS earnings from its important United States subsidiaries to the sterling devaluation in 1967 (which event was partly attributable to the p/e re-rating of BATS from its relative 60 at end 1967 to nearly an 80 relative at the end of 1968, which re-rating, compounded by a growth in earnings, led to a rise in the BATS share price from £2.25, in late 1967, to £3.75 at the end of 1968 , a rise of no less than 66 per cent in a year).

Breweries were re-rated from a p/e relative of below 80, at end 1968, to 120 in mid 1971. The re-rating took place when the market paid greater attention to the quality of brewery profits, to the inflation-hedge nature of the breweries' massive investment in freehold property, and when it

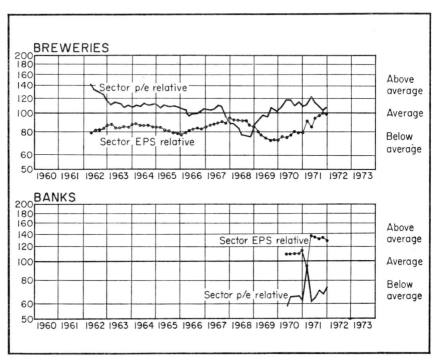

Figure 16:5   Sectors of Stock Market re-rated upwards

became more apparent that management in the sector generally was improving, particularly as regards achieving more realistic returns on capital employed. The sharp rise in bank share prices in 1971 was caused primarily by the upward re-rating of the p/e multiple following publication of "true" profits for the first time, compounded by profits better than generally expected.

The graphs in Figure 16:6 show the effect on companies as a result of re-rating upward of the brewery and banks sectors. Share prices of all three companies more than doubled in 1971.

The volatile earnings relative demonstrated in Figure 16:7 shows the relatively cyclical nature of these companies' profits (in the past at any rate). This has resulted in volatile p/e relatives, which in absolute terms are even more volatile. Valuing cyclical earnings always presents a problem to the professional investor, who knows through experience the risk exposure if stocks are bought on high p/e's based on "top of the cycle" earnings, or if such stocks are sold on low p/e's based on "bottom of the cycle" earnings.

The company director who wants to make an assessment of his company and of his competitors can prepare a *relatives* graph of the sector of the stock market in which he is interested and apply it to any long-term or short-term period as best suits the need. By taking the average of the sector as the base line of 100 he can compare his own company and his competitors relative to the average over the time-period of his choosing.

He can similarly prepare sector information on share prices and proprotion of profit distributed as dividend on a *relative* basis.

Clearly, what corporate management wants to achieve is a high p/e rating on the company's stock (to enable growth by acquisition, to resist takeover approaches and to maximise shareholders' returns—including corporate management's where stock options exist).

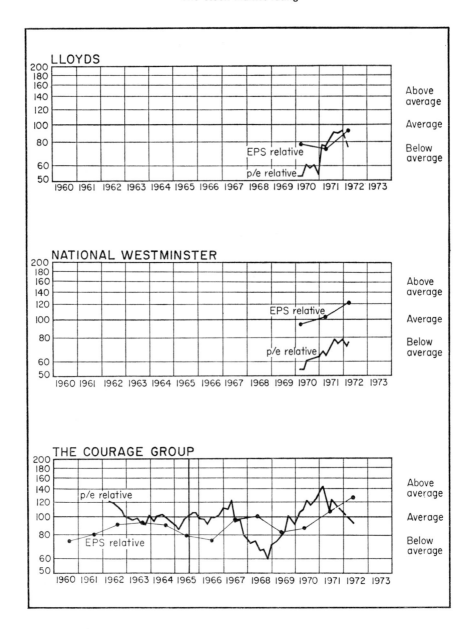

Figure 16:6   Effect on stocks of upward rating of sector

Vertical black line represent introduction of corporation tax
Comment is restricted to period after introduction of corporation tax

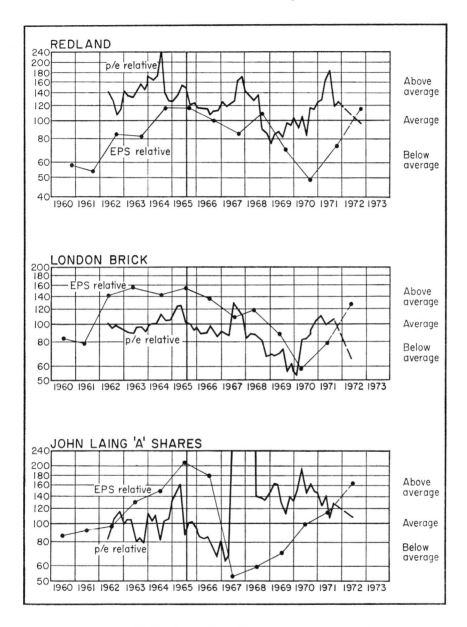

Figure 16:7   Examples of p/e ratios on companies
on cyclical earnings

Vertical black line represents introduction of corporation tax
Comment is restricted to period after introduction of corporation tax

345

16:8   Summary of steps to improve the price/earning ratios

16:8:1   Maximum disclosure

Maximum disclosure, as emphasised in the first part of this chapter, is essential. A Source and Application of Funds Statement, together with the *earnings per share* figure highlighted both for the current year and previous year's trading and in, say, a five-year table, is helpful in this respect.

16:8:2   Indication of awareness

Be sure that the professional investment community know that the management recognises its objective and responsibility in seeking to achieve growth in earnings per share and, to a lesser extent, in assets per share. Too many public companies still highlight pre-tax profits (absolutely) and the *dividends* declared without highlighting the per share earnings.

16:8:3   Emphasis on steady growth

Above average growth in EPS will *ultimately* lead to an above average rating, but that steady growth is better than highly volatile growth.

16:8:4   Proper accounting

Odd accounting should be avoided—for example, excessive use of reserve accounting, of capitalising revenue expenditure, of taking dealing profits through the profit-and-loss account, and dealing losses against reserves. Remember the really professional investor recognises that a dealing profit is worth a multiple of one (that is it is non-recurring) and that the company's p/e could be affected.

16:8:5   Quality of earnings

The quality of the company's earnings is important; the higher the quality of earnings, the higher the p/e.

16:8:6   Public relations

Good relations with the financial press should be cultivated, as with investment analysts and other opinion formers, including the instututional investors themselves.

Chapter 17

Managing Acquisition and Merger Situations

Eric Izod, Executive Director, Industrial Mergers Limited and Manager, Industrial and Commercial Finance Corporation, Merchant Banking Services

In its essential arguments this chapter does not attempt to make a fine definition between an acquisition (colloquially a takeover) and a merger. The reason, quite simply, is that the border-line between the two can be extended, according to who is arguing the case, so as to verge on the extremities.

At one extreme the "true" merger is one in which two companies engaged in identical or complementary business, with approximately equal assets, profits and capital structures have managements which, at a given point in time, are eager to talk about getting together.

In practice this is a situation which seldom happens. What is usually called a merger arises when the management of one company approaches another with similar interests and finds that its view of the advantages of a marriage is echoed by the other side. In such a case it is relatively easy to call in an independent firm of accountants to recommend an exchange of shares (plus adjustments in cash on fixed interest stock) which is acceptable to both managements, if they are principles, or which both managements can recommend to outside shareholders.

At the other extreme is the really aggressive takeover bid which succeeds in spite of the most bitter objections of management, workers and a substantial minority of shareholders of the company subjected to the bid. In cases when such an operation is carried out through the offer of an exchange of shares it can still be regarded as a merger because accepting shareholders still have an interest in their original business as well as in the business of the company making the bid. The pure take-over bid is one in which the offer consists entirely of cash and accepting shareholders have no further interest either in their original company or in the bidding company.

At this point it is important to examine the basic considerations attaching to mergers. In the 1950s companies were acquired by the business tycoon at prices far below the real value of their assets. By the mid 'sixties, the trend was reversed, and the purchase price of companies acquired contained a large element of so-called "goodwill"—and this prompts one to ask how permanent in fact is the goodwill passing from the seller.

17:1   Why do companies merge?

It is important to ask the question: *Why do companies merge?*

17:1:1   Seller's reasons

The seller's reasons may be listed as follows: frequently they are not reasons at all but an inevitable consequence of *management failure*. This often occurs when a management has failed, through one cause or another, to earn adequate profits, or to foresee and thus forestall a falling demand for the company's products, or to provide for management succession.

A frequent reason is the *sudden crisis*. This may cover a loss of turnover, resulting from external or governmental policies. It may be due to over-trading, which is often occasioned by lack of budgeting, or by external pressures in times of a credit squeeze.

There is also the *urge to cash in*, which grips the directors or shareholders of the family business who are influenced, and probably bewildered, by government legislation making more and more complex, for example, the close company situation.

Then there is the problem of *estate duty provision*, especially for a majority shareholder in a private company.

Lastly, *growth opportunities*, where the successful management of a small company is attracted by the chance to merge—but not submerge— its identity with the management of the acquiring company and, in fact, provide the management succession needed there.

17:1:2   Buyer's reasons

The acquisition criteria of the buyer might be answered under the following heads:

The *sudden bargain:* while many directors over-estimate the value of their companies, conversely there are frequent instances of directors who, by not seeking professional advice, sell on an assets basis without being aware of the true potential, or without realising that the profits being earned would justify the inclusion of a substantial "goodwill" element in the purchase price.

There is the *surplus cash* situation, where a judicious acquisition can profitably utilise funds which might otherwise lie idle or, at best, earn only a small return if invested in securities.

There may be lacunae in the buyer's own facilities—perhaps in management, or the product range, the marketing or research and development departments; or there may be processing or purchasing problems, all or any of which could logically point to the advisability of a vertical or horizontal merger.

Another reason is *falling return on investment.* When directors, in their forward planning, predict a decline, they may diversify by acquisition, or forestall serious competition in their product mixture by buying out the competitor.

Lastly, *growth opportunities:* the successful management with its five-year plan, including budgetary and cash flow controls, is in a position to look forward for merger proposals to dovetail in with its forward planning for growth.

17:2   Managements' duties

The merger field is one in which it is very difficult for individual managers to be entirely objective. Human ambitions, reputations and livelihoods are involved.

It is natural for an able management to seek successful growth for its company, since to be associated with growth enhances reputations and to be in charge of a large organisation means prestige as well as remuneration. And growth can be achieved rapidly through mergers and take-over bids. The danger is that the prospect of growth through acquisitions can become so alluring that insufficient thought may be given to other considerations.

It is even more difficult for managements confronted with a takeover bid, or which is presented with the prospect of a junior role in a suggested merger, to be entirely objective. Few managers accustomed to autocracy relish the prospect of a deputy position. Even fewer welcome the idea of early retirement or unemployment. Confronted with such prospects it is only natural for people to allow their personal positions to dominate other considerations.

The Stock Market list includes a number of companies which, through acquisitions, have grown enormously in terms of profits and assets, but which show a disappointing, or even a declining trend in earnings per share. Equally, it contains companies the shares of which stand substantially below the past or present day value of a bid which the management succeeded in defeating.

In both types of case the cause of such poor consequences was usually a lack of objectivity on the part of the managements concerned. While there may be many other things to take into account, the main criteria to be considered in merger decisions are as follows:

17:2:1   Buyer's duties

The buyer should be convinced that an acquisition will result either immediately or prospectively in a better earnings per share performance by his company than would otherwise be the case. This is true whether the acquisition represents a complementary business, a diversification in order to make the buying company less vulnerable to fluctuations in its own trade or a simple purchase of under utilised assets which can be sold subsequently at a substantial profit.

In other words the management of a bidding company should be satisfied that any acquisition will be beneficial to its existing share-holders. Such an objective may seem elementary but it can be, and frequently is, lost sight of very easily. This is because, whereas a venders' shareholders have to be persuaded into acceptance, a bidding management has no serious need to win the approval of its own shareholders. In fact, its own shareholders only have to be consulted if the bid requires additional authorised capital or borrowing powers. In the case of a Stock Market quoted company, it is almost unheard of for shareholders to refuse. In practice they have no say in the matter.

Obviously, if a buying management is to fulfil its duty to its shareholders it has to get the terms of its bid right. Equally obviously, the right terms are the cheapest which will win acceptance. It may be that an initial bid price has to be raised in the light of a spirited defence or the emergence on the scene of one or more other bidders.

It is in the latter case when a bid battle begins that it is all too easy for management to lose sight of the simple objective that acquisitions should represent good value for money. There is only one answer. The bidder should always have a maximum price established in its mind before making an approach. That price should never be exceeded.

There are numerous other things to consider. Among the main ones are: will there be sufficient total management capability to make the best of the acquisition? Will employees be co-operative, particularly if redundancies are going to be involved? Will customers object? Will the terms strain cash resources? The problem of getting bid terms right depends on the answers to these and many other questions.

17:2:2   Seller's duties

The seller's duty is also to give prime consideration to the interests of shareholders. If management accepts an initial offer it should be sure that it is the best obtainable. The difficulty is not to be motivated by personal considerations such as when a chairman and managing director is offered financial remuneration and added personal prestige in the organisation which will result from the merger.

If, as is commonly the case, a management advises shareholders to reject a bid it clearly has a minimal duty to do one of three things:

1   To provide a convincing argument that the prospects of the company under the existing management are better in terms of probable earnings per share than are likely as a result of acquisition where a share exchange is concerned. If the bid is in cash, the onus on the management is to produce a plan which will produce a share price higher than the cash offer. It has to be realised, of course, that any such

argument is bound to be faced with the question: "Why did you not tell shareholders of this potential before a bidder appeared?"

2 To produce an argument which is convincing enough for the bidder to raise his price

3 To find another bidder who is prepared to pay more

If defending managers can satisfactorily cover one or more of the above points, they will be in a strong position to look after the next prime interest, that of their employees, and even to get the best terms, as individuals, for themselves.

A management which cannot respond to a bid in one of the three ways listed above should recommend acceptance. If it fights it is bound to lose without even salvaging its own dignity.

17:3   Planning the merger

Whether a company establishes its own acquisition department, or consults its professional advisers or a merger specialist organisation, the board of directors must:

1 Specify the investment resources available and, as a corollary, the appropriate method of financing

2 State what return on investment is sought

3 State the product range requirements—whether they should be complementary or additional to the existing products

4 Identify their own strengths and weaknesses in management, technical and marketing skills and so on

5 Mention the location preferred

6 State the operational aims

7 Agree on the compatibility of the various people concerned

Equally, the selling company must define:

1 The degree to which it wishes to participate after the merger has taken place

2 What guarantees it requires on the continued employment of the staff and workpeople

3 The asking price

4 As with the buyer, the compatibility of the people involved

It cannot be over-emphasised that mergers involve people, and often an independent view on the compatibility of the merger partners should be sought.

17:4   Finding the right partner

With the specifications of the *buyer* or the requirements of the *seller*, the function of the management or its professional advisers is to search for, screen and identify likely candidates to fulfil the requirements.

In many cases this is achieved by personal contacts between individuals who have become friendly rivals in competing businesses in the same or allied trades. The advantages of merging either because of "economies of scale", savings in research and development costs per manufactured unit, a rationalisation of factory sites or a rationalisation of marketing through increased product ranges or a joint extension of geographical areas can all become evident enough to appeal to both sides.

17:4:1   Registers

In other cases it may be achieved from the registers maintained by merger organisations, or generally from research into industry, and from information obtained from accounting data available from the Companies Registry and Extel Cards, and comparison with similar companies in the required industry.

Most merchant banks keep registers of potential buyers and sellers. So do two semi-official, City-sponsored organisations, The Finance Corporation for Industry and The Industrial and Commercial Finance Corporation. The latter has a subsidiary, Industrial Mergers which specialises in introducing suitable merger parties.

Before approaches are made, it is important that the short-list of companies appearing *prima facie* to fit the requirements should be discussed.

17:4:2   Method of approach

Approaches can be made in various ways, but personal interviews are indispensable. In many instances, the auditors of companies are known and this is preferable to the direct approach since, if negotiations prove fruitless, the directors would obviously not take kindly to repeated approaches which may in turn come to nothing, and, indeed, may even discourage such further approaches, thereby closing the door on what could have been a successful operation.

If the approach is successful, then it is important to secure information about the company in considerable detail. Reluctance to press enquiries and requirements in the early stages can prove expensive later for both parties.

The requirements of the Takeover Panel must be observed, and the professional advisers must have authority to make disclosures. Indeed, the rules of the Panel require that if an offer, or even an approach with a view to an offer being made, is not made by a principal, his identity must be disclosed at the outset.

17:5   The purchase price

In valuing the share capital of the company, the following factors must be taken into account:

1   The cost of the time which can be saved by the operation
2   The interest to be retained by the seller
3   What guarantees on continuation of employment the seller requires for his employees
4   The permanency of the goodwill element

There are various techniques for evaluating mergers, namely:

1   Appraisal of assets
2   Discounted cash flow—calculating an interest rate which discounts an estimated future rate of profits to a present value
3   Past profits on a simple or weighted average multiplied by an agreed multiple

The generally accepted basis of valuing a successful company is a price earnings ratio, that is, an agreed multiple of the profits after deduction of corporation tax. Whether or not the multiple is geared to a profit forecast of the current year, a simple or weighted average must depend on many factors, including whether the selling company is a growth company in a growth industry and whether the industry is subject to profit fluctuations due to competitive conditions or political influence.

The price/earnings multiple which is used in the calculation also reflects the quoted market conditions pertaining to industry and management. The *Financial Times Index* will indicate the industry rating.

Companies earning an inadequate return on capital employed may as *sellers* have to accept a purchase price based on a discounted assets basis. This does not necessarily mean discounting on the book values as disclosed in the balance sheet; it may require an appraisal value of the fixed and current assets. The amount of discount will vary with the company's activities and location. It will also depend upon stock and work in progress—whether it is in balance with orders on hand, and whether the orders are profitable. One of the many functions of a merger organisation is to seek buyers requiring certain locations, urgent production requirements and so on, which can reduce the size of the discount.

Sometimes research and development expenditure contribute towards an inadequate return on capital employed being shown. The purchase price may then be based upon assets plus goodwill representing the value of the product development. The valuation for goodwill will depend upon finding the right buyer; often the sale of a controlling interest, with an option for an agreed period and the price geared to profits, may be advantageous to the *seller*.

17:5:1 Examples

Two examples of companies sold on a price/earnings ratio are shown below. In the second example, the effect of this acquisition on the quoted price of the acquiring company is worth noting.

Example 1. A United Kingdom company acting as agents for import and distribution of engineering products.

The European manufacturing company has been acquired by an American company which now wishes to control distribution by acquisition of the United Kingdom company and other European distributors.

The United Kingdom company's net tangible assets (NTA) at 31 March 1968 amounted to £288 800.

The profits before taxation from 1964/68 inclusive showed substantial improvement: 1964—£49 200, 1968—£150 800. The United Kingdom directors were forecasting pre-tax profits of £230 235 000. After negotiation during January 1969, a price/earnings ratio (p/e) of 11 was agreed, based upon pre-tax profits of £233 000 after deduction of corporation tax at the rate of $42\frac{1}{2}$ per cent:

	£
Profit before taxation	233 000
Deduct: corporation tax at $42\frac{1}{2}$ per cent, say	99 000
	134 000

p/e 11 × £134 000	£1 474 000
	for 162 400 ordinary shares of £1

A final compromise with the United States financial advisers was a purchase price of £1 460 000 plus compensation payments of £5000 each to three non-executive director/shareholders.

Example 2. A knitwear company in the East Midlands. The two specific reasons for selling were:

1 The cash resources available within the company without any capital expenditure commitments permitted no defence against shortfall provisions of the Finance Act 1965
2 The only two directors and shareholders were a man in his mid-sixties and his wife (non-executive) with a need to provide for estate duty

The asking price for this company was £525 000 and it is interesting to note how this purchase valuation was calculated by the seller:

	£
Net tangible assets (Note 1)	450 000
Goodwill—representing the average of the last three years, namely, the audited accounts of 1966 (£82 000), 1967 (£69 000) and the then forecast for 1968 (£75 000), say	75 000
	£525 000

Note 1: The NTA was adjusted for the retention of profits after taxation for 1968 and included liquid resources of £135 000.

While, perhaps, one might not agree with the basis of calculating the purchase price, it seemed reasonable. However, it was necessary to determine:

1 Had the "goodwill" any permanent value, having in mind that the individual who had founded and built up the business wished to retire after an agreed period for handing over?
2 What other management resources were available in the selling company?
3 What was the real goodwill figure, having studied the balance sheet and ascertained that freehold property was shown at cost?
4 Was the customer relationship with the individual such that there could be a reduction in sales, and were they directed to wholesale or retail?
5 The basis of depreciation of plant and machinery. Was it over-valued at the balance sheet figure?
6 The basis of valuing stock and work in progress

The following factors were ascertained:

1 The freehold premises were valued at £70 000 in excess of the balance sheet figure on a "going concern" basis; this included the item "Dyeing and Finishing", which formed part of the freehold and is difficult to value except on this basis.
2 The sales were mainly to the wholesale sector.
3 The management could not be regarded as policy makers; they were of reasonable second-line quality, and mainly in their fifties.
4 There had been no plant replacement programme of any consequence over the past five years and on a modern depreciation basis the plant was over-valued by, say, £30 000.
5 On the credit side, it was reasonable to expect a saving of, say, £5000 on the existing directors' remuneration of £12 000 with the appointment of a replacement. Production was mainly against firm orders, and stocks and work in progress were valued on a conservative basis.

This proposal can be examined on a price/earnings basis calculated on an average of profits over three years. This is reasonable in the case of textile companies, where profits can fluctuate with competitive and

359

credit squeeze conditions. The average is adjusted in respect of the profit forecast of 1968 for future adjusted management remuneration, and the draft results for the first nine months based on the accountant's report, with the following result:

	£
Profits—1966	82 200
Profits—1967	69 100
Profits—1968	89 000/90 000
	240 300
Average, say	80 000
Deduct corporation tax at 42½ per cent	34 000
Available for distribution	£46 000

	£
A p/e of 8·5 values the average earnings at:	391 000
plus cash availability of, say	134 000
Asking price	£525 000

Now examine the effect upon the small quoted company which acquired this textile company for £525 000. The purchase consideration was satisfied as to £400 000 in cash and £125 000 in 25p ordinary shares at 46·25p per share. It was also agreed that £75 000 of the proposed share issue would be renounced by the vendor for cash in favour of finance companies, who also advanced £300 000 by way of secured loan.

	£
Profits before tax—acquiring company	100 000
Profits before tax—vendor company	90 000
	190 000
Deduct interest on £300 000 loan	26 250
	163 750
Deduct corporation tax at 42½ per cent	69 600
	94 150
Deduct preference dividend	900
Available for distribution	£93 250

The vendors were seeking a transaction wholly in cash, but were advised that £475 000 in cash and the balance in shares (£50 000) could be attractive. It is customary to place a restriction on vendor share-holders not to sell acquired shares for a defined period. In this case no such restriction was imposed, as it was desired to create a less restricted market in the quoted shares of the acquiring company.

The market value of the equity capital of the acquiring company at 46·25p per share was £600 697.

Divide the profits available for distribution by the value of the equity at 46·25p per share = 15·5 per cent earnings yield or a p/e of 6·4.

Within a short period the 25p ordinary shares were quoted at 60p per share valuing the equity at £779 284. Using the above formula this gives a 12 per cent earnings yield or a p/e of 8·3.

The two examples shown above are takeovers. Whilst the trading names are retained for the established goodwill, the management is partially submerged. Future policies and the conduct of the business will be directed by the board, or the group or divisional management of the acquiring company.

17:6   Consultations

This section should be read in conjunction with the chart in Figure 17:1. It is assumed that a professional merger organisation is involved. However, the basic principles apply in cases where negotiation is entirely between one management and another.

17:6:1   Preliminary consultations

Preliminary consultations can be achieved by directors making personal contact with their opposite numbers in a company comple-mentary to their own, or by a merger organisation initiating the ap-proach. Visits to each company's factories can often assist in the appreciation and understanding of the objectives of both parties. The proper use of the merger organisation's register and advice at this stage can save a great deal of time and effort.

17:6:2   Getting to grips with the merger

It is often necessary to disclose certain financial and trading informa-tion about the companies concerned, to ensure that they are both in

361

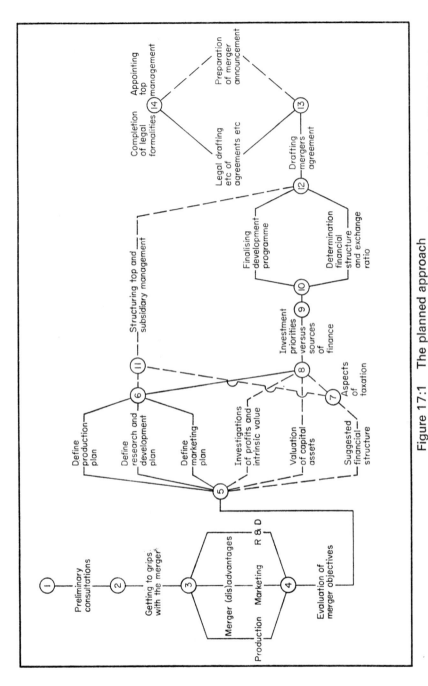

Figure 17:1   The planned approach

This chart is based on a network plan which appears in *Mergers: A European Approach to Technique* by N R A Krekel, T G van der Woerd and J J Wouterse, Business Books, 1969.

agreement to hold meetings to review stages 3 and 4, and to discuss the advantages and disadvantages of merging under headings such as production, marketing, research and development. These headings can be adjusted to meet the requirements of the trading activities of the companies concerned, and such a meeting should be attended by directors of both parties, their financial advisers or auditors, and the merger organisation, if involved. The latter should then evaluate the merger objectives, referred to under stage 4 to recommend whether the advantages of the rationalisation are attractive to the interested parties. It may, at this stage, be necessary for the merger organisation and the professional advisers to the companies concerned to give some broad outline as to how the companies could be fitted together financially, and also to appreciate whether part of the purchase consideration needs to be satisfied by a cash contribution, in order to assist in possible future estate duty requirements. It may also be necessary, if a public company is involved in the negotiations, for some preliminary announcement to be made in the press.

If it is agreed that the negotiations should continue, it is necessary that the parties to the merger instruct members of their individual management teams to co-operate in defining the future production, research and development, and marketing plans of the merged group (stage 5), and they should produce a report setting out the future intentions, and also the investment requirements to implement their recommendations (stages 6 and 8).

At the same time, the merger organisation, with the co-operation of the auditors or financial advisers to the companies, should prepare financial information with regard to previous profits earned by the merging companies, and if necessary, instruct valuers to prepare valuations of capital assets—this can be very important if, in the merger proposals, certain premises or factories are to be disposed of—and to recommend the financial structure for the new group.

Under stage 7 aspects of taxation will have to be carefully considered and it may be recommended that clearance under Section 28 of the Finance Act 1960 should be obtained from the Inland Revenue, or, if the financial proposals are very complicated, it may be necessary to obtain the opinion of legal counsel.

The structuring of the top and subsidiary management under stage 11 should not be rushed, as it is difficult to undo hasty decisions and, often, time is required by the directors of the merging companies to appreciate the various counterparts of the merged organisation to ensure that the right appointments are made. The critical path approach has been drawn through stages 5, 7, 8 and 11 in view of the fact that instructing valuers, obtaining clearance on matters affecting taxation, will determine the time-factor for completion of the merger proposals.

Under stage 9 it is important that the investment priorities, recommended by the management team defining the future programmes on production, marketing and research and development, are carefully considered against the background of the present borrowing structure. It should be decided whether the group reconstruction will permit additional borrowings, or whether the equity capital should be enlarged to ensure a correct gearing. It is senseless to group "over-borrowed" companies with further plans for expanding their combined activity without a sound equity base.

Provided the investment priorities and the financial strength of the new company can be reconciled, one can proceed to stage 10, which deals with the finalising of the development programme, the determination of the financial structure and the exchange ratio of shares and/or loan stock.

Under stage 12 the merger organisation, in conjunction with the professional advisers to the parties, should draft the merger agreement for approval and signature by the parties concerned.

Stages 13 and 14 are self-explanatory, but it is important that the merger organisation and the directors of the companies concerned should not consider that their functions end with the completion of the legal formalities and the appointing of top management. It is essential that there should be harmonisation of personnel (which will often require the co-operation of trade unions), information relayed to suppliers and customers of the merged companies making them aware of the personnel with whom they will have contact in future. The re-grouping of administration, manufacturing departments, sales departments and the re-orientation of marketing policy of the merged group, defined under stage 6, should proceed to ensure that the advantages discussed at earlier meetings of the directors are implemented.

Chapter 18

Managing Corporate Taxation

John Reynolds, Tax Adviser, Esso Petroleum Company Limited

I hope you will not trouble your head further with tax matters, because you seem to have spent a lot of time in going through these various Acts and if you go on spending your time on Finance Acts and the like, it will drive you silly.

Most executives would probably not become litigants in person even if their own personal tax affairs reached the stage of litigation, but today none can follow the advice of Mr. Justice Singleton to a litigant in person and ignore tax matters entirely.

18:1 The influence of taxation on business decisions

It is still a matter for dispute amongst economists as to how far business decisions are influenced by taxation. The Richardson Committee on Turnover Taxation came to the conclusion in 1964 that investment decisions were generally reached without regard to the after-tax results in all but a handful of the cases surveyed. The abolition of investment grants marks the end of an era which offered both cash grants and free depreciation at one and the same time to stimulate certain types of capital investment. The 1971 Finance Act reintroduced, with modifications, the old system of capital allowances and the Finance Act 1972 increased them; these changes appear to indicate that the Government (except in regard to development areas) now regards even cash grants as an unsatisfactory incentive to capital investment. On the other hand, the 1971 Act also introduced provisions to be effective for 1973/4 and subsequent years to simplify the personal tax system in the United Kingdom. Central to these proposals is the replacement of the standard rate of income tax, coupled with earned income relief, by a basic rate of tax, probably of thirty per cent. In this way the Government hopes that taxpayers will identify clearly the marginal rate of tax attaching to their incremental earnings. If the Government feels that the employee can be motivated more directly by having an accurate knowledge of his marginal tax rate it seems strange that business investment decisions cannot be accorded similar treatment in the Government's taxation policies.

In practice it is probable that since 1964 business has increasingly *looked* at the after-tax results of its projects and that the findings of the Richardson Committee in this respect are no longer valid. It is a quite different question whether business is *influenced* by what it sees. Much of the blame for the failure of business to be motivated by tax incentives must be laid at the door of both major political parties who, in recent years, when taking over the reins of government, have regarded themselves as the first tax reformers of the twentieth century. No industrialist would care to wager that the tax incentives recently introduced will still be operative in five years time: a week may be a long time in politics, but five years can be a relatively short time in a capital investment programme. As a result industry tends to take what cash grants and tax reliefs it can, as it goes along, but not to base its major investment decisions in incentives which can disappear literally overnight.

18:1:1 Timing of payments and receipts

In looking at after-tax results a business must look at both tax costs and tax incentives in numerical terms and also at the *timing* of both tax payments and the receipt of grants and allowances. There must be awareness not only of the amount of the allowance but also of its timing. If the granting of an allowance is delayed for one year because, although the expenditure has been incurred, the plant is not brought into use, then its value to the taxpayer is reduced by whatever percentage should be used for discounting purposes. In a capital-intensive business the effect of tax allowances on capital expenditure will either be to reduce the taxable profits of the period or to eliminate them entirely and to create a loss. Both costs and timing can have a marked effect on the return from an investment project. Tax avoidance is a much more difficult exercise and, whereas a company may not have at its disposal the expertise necessary to avoid the payment of tax completely (even assuming that to be possible at all), its own employees should be able to evaluate an investment project or a selling price by reference both to the *quantum* and *timing* of its tax payments and tax allowances.

18:1:2 Example

The changes now being introduced into the capital allowance system and into the corporation tax system itself will not remove the need for industry and commerce to appreciate the after-tax results of its business decisions. Tax plays a part in the very first decision of all: how should a new business enterprise be financed? For example, after a nominal capital of £100 to cover formation expenses, two companies, A Limited and B Limited, require a further £1000 of working capital with which to start the business. Company A raises £1000 by the issue of ordinary share capital, while B raises the same sum by means of a debenture. If both A and B regard ten per cent as an appropriate return to those investing in their companies and both companies make pre-tax profits of £2000, their respective positions will be:

A Limited		B Limited	
Pre-tax profits	2000	Pre-tax profits	2000
Corporation tax at 40%	800	Less interest	100
	1200		1900
Dividend gross 10% × £1000	100	Corporation tax at 40%	760
	1100		1140

Both companies will have returned £100 to the investor, but while B will have £1140 with which to continue its operations, A will have only £1100, not receiving any tax deduction for the dividend paid.

18:2   The change to the imputation system

This difference between A and B will generally be present under most systems of corporate taxation and remains as true under the imputation system as under the classical system. The change to the new imputation system from April 1973 was introduced in the Finance Act 1972 following discussions with industry and a select committee of the House of Commons. It was a characteristic of the classical system introduced in 1965 that a company's tax bill increased if it paid dividends, for, in addition to a corporation tax charge on the profits, there was an income tax liability on the gross dividends. Under the new system, the tax charge of a company is unaffected by whether it pays dividends or not. When a dividend is paid a tax liability called *advance corporation tax* is payable. The rate is thought likely to be three-sevenths of the dividend. This advance corporation tax is allowable against the corporation tax liability on profits.

It is still necessary for a company to consider tax in paying dividends, however. This is because dividends paid may produce a liability to the higher rates of tax (and possibly a surcharge) when received by the shareholders. On the other hand, surplus funds retained by the company may well produce a capital gains tax liability in future, in addition to the full corporation tax charge.

Due to the mechanism employed by the Revenue to recover income tax on payments of both dividends and annual interest it is important in negotiating loan agreements to keep a close watch on the dates on which interest will be payable by a company or to a company under such agreements. At present the basic procedure is that throughout the tax year—that is, from 6 April to the following 5 April—a running account is kept on a monthly basis in which are mixed payments of both dividends and annual interest, whether paid by or to the company. If at any time during the year when a company makes a payment of either kind it has paid more tax than it has suffered on dividends and interest received, it can take a credit for the excess tax suffered and only pay over to the Revenue the balance of tax due. In the case of a receipt from which income tax has been deducted by the payer, the company can claim repayment of any excess tax suffered. At the end of the year the company must separate its dividends paid and received from its annual payments made and received. It is not always in the interest of a company to take the apparent advantage offered by the provisions for monthly accounting and retain tax deducted or seek immediate repayment of tax suffered. In computing the position at the end of the tax year when dividends have been separated from annual payments, credit for tax paid or suffered is only given where settlement with the Revenue takes place in the same accounts year in which the payments are made or received. By postponing payment to the Revenue of income tax deducted a company may be deferring by twelve months a credit for tax, while delaying by only three months actual payment to the Revenue of income tax deducted.

Under the imputation system, the periodic returns of interest and dividends will be on a quarterly basis and these items will be kept quite separate. Once again, it is necessary to pay attention to the timing of dividends. A dividend paid on the last day of a quarter means the payment of advance corporation tax almost at once, whereas payment on the first day of the quarter gives an extra three months delay effectively.

18:3   Close companies

Once a decision has been taken on the mode of financing an enterprise and it has been decided that a limited liability company is the most suitable form, the position of the shareholders will depend on whether or not the company is a "close company". A close company is one which is under the control of five or fewer "participators". A participator includes persons other than ordinary shareholders, but a company can escape the penalties of being a close company if at least thirty-five per cent of its voting shares are held by the public and are dealt in on a recognised stock exchange. It is not always a simple matter to determine whether or not a company is a close company and expert advice should be taken if any doubts exist as to its status. The penalties of being a close company are severe in that the Revenue can exercise its rights under what are colloquially known as "the shortfall provisions" and deem a dividend to have been paid to the shareholders even though this has not been done. The result is that a close company can incur a liability to income tax at the standard rate in addition to its ordinary corporation tax liability. Where the shareholders in a close company pay surtax at the top rate, the total tax liability on the profits of that company can reach ninety per cent before those profits finally reach the pockets of the shareholders.

There are now mitigating factors in the position of a close company. No arithmetical restriction is imposed on the remuneration that can be paid to its directors, but those directors must be actively engaged in the work of the company and justify the amounts paid. The Revenue will attack cases where they feel this does not occur. Where the Revenue has used its powers to deem the payment of dividends, the income tax assessed in this way will be credited against the liability that arises when a dividend is actually paid. Again, if the company is a trading company, as opposed to an investment company, not more than sixty per cent of its income will be subject to the shortfall provisions and this maximum may be reduced under a formula made still less restrictive under provisions of the Finance Act 1971.

The position has been improved yet again under the new imputation system. The shortfall provisions now apply to far fewer companies because the limits have been substantially increased. Furthermore the maximum percentage distributable has been reduced from sixty per cent to fifty per cent, and there will be a special lower rate of corporation tax for small companies.

As a result of the statutory provisions relating to close companies it has generally been in the best tax interests of a small business to cease operations as a limited liability company and function instead as a partnership. There may, however, be sound commercial reasons for preserving the corporate status of the business.

18:4   Overseas companies operating in the United Kingdom

An overseas company wishing to operate in the United Kingdom may either form a subsidiary company resident in the United Kingdom or operate through a branch. In the latter case it will incur only a liability to corporation tax, whereas the United Kingdom subsidiary of a foreign company will, additionally, be subject to a withholding tax on its dividends. If the foreign parent is resident in a country with which the United Kingdom has a tax treaty, the precise rate of withholding tax will depend on the terms of the treaty. If not, tax must be withheld at the standard rate and the foreign shareholder could be also subject to surtax.

The position of overseas companies operating in the United Kingdom, whether through a branch or a United Kingdom resident subsidiary, will be radically altered when the proposed reform of corporation tax takes place. The corporation tax charge for a branch will clearly increase as there will be no advance corporation tax credit. The position for a subsidiary company may not be significantly worse, but this will depend on the results of re-negotiation of double tax treaties.

18:5   Grants and allowances

Having established a suitable corporate structure, the next stage will be the acquisition of buildings, plant and machinery necessary for the proper running of the business. No question of investment grants will arise unless expenditure was incurred under a contract made on or before 27 October 1970, on assets of a kind which would have attracted grant under the terms of the Industrial Development Act 1966. Cash grants have been available from 22 March 1972 for plant and machinery or buildings in the special development and development areas wholly or mainly used for manufacturing, mining or construction, and the availability of a cash grant should always be checked in evaluating a project. The grant rates vary according to the part of the country in which the asset is situated, a higher rate being available in special development areas.

18:5:1   Depreciation on ships

There are two types of "free" depreciation: only in the case of ships is the tax depreciation granted truly "free". The taxpayer can take the whole or any part of his expenditure as an allowance in the accounting period of his choice, provided that in the period in question, or an earlier one, he has satisfied certain conditions in regard to the ship. The importance of free depreciation of this kind is seen in considering tax losses (see below).

18:5:2   Depreciation on other plant

The "free depreciation" granted in respect of other expenditure on

371

plant is not "free" in the same way. In the first year a percentage (currently 100 per cent, but it can be anything between 100 per cent and nil) of the expenditure must be claimed and thereafter only twenty-five per cent of the declining balance can be claimed in each subsequent year. In this way it is much more difficult for a taxpayer to build up a "pool" of losses by the use of free depreciation. The first year allowance is given in the year in which the expenditure is incurred and the first writing-down allowance of twenty-five per cent will be given in the next year, provided the asset has been in use. Thereafter the twenty-five per cent allowance will continue in each subsequent year on a declining balance basis. The table below shows that it is in the early years, and most significantly in the first year, that the benefits from tax allowances are most marked. By the end of the third year £35·5 out of the £40 of tax allowances (assuming a corporation tax rate of forty per cent) available on £100 of capital expenditure will have been received:

(Assuming a first year allowance of 80%)

		£			£
1st year	First year allowance	80	at 40% corporation tax		32
2nd year	Writing-down allowance 25% × 20	5	,,	,,	2
3rd year	Writing-down allowance 25% × 15	3.75	,,	,,	1.5
	Expenditure allowed	88.75	Value of allowances		35.5

18:5:3   Industrial buildings

Industrial buildings, which never attracted investment grants, now qualify for cash grant if situated in development areas. They continue to qualify for the old initial and writing-down allowance, except that the rates for the former have been increased. There is now an initial allowance of forty per cent for expenditure on industrial buildings in special development, development and intermediate areas and in Northern Ireland, and of thirty per cent elsewhere. The initial allowance is granted in the period in which the capital expenditure is incurred. There is a four per cent writing-down allowance on a flat rate basis given for that and subsequent years in which the building is in existence as an "industrial building or structure", until it is sold.

In addition to the tax allowances already mentioned there is relief in the form of allowances for other types of expenditure, such as that on mines and oil wells, dredging, agricultural land and buildings, scientific research, patents and know how. There are special provisions relating to expenditure on motor cars. It is also important to remember those assets which do not qualify for tax allowances. These include freehold land and leases of land, goodwill, office buildings, shops, hotels and places of entertainment. Exceptionally, some relief is due for premiums paid for business premises.

18:5:4   Disposal value

Where capital expenditure is incurred on or after 27 October 1970, different rules now apply when those assets are sold or scrapped. The disposal value up to the amount of the capital expenditure incurred on the asset is set against the balance of expenditure incurred on plant and machinery used in that accounting period and the writing-down allowance of twenty-five per cent is applied to any excess over the disposal value. In this way the impact on a company's tax position where large assets are sold or scrapped is now more evenly spread than under the previous system of balancing allowances and charges. Only if the asset fetches a higher price than its first cost (plus the cost of any additions to it) will there be any liability to corporation tax on a capital gain. The distinction can be important in that, where proceeds of sale are taxed as a capital gain, the company may be able to exercise its right of "roll over" (see below) and avoid or defer the payment of tax.

18:6   Liability for capital gains

Every transaction involving the receipt of a capital sum, whether from the disposal of an asset or not, has to be considered and the gain or loss computed. Sometimes a computation will be required even though no capital sum is received, for example, on the demolition of a building. When the taxation of capital gains was introduced on a broad scale by the Finance Act 1965, special rules were necessary to ensure that gains arising before 6 April 1965 were not assessed to tax. For assets acquired before that date, the normal basis of assessment is by time apportionment by reference to the period for which the asset was owned between 6 April 1945 and 6 April 1965. In all cases a company has the right to elect for the asset to be valued as at 6 April 1965 and to pay tax on any gain arising between that date and the date of disposal. Where a quoted security or land having a development value is sold, the company has no choice at all and the capital gain must be determined by reference to the value of the asset at 6 April 1965. In some cases companies went to the lengths of valuing all their assets at 6 April 1965 and heavy fees were incurred, but in practice disputes with the Revenue over 1965 values have been comparatively rare.

Frequently the liability of a company in respect of a capital gain will arise on the sale of assets used in its trade. If the company can show that it has invested the proceeds of sale (or a greater sum of money) in certain assets within a year either side of the sale, then payment of corporation tax on the gain can be deferred and sometimes permanently avoided. Assets which can be used for this purpose are: land and buildings occupied by the company for the purposes of its trade, fixed plant and machinery, ships, aircraft, hovercraft and goodwill. The original effect of the "roll over" provisions was that a company with a continuing investment programme could be virtually certain of avoiding for ever any liability to tax on its capital gains by "rolling over" the assets against depreciating assets such as plant and machinery. Restrictions were introduced in 1969 to prevent this device and it is no longer possible to "roll over" indefinitely gains on non-depreciating assets (for example, land) against the purchase of depreciating assets such as plant and machinery. If a gain is "rolled over" against a depreciating asset the maximum period for deferring the liability to pay tax is generally ten years, but it may be less in certain circumstances.

18:6:1   Rate of tax

The new corporation tax system will introduce a lower rate of charge on capital gains, expected to be only thirty per cent instead of fifty per cent. This prevents the high double charge which would arise otherwise. The advance corporation tax suffered on dividends is not available as a credit against gains charged at the reduced rate.

18:6:2   The grant of a lease

If a company grants a lease of more than fifty years, the proceeds from the grant will be subject to tax in the ordinary way as a capital gain arising from the part disposal of the land. If a lease is granted for fifty years or less at a premium (whether rent is also received is immaterial) the landlord is subject to corporation tax on the premium received with a deduction of one-fiftieth of the premium for each complete period of twelve months other than the first twelve months comprised in the lease. Any rent will be subject to corporation tax as ordinary revenue. The following example illustrates the way in which such premiums are taxed:

> A Limited grants a lease for 21 years for a premium of £10 000 and an annual rent of £400. The amounts subject to corporation tax in the first year are as follows:
>
> $$£10\,000 - \frac{(21-1)}{50} \times £10\,000 = \qquad £6000$$
> One year's rent at £400 $\qquad$ 400
>
> $\overline{\qquad\quad}$
> £6400
> $\overline{\overline{\qquad\quad}}$
>
> In subsequent years the only liability of A Limited will be on the annual rent of £400. (There may also be a capital gains tax liability on part of the £10 000.)

"Premium" is widely defined and includes:

1 The cost of improvements which a tenant is required to carry out under the terms of the lease
2 Any lump sums paid in lieu of rent and
3 Sums paid for the variation or waiver of any terms in a lease

18:7 Losses

Various adjustments to the trading profits of a company may help to create a loss and, indeed, the trading results may be so poor that a tax loss is present even before tax allowances are taken into account. There is no limit on the period for which losses may be carried forward, but a tax loss arising from a trade may either be applied against other income (for example, investment income) of the same period, or the profits and other income of the immediately preceding corresponding period. If not used in any of these ways, a trading loss can be carried forward for an indefinite period but can then only be used against future profits of the same trade. If losses are used against the profits of the current or immediately preceding corresponding period, they can be applied against capital gains of the same period. Capital losses, however, can only be used against capital gains of the same period. If the gains of the period are insufficient to use all the capital losses those losses can be carried forward but are only available to offset capital gains of a future period.

18:7:1   Groups of companies

The use of tax losses can be extended if a company is a member of a group of companies. For this purpose two companies are treated as members of the same group if one is a seventy-five per cent subsidiary of the other, or both are 75 per cent subsidiaries of a third company. To constitute a group for this purpose each company in the group must be resident in the United Kingdom for tax purposes, a company being so regarded if its central control and management is exercised in the United Kingdom. Within such a group, one member which has incurred a tax loss in its trade can surrender that loss to be used by another company in the group which has made a taxable profit in the same accounting period. If the accounting periods of member companies in a group do not correspond, some apportionment of the loss available must be made. A "pool" of free depreciation may be especially useful to create a loss in a particular tax year, because companies within a group are only permitted to surrender losses on a current basis and losses brought forward from earlier years cannot be used in this way. For example:

A Limited and B Limited are members of a group. The results for tax purposes of the two companies are:

	1971	1972
A Limited	400	800
B Limited	(900)	(600)

On the assumption that the 900 loss of B includes 300 of free depreciation, B need only surrender 400 of its loss to prevent A from making a tax payment in respect of 1971. In these circumstances B should surrender 400 of its loss, not claim the 300 of free depreciation and carry forward a loss of 200. In 1972, B has a current loss of 600 which is not sufficient to offset the 800 profit of A and the loss of 200 brought forward is not available for this purpose. At this point B can claim 200 of the 300 free depreciation available to it and in this way increase its loss for 1972 to 800, the level required to offset the taxable profit of 800 made by A in that year. In a similar way, losses of a company which forms part of a consortium of five or fewer companies can be used by member companies of the consortium in proportion to the respective shareholdings in that company. This remains true, in principle, under the new imputation system.

There are also provisions enabling a subsidiary company to pay dividends to its parent without any deduction of advance corporation tax. This can improve cash flow. Similarly the credit of a parent company for advance corporation tax can be surrendered to its subsidiary.

At this point those analysing a particular investment decision will have considered the appropriate corporate and capital structure of the company and its relationship with other members of a group of companies, availability of cash grants, and the capital allowances due on any capital investment involved, and they will be able to relate these factors to the sales proceeds forecast to arise from the enterprise. The analyst will also have calculated the incidence of corporation tax on the profits, and if the project is a capital-intensive one, the year in which the profits will become liable to tax after the allowances have been absorbed. Corporation tax will generally be due between nine and twenty-one months after the end of the accounting period in which the profits arise. The analyst can then apply to those figures the discount rate regarded as appropriate by his management. Where payment of tax is delayed because of the high level of capital investment or the utilisation of past losses, caution is needed. In the first place, recent legislation has curtailed the use of accumulated trading losses against current profits and led to a marked decline in the market value of tax losses. Secondly, where payment of corporation tax is forecast to be postponed for a significant period, and certainly in cases where that period exceeds two years, there are bound to be a large number of uncertain factors which could alter the position radically. Political changes are always likely and within the company other business decisions could lead to dramatic changes in the tax-paying outlook. It is vital that the board of a company should be aware of the impact of taxation on its projects but equally important that it should realise just how far the present value of future tax payments can be varied by circumstances within, and outside, their control.

18:8   Salaries and pensions

No business can function efficiently without employees of sufficiently high calibre to produce the profits expected from the capital invested. A continual turnover among employees is just as costly as a faulty investment decision and may contribute to it. Many businesses believe that if their salary scales are pitched at the right levels then they have solved the problem, and express surprise when employees leave their service. In fact a proper remuneration policy requires a remuneration *package*, which must take account not only of salaries but of all other fringe benefits and, in particular, of the pension needs of employees. It is obvious that A can receive a higher salary than B but still be financially worse off than B, who may have the advantage of a much better pension scheme and, perhaps, other fringe benefits as well. Where the executive's salary is subject to surtax, these considerations become even more important. Indeed, it is the very high level of tax on earned income which has led to the United Kingdom becoming more concerned with fringe benefits than almost any other country.[1]

It is particularly important at the present time that a company should give thought to its pension policy. If it has no pension plan, then it must realise that recently legislation has (with one or two important exceptions) liberalised the benefits which can be paid to employees on retirement. An employee can now receive the maximum pension permitted under a Revenue-approved scheme—two-thirds of final salary—after only ten years service, and the maximum right to a lump-sum payment on retirement after twenty years service. These changes will result in greater pressure from employees for better benefits more closely in line with the maxima permitted by the Revenue. New rules, to be observed if pension plans are to enjoy the benefits of Revenue approval, will be mandatory on existing schemes by April 1980, but such schemes cannot make alterations after April 1973 without complying with the new requirements, unless such alterations are "immaterial . . . in the opinion of the Board of Inland Revenue." One of the limiting provisions in the new legislation is that members of a plan will no longer be able to commute up to twenty-five per cent of the value of their pensions. Instead they will be able to receive, under an approved plan, a lump sum not exceeding three-eightieths of their final remuneration for each year of service, up to a maximum of forty years. Although under the new rules the period of service to qualify for the maximum lump sum payment is twenty years, many executives will suffer a reduction in the amount payable to them on retirement in lump-sum form and for this reason employers may wish to defer for as long as possible the change to the new rules and practice.

18:9　Share-purchase schemes

The good employer will also be concerned to motivate his key employees. Following the Finance Act 1966, stock options ceased to be attractive because the entire gain made by the employee on the exercise of his option was taxable under Schedule E at the employee's marginal rate of tax. As a result, share-purchase schemes replaced share-option schemes as a form of incentive. In a share-purchase scheme the employee is permitted to buy the shares at once, although his rights to dispose of the shares may be restricted for a period of time. If there are problems in financing the purchase of shares in a scheme, partly paid shares can be issued. Between 1966 and 1972 a large number of share-purchase schemes were launched, and at that time the Revenue could only tax the employee under Schedule E if the shares were issued at a price below market value. The "market value" was often drastically reduced, due to the restrictions placed on the shares. These might take the form either of making the future value of the shares depend on the attainment of specified profit targets or of imposing restrictions which precluded the purchaser from enjoying his full rights as a shareholder for some years to come. All these factors reduced the market value of shares and in addition the shareholder was only liable to capital gains tax at a maximum rate of thirty per cent. This compared favourably with a maximum rate of just over seventy-five per cent if the same shares had been offered to him through a stock-option scheme and he had sold the shares immediately after acquiring them through the exercise of his option.

Employees who had been caught holding un-exercised options when the Finance Act 1966 was passed, assiduously pressed for a change in the law to enable them to exercise their existing options at a lower tax cost. The Government, too, became increasingly concerned at the proliferation of share-purchase schemes and in the Finance Act 1972 it took steps to control both stock-option schemes and share-purchase schemes. Provided rights granted under either type of scheme conform to the requirements of the Act, liability under Schedule E is avoided and the employee is only taxable at rates appropriate to capital gains when he disposes of the shares. This offers a useful additional incentive to the highly-taxed executive.

18:10   Managing taxation

Enough has been written to show the wide implications of direct taxes on the running of a business, regardless of its size. Successive governments have increasingly placed the onus of administering the tax system on the taxpayer himself and no John Hampden has arisen to throw off the burden, although some have tried to do so. One taxpayer went so far as to withhold from the Collector of Taxes part of the PAYE deducted from his employees to reimburse himself for the administrative costs incurred in operating the PAYE system, but the Courts made it plain that he had no right to do so. Value added tax (VAT) is planned for April 1973 and this will provide a further administrative shock to those businessmen now accustomed to take corporation tax and PAYE in their stride. The size of the administrative burden will depend to a great extent on the way in which it is to be operated by the Customs and Excise, but already the advent of VAT has provoked a great deal of discussion in business circles on the subject of tax administration.

This in turn focuses on the problem of tax management. How should tax be *managed* in a business? The answer lies in two areas: *tax planning*, which is the arrangement of the affairs of a business to minimise the impact of taxation by reducing or eliminating the amount payable or deferring payment and *tax compliance*, which involves the computation of the tax liabilities of a business arising over a period of time. Broadly the former will generally look to the future and the latter to the past but this is *not* an invariable rule and they frequently become interwoven. For example, a decision may have to be made whether for a capital gains computation an election should be made to take the value of that asset at 6 April 1965. Whether or not the election is made affects the amount of tax actually payable—that is *tax planning*. The election is in fact made when the computations of the company are submitted to the Inspector and forms part of the computation—that is *tax compliance*.

A small manufacturing company employing 200 people will not run to its own "in house" taxation adviser. It will probably have a very overworked chief accountant responsible for everything from the canteen accounts to the chairman's personal tax return. This harassed individual will probably try to deal with every kind of tax problem affecting his company, but he will be very foolish to make the attempt and his employers will be equally foolish if they permit him to do so. He must get help outside the company and, just as it is impossible for him to cover the whole range of tax problems affecting the company, so no accountant or solicitor practising on his own without adequate professionally qualified support staff will be able to provide the service needed by the company. Having got outside advisers of suitable calibre, the next rule is to use them. If the advice is good, it may not be cheap, but it will show a profit in the long run if it is properly used, and a company should not be afraid to change professional advisers in the way that suppliers of raw materials may be changed; an adviser of many years standing will have the advantage of knowing a business thoroughly but he can also become complacent and old fashioned.

" 'Big-company tax men' are murder. They judge themselves by how many pros and cons they can dream up, and how many alternate methods might be 'worth investigating'. You need a man who will say, 'If I were you and had to make a decision and then get back to minding the store, I'd do this.' " Robert Townsend's very sound advice in *Up the Organization* is worth bearing in mind. There is no reason why a big-company tax man should not give advice in these straight forward terms. Equally it is vital that his advice shall be heard if not always followed. To do this he must have the ear of the board of directors and he must report direct to a board member. Only in this way can tax advice be kept free of company politics and the risk of distortion minimised. No board of directors wants to be assailed with a string of sections from the Finance Acts and the company tax man should always aim to present his advice in conclusive terms to management without reciting the legal arguments on both sides of a question which contributed to his advice. Having said that, management may well wish to have an indication of the strength underlying a particular piece of advice but an adviser can indicate this without a dissertation on the underlying legal niceties.

18:10:1   Choice of adviser

What kind of a man should a board of directors look for to give tax advice within their organisation? In the United Kingdom the general tendency is to seek out an Inspector of Taxes and if only one man is to be used in that function, then the Inland Revenue is probably the best source from which to recruit. The Revenue gives its Inspectors first class training and an Inspector who has had charge of a district and some experience at Head Office will generally be an attractive proposition to industry. Despite his previous experience, both he and his management must recognise the big transition involved in such a change. A very large organisation may have a taxation department employing a number of men (or women—this is a particularly suitable field for the employment of women) and in that case there is much to be said for blending the experience of a former Inspector of Taxes with that of the legal and accountancy professions. The spate of legislation in recent years has increased the need for lawyers in this field and it is noticeable that barristers, solicitors and other specialist consultants are increasingly moving into areas previously handled by the accountancy profession.

It may not be cheaper to engage such a man if his entire time is spent in preparing the corporation tax computations of the company. The time required to prepare computations will vary considerably from one company to another and will, in part, depend on the nature of the business. Much will also depend on the quality of the information supplied to a tax department from other parts of the organisation. A tax manager should say clearly what information he requires for the computations and other departments should supply it in that form. Equally, a company ought not to be submitting to the Revenue computations containing detail not required by the Revenue. This creates additional work within several departments of a large organisation.

In addition to handling tax computation work, a tax manager or tax adviser must be encouraged to get to know his organisation. His job cannot be satisfactorily performed from an ivory tower and he will be much more valuable when once he has acquired a sound knowledge of the company's operations and some valuable contacts outside it. Within his own organisation he must be concerned both to acquire information and to impart it. It is part of his function to educate the executives of the organisation to an appreciation in outline of the impact of tax on their business decisions. If he is encouraged to develop the tax planning side of his function, he will need outside contacts. Very few tax planning schemes are wholly original: they usually develop from other thoughts and ideas. He will also derive considerable value from others engaged in the same line of industry or commerce through a trade association to which his company belongs. Equally, he will not develop his own ideas without opportunity for reading and creative thought. In summary, there are three rules which should govern the position of tax manager or tax adviser in a large organisation:

1 It must be both a senior and an independent position
2 Management must appreciate that tax planning requires spells of concentrated thought and reading
3 The tax manager must get out and about, both to secure a knowledge of his own organisation and to spread among his fellow executives an appreciation of tax considerations affecting their business

With this basis, the man appointed will have a good start towards avoiding the pitfalls which can surround the "big-company tax man."

18:11   Reference

1 See *Inflation Taxation and Executive Remuneration* (Merrett and Monk, 1967). Despite the higher rate of earned income relief introduced by the Finance Act 1971, the recent levels of inflation have made the point even more valid than when the book was first published.

Index